Liam Neeson

The First Biography

Ingrid Millar

St. Martin's Press ✖ New York

Library of Congress Cataloging-in-Publication Data

Millar, Ingrid.
    Liam Neeson : the first biography / by Ingrid Millar.
        p.   cm.
    ISBN 0-312-14002-9
    1. Neeson, Liam.   2. Actors—Ireland—Biography.   I. Title.
PN2601.N46M56   1996
791.43′028′092—dc20
    [B]   95-36226
                                                           CIP

First published in Great Britain by Hodder & Stoughton

First U.S. Edition: January 1996
10   9   8   7   6   5   4   3   2   1

Contents

For Roar and Lion. Semper fidelis.

Glamis thou art, and Cawdor, and shalt be
What thou art promis'd: yet do I fear thy nature:
It is too full of the milk of human kindness
To catch the nearest way: thou wouldst be great,
Art not without ambition; but without
The illness should attend it; What thou wouldst highly,
That thou wouldst holily; wouldst not play false,
And yet wouldst wrongly win.

William Shakespeare, Macbeth, Act I, Scene 5

Author's Preface

I am indebted to the many friends, neighbours, colleagues, relatives and acquaintances who talked to me and confided their memories and reminiscences about Liam Neeson. Some did not want to be named, virtually all wanted no thanks for their unstinting generosity and hugeness of spirit. They are, mostly, Irish. There can be no greater commendation than to go there and see for yourself what unfailing hospitality they offer. If there are those who have overlapped, and those whom I have not been able to get back to and thank again, then I take this opportunity to do so.

Thanks go to . . .

In Ireland, north and south: Alannah Boyle, Maureen Caves, everyone at the All Saints, Martin Delargey, Frank and Julie Egan, everyone at the Cushendall Golf Club but especially Mary Dunlop and Gerry, Sean Harvey, Tony McAvoy, Pat McCambridge, Charlie McCurry; in Cushendun, Randall McDonnell and Theresa McKeegan; Gerry McKeown, Duncan McKinnon, Oliver McMullen, John McNeilly, Tommy McReynolds Jnr, Pat McRory, Mary Mulholland, Joe O'Neill, Maurice O'Neill, Des Rafferty, Malachy Skelton, the staff at the Leighinmoor and the Adair Arms Hotel.

In England and Scotland: Duncan and Miki, Josephine Fairley, Chris Moore, Philippa Kennedy, Richard Barber, Quinn Donahue, Alison MacDonald, George Lucas, Annabel Ossel, Stuart White, Mansor, Ian and Chris at the wonderful Media Aspects, and especially Judy Chilcote, Jane Adams and Kay Goddard. Nil desperandum!

Liam Neeson

In the USA: Gabrielle Donnelly, Owen Bjornstad, CG in New York (simply the best), Niki in Beverly Hills, the Reerstadts in Venice Beach, Adam Pensotti.

And last but not least to my children, for putting up with this Irishman, lovable thought he might be, in their home and their lives for so long.

Thanks and love to you all.

Prologue

Women adore Liam Neeson. All women, all ages, shapes and sizes. Whatever their taste, Liam Neeson fits the bill.

He is the Holy Grail of all that's desirable in a man – where the physical meets the emotional in perfect harmony. Rugged good looks, immense physique, all his own hair and teeth, just the right crinkles round the eyes . . . all that, married to an inner core of apparent spiritual depth, sensitivity, awareness. And the lot topped off with the gloss of charm and good manners. Add to that potent mix success, power, money, glamour and status in the most glittering of all professions – the film industry, and you have a Colossus at whose feet women feel bound to fall (so he will sweep us up, as if we were feather-light and fragile. Yes, even those of us who will never see the needle dip under ten stone again).

He is six feet four inches, a former boxer from a solid working-class Irish background, who is yet prone to losing himself in lyrical books, the music of Van Morrison and lonesome strolls through the glorious hills of County Antrim.

Liam Neeson is the epitome of woman's fantasy, a legendary Goliath whose sum of parts is actually greater than the whole. He fuels gossip of the kind which women adore. We can closet ourselves away, compare notes and share dreams of this giant among men. Discuss in depth his one-time womanising track record, criticise his past aberrant (of course) choice of glossy, glitzy women, thrill to the stories of his legendary lovemaking and speculate on the supposed enormity of his credentials. Oh all right, as we're among girls – his wedding tackle. And just because he's married now, it doesn't stop us speculating . . .

But behind the fantasy, there hides another Liam Neeson. A loner and an outsider, a boy who might have been a loser all his life, a man they said was too 'nice' to succeed at anything other than, well . . . simply being nice. A failed student turned fork-lift truck driver whose only outlet for the passion that burned within was an amateur dramatic society in a small town with mean streets and a citizenship with a reputation for being even meaner.

Liam Neeson could have been stuck there. But he made his escape, one calculated move at a time, to a place of glory, to megastardom, with a matching astronomic bank balance.

So how did a dreamer and a drifter scale those giddy heights? This book charts the exceptional path of an exceptional man.

1

The Childhood Shows The Man*

'I like to kid my mother, I think I'm a strain. My mother's family were originally from Waterford, which was a town forced and fashioned by the Vikings; that's where they landed.

'I'm convinced there was rape and pillage in our family way back then because they're all built the same, these wee Irish folk and then suddenly I come along, six feet four inches and built like a block of flats.

'There's a gene strain that repeats itself every two hundred years – that's me. So in all the family pictures, people are looking at this line-up and saying, "Who's Liam? That's him there? And who was your milkman way back then?"

'I was always different.'

Funny thing, ambition. But Liam Neeson was born with it coursing through his veins. Ever since he bounced into the world on 7 June 1950, he was marked out to be special. To his parents, Barney and Catherine 'Kitty' Neeson, this child was indeed a gift from God, their third child but their first and only son.

Kitty, as she held him, fed him, bonded with him, knew her son was different, special. She had secretly longed for a boy, now here he was, ten tiny fingers, ten tiny toes, perfect in every way, to join his two big sisters. But he would always have a special place in her heart. There is no love in life like a mother's love for her son.

*The Childhood shows the man,
As morning shows the day. Be famous then
By wisdom; as thy empire must extend,
So let extend thy mind o'er all the world.
John Milton, *Paradise Regained*, Book 4

For Barney, the gift of a boy was a bonus; here at last was the keeper of the flame, the son and heir who alone would carry the family name. He had his dreams and ambitions for his son, the aims he had never been able to achieve himself, but even in his wildest fantasies, he could never have anticipated just how far and wide this infant boy would see his name travel.

He was, if you believe in astrology, a typical Gemini, from the start, warm and sweet. A lovely, happy baby, a charming, biddable child, he crept up on you, touched you, left his indelible impression on your soul.

As they watched him grow, the family noticed Liam was a loner, but he was happy with that. Solid, dependable, he did not take kindly to sudden changes. He liked to do things his way, and in his own time. You could never shove him around. He was determined to hold his own ground. If the other kids did not take too kindly to that, then it was all right by him. He found his own space and he stayed within it, preferring not to mix and mingle and indulge in the rough and tumble of the other kids' games. He knew who he was, and what he was, right from the start. Above all, he was a dreamer.

Where did he come from? Little Ballymena (population 30,000) a predominantly Protestant town in Northern Ireland, produced only one other famous son: the Reverend Ian Paisley. They don't come much more Protestant than that.

Ballymena is indistinguishable from a thousand other provincial, parochial, inward-looking little towns. Blighted by sudden and unlovely expansion in the industrial nineteenth century, there is little in the way of cultural heritage or beauty to commend it, save the enchanting hills of Antrim in which it nestles. Its focal point is the Tower Centre, a small, centrally situated concrete shopping mall. There is no museum, art gallery or theatre, and anyone wishing to put on local entertainment must first persuade the councillors that they will generate enough revenue to warrant freeing up the Town Hall for a night or two. There is one tiny, antedeluvian cinema, the State, and this was where young Liam Neeson would retreat into his own little world and feed his fertile imagination. Often, he was the only punter in the place. Even now it stands, peeling paint and moth-eaten flock-covered seats, like a living testimony to the fifties. Ballymena, the town, feels as if it's stuck in a timewarp.

The Neeson family were well known around Ballymena, even though they liked to keep themselves to themselves. Being Roman

Catholics in a town that declared itself to be staunchly Orange meant they did not care to make their presence felt too much. The Catholics here, in the minority, formed a close-knit community, turning to each other and their Church in times of trouble.

The Neesons did not court trouble, nor did any come their way. They were, above all, eminently respectable, solid and working class. His father, a school caretaker and later a 'lollipop' man, his mother, a school cook, were a complimentary couple: he, self-effacing and not given to gab a lot; she, warm and strong, the canny Irishwoman with a love of life and family. In true Catholic tradition, they had produced four children in six years. Two girls in quick succession, Elizabeth and Bernadette, two years later a boy William John and finally, their baby, Rosaleen.

William John, the only boy, became Liam for short, abbreviated because his sisters could not get their toddler tongues around William – and also in respect of a dearly loved friend of the family, the local priest.

So there were six of them, all crammed into a tiny terraced home in Corlea Gardens, on the Demesne council estate, round the corner from the sprawling St Patrick's army barracks and just up the road from the town centre.

Here, in their spotless, net-curtained home, Kitty was in charge, running the household with rules and restraint. You needed routine and discipline with four weans in a house not much bigger than a box. She identifies herself, even today as 'a Ballymena woman'. And, you should know, Ballymena women do not 'blow' – especially not about their children. Praise is hard won round these parts. You are expected to work diligently, do your best, behave impeccably and respect your elders. In fact, show some respect for everyone.

It is a repressed and repressive community where the women are fastidious and the men are down the pub. Union Jacks fly proudly from flagpoles in the garden or strapped precariously to windowsills at a dodgy angle. This is a Protestant town and proud of it.

The Catholics quietly go their own way and, above all, have to appear law-abiding and conscientious. The Neesons were nothing if not that, crammed into their three-bedroom home, Barney and Kitty in one room, the three girls in another and wee Liam – who would still be cramming his six-foot-four frame in there at the age of twenty-one – in the little box bedroom. He never did leave home until he left his home town.

Barney was a dreamer too, gentle, quiet, abstemious. His own father had run a pub and as a consequence, watching the hardened boozers pour their every last penny down the drain, had renounced alcohol himself. Kitty, a teetotaller, also frowned on those who let the devil drink take hold of their lives. 'Ours,' says Bernadette, now in her mid forties, a teacher in Worthing on the English south coast, married to a headmaster and herself a mother of six who understands the need for discipline in the home, 'was a temperate household.'

Young Liam grew up to witness his father's only indulgence: poker, a once-weekly treat played not in a gambling den, but against parish priests in a local church hall. Members of the Church or not, they still managed to deprive him of the odd fiver most weeks. And Kitty would be upset over that. Barney would come home in the wee small hours, having lost the spare housekeeping that should have been put to one side. He would shrug. What was the matter, saving for a rainy day? It was always raining in Ireland.

Sure, thought wee Liam, lying in his bed at night, listening to the whispered debate through the partition walls, and it's harmless enough.

His Auntie Mollie McKeever he loved especially. She had a soft spot for this wee boy, so much quieter than the others, an intense child, very deep. 'He always liked to keep himself to himself,' she notes. 'But he was always so willing to please. You never saw a child who was so helpful and conscientious.'

A special little boy, wee Liam. But when he wanted something, right from when he was a toddler, he aimed for it – and he always got what he was reaching for. He wasn't one to be put off. She recalls: 'He always knew exactly what he was after and he made up his mind to have it. Whatever he started, he gave it everything he'd got. But he would never have walked over anyone to get it. He was considerate of others, always.'

Elizabeth, the eldest sister, watching, wary, observed how her brother was left out to some extent by the throng of strong, garrulous women around. Sure, and who wouldn't be quiet when you had to yell to be heard above a battalion of women? Liam was inevitably shy, sometimes painfully so. His only role model, his father, was silent and, within the home, acceded to the women who outnumbered him.

Elizabeth, now in her mid forties, married to a dentist with two teenage children, Rory and Julie, lives in the little coastal village of Cushendall. Just a few miles up the road from Ballymena, it could yet be a million miles away. Friendly, peaceful, quaint, with low-beamed pubs like Johnny Joe's dating back 300 years, it is here Neeson returns when he comes home, to take in a few pints with friends and family at the Golf Club. Here, Elizabeth remembers how being brought up with so many women affected her baby brother. 'It wasn't a typical family, one boy and all these females around. I think Liam truly was a bit intimidated by it. Especially when all our girlfriends came round, he would take off for his room and you wouldn't see him till there was some peace in the house again.'

If it was difficult for one boy to fit easily into that sort of environment, as with every downside, there was a corresponding advantage. What a training ground, a precedent for understanding just how women's minds worked.

Liam was there, a prisoner of his circumstances, trapped by it yet thriving on it, growing through it. While his father, should he choose to do so, could exercise his authority, invoke his male stance, Liam could sit back and soak it all up. Barney elected at odd moments to make his escape from all this bantering madness. He would quietly exit, take off for his flutter and the sanguine, peaceable company of priests.

The family was close-knit and God-fearing. Kitty, in particular, was apt to worry about her only son. It's a habit she has never lost to this day. 'I still fret about Liam. Tell me, what mother doesn't worry about her children? You bring them into the world, you want the best for them and you worry about them. It's human nature. He's whatever he is, but he's still my son.'

In the way of the fifties, the Neesons were typical parents. They fussed and they fretted, they ploughed their lives into the family and willed them to do well. The war had taken so much from them, their chance of continued schooling, a white-collar career for Barney perhaps, a bettering of themselves, but God be blessed, they had a roof over their heads, a home and their health. For that alone, they should be grateful. But the children, well, *they* could truly achieve, given the right grounding, the correct code of conduct. And, above all, an education.

It would be a long time hence before psychologists would begin to argue that the whole point of raising children is a process of building them up and letting them go to find their own strengths and live their own lives. In the fifties families came first. And among the Neesons, the ties that bind were more like steel hawsers.

Liam would grow, then, brought up to believe you never turned away from those who loved you and raised you. You paid them your dues and in return they stayed constant, adoring, a retreat without change in an ever-changing world. That, for him, was home. His family did not change, and Ballymena does not change. It is still much as it was in 1952.

Kitty was protective and her biggest worry was that Liam studied too much. He was a model child, well mannered, polite and beholden to authority, to parents, to neighbours and even to friends. So his sisters, confident in their united front, would fight his battles for him.

Of his own volition, he would have preferred to be on his own in the peaceful sanctuary of his bedroom, his head in the clouds. Or sitting in front of that miracle invention, the television, which was only now, in the fifties, beginning to creep into people's homes.

Kitty keenly restricted time spent in front of the television in her home. There was *Children's Hour*, there was *Dixon of Dock Green*, but there was much more besides that she denounced as quite unsuitable for family viewing. Liam, entranced by the grainy black and white scenes that flickered from the box in the corner of the living room, found an outlet for his fertile imagination.

As soon as he was old enough, he relentlessly pestered his mother into letting him go to the cinema. Saturday mornings, regular as clockwork, he took himself down to the State and lost himself in the world of film fantasy. He was safe there, and Kitty approved. Soon he was addicted, spending all his pocket money on cinema tickets, and doing odd jobs for spare pennies to finance his habit.

'When I was a kid watching matinees,' he recalled thirty years later, 'I was just so into it. Maybe it was just pure good luck that I found what I wanted to do and found myself in it and eventually ended up here. But there's times when I feel I almost willed my career into existence, way back then in the State cinema. They had a double bill and they changed it every two days. You could see fourteen films a week, which I often did.

'I was usually the only one in the place, and I'd be taking in a Sergio Leone western along with *Women in Love*. It was quite an education for a boy like me.'

But all good things must come to an end, and the State cinema realised it was not likely to stay a viable concern when its income relied largely on Liam Neeson's pocket money. 'Eventually, at some point in my teens they began showing porn because they figured that's where the money was. I went a few times but I'd got friendly with all the people working there and it got too embarrassing to go in and watch *Lust in the Dust* or whatever. So I'd go home and read instead. I was dead boring as a child. Really, dead boring.'

They do not remember Liam Neeson like that round these parts now. He is fêted and toasted as one of their own, one who made good and got away, but whose heart still lies at home. With his elevation to star status, the memories have become tinged with a rosy glow. They will raise their glasses to him in all the pubs, and as one toast follows another, they become even more fulsome in their praise of the Ballymena Boy. And the conversations will turn, with typical Irish sway, to how much their town and yes, they themselves, had to do with his ascent to greatness . . .

In the bar of the Leighnmoor Hotel, now owned by one of his oldest friends, Pat Falls, when the subject of Liam Neeson is considered the conversation flows like the Devil's Buttermilk, as Guinness is known.

The editor of the local *Ballymena Guardian* newspaper, and a long-time friend of the Neeson family, Maurice O'Neill, has tipped me off that Liam is wont to stroll into the Leighnmoor unannounced on his visits home. Why, just last summer, says Maurice, he walked in while all the regulars were watching the World Cup on the pub telly and said the drinks were on him. It was his stag night. So protective are the locals of their Liam that no one breathed a word of what would undoubtedly have been a great scoop story.

They will wax lyrical on him till the Erne runs dry but they will never, *ever* let you in on his secrets. Theirs is a close community, with a shared history, and now the shared glory of a famous son of their own.

'Sure, you can't imagine our Liam being cruel to or about anybody. He was the epitome of decency, a nice boy from a respectable family. He was always very courteous, too, exceptionally well mannered. "Well reared" as we say around here,' offers one local.

'Aye, we were lucky then, having a good community round us. Liam benefited from that,' vouches another.

And someone else, more expansive: 'Society has changed in the last thirty years, you see, and all the worse for it. Neighbourhoods have become suburbs and the town centres have been turned over to business and most of it lying empty and boarded up, it's diabolical. But in those days, people lived in the streets of the town, around the centre, and everyone knew everyone else. Liam was of that generation.'

Ah, the good old days, they muse, when, 'We had friendship on our doorstep, and decency. Doors were left unlocked and neighbours could walk in and out of each other's homes. There was a code of neighbourliness and good behaviour. When you're raised with that, you don't forget it. It becomes part of the fabric of your nature.' As one, they're agreed: 'Liam had all that, and he still does.'

In those glory days, they say, 'If you ever cheeked someone in the street, your mother would have clashed your ears for you. There was discipline. You learned how to behave and you stuck to it. Liam has just brought that discipline to his craft and found a world where he's exceptional, because for sure few people in the film industry were raised with that kind of basic decency towards your fellow man. Or the ability to adhere to rules, rules you set yourself.'

Round here, it is clear, Liam Neeson is testimony to all that is good and right and just, all that can rise glorious and exultant from this drab little town. It might be unprepossessing, but Ballymena has its priorities right, and its heart in the right place. Family comes first, and they all look after their own.

'No matter how far away he was, nor what different a world he moved in, he was always surrounded by his family. He took them along, in a way of speaking. They were *that* close, the Neesons. He might be thousands of miles away, but they've always been with him.'

Aye, they are agreed, 'Even now, you'll catch Kitty in the street and she'll tell you, if she's pressed, because she never likes to blow, about our Liam. He's never really left here. It was always, still is always, *our* Liam.

'And he did stand out, even as a boy. The others were all kidding around in little gangs but Liam stood apart. He was never one of the crowd. He was a loner, on his own, sort of contained within himself. Of course, his mother is like that. She's quiet, too.'

In this closed-in community, they do not welcome outsiders, do not trust you not to condemn them for having lived their narrow lives. But they will happily let you know what you are missing if you have not lived the small-town life. It might be narrow, but it is full – and full with the things that matter.

'The thing about Liam, you see, is that he was always happy, he was never a boy in torment. There was always a big, open, happy grin on him, it fair bowled you over. Everybody fell for it. And when Liam smiled, his eyes lit up.

'You'll often hear people round here saying, "Oh yes, so and so is very nice . . ." and they don't mean it, not at all, but they'll say it because that's the sort of place Ballymena is. You wouldn't want people thinking you had a bad word to say about others. The truth can be awful hard to come by in a place like this. But, in Liam's case, it was the God's honest truth. He really, truly was the loveliest lad.'

And why should they not be fans? There is little else round here for Ballymenians to lay claim to as something to be proud of. And if it wasn't that the days of knocking on your neighbour's door and just walking in were long gone, they might be forming a steady stream of visitors to Kitty's home these days.

Because there, in pride of place in her living room, in this smart, spanking new apartment which Liam has bought her, is testimony to how far her son's talents have taken him. Framed on the wall is the following letter:

> *I deeply regret that we didn't have a chance to meet when you were here [in Washington DC] recently.*
>
> *Your portrayal of Oskar Schindler is brilliant and I hope I will soon have an opportunity to tell you personally how much I admire your work.*
>
> *Best wishes for a wonderful holiday season.*
>
> *Sincerely,*
>
> *Bill Clinton*

Even Liam Neeson, lost in his world of childhood dreams, could not have foreseen that one coming.

2

Boxing Clever

'I was a boxer for nearly ten years, from the age of nine right up to seventeen, but truly, I didn't have the killer instinct.

'They said I was good but before every tournament I was the same, shit-scared. I'd be thinking, What am I doing here? Why am I doing all this? Who's it for?'

From the age of nine, Neeson started to box under the expert eye of Father Alec Darragh. The priest, a long-time family friend, had often sat up into the early hours playing cards with Barney, the pair of them setting the world to rights.

In the intimacy of their card-playing circle, Barney Neeson broke down the barriers he normally put up when it came to baring his soul. Reticent by nature, trading confidences was not his style. You saved that for the confessional. Much more to Barney Neeson's taste was the 'Get On With It' philosophy. You're not much of a man if you go mithering about your troubles. That was women's stuff. But here, in their card den, he felt he could confide in the priest about a matter that had been worrying him.

Barney Neeson was concerned for his only son. A gangling, shy lad, he was a natural loner, preferring to spend his time holed up in his room doing who knew what, or whiling away lonely afternoons with flights into film fantasy at the State cinema.

Barney knew that Liam wore the badge of the outsider. He was at a disadvantage anyway, being a Catholic in this tight-knit community of staunch Protestants. You had to work hard at fitting in here, keep your nose clean, be a good neighbour. By doing just that, Liam had singled himself out from the crowd. Fine to be an upstanding citizen when you're grown up and just looking for a quiet life.

But tricky when you're adolescent and your peer group look for anything to hold against you, pick on you for. Children, too, can be cruel to those who don't fit in.

His character, even more than his religion, set Liam apart from his peers. Aimless, jobless teenagers with too much time on their hands and too little money in their pockets were no different in Ballymena to anywhere else. Fired up with a few pints and a burning resentment that they had no work and no future, they targeted those who did not fit in with their malaise.

At nine, ten, eleven, he would soon be open to influence from all sides. Boys in their teens, Barney knew, often rejected their families, favouring a rebellion from discipline. He was sure this would not happen to Liam. He would make sure this did not happen to Liam.

Father Darragh had the answer. What the lad needed was a bit of direction and some self-defence technique. At the All Saints youth club, where he presided over the social and sporting activities, they ran boxing classes. Liam was a tall lad, but skinny and all arms and legs. Boxing would put a bit of muscle on him, give him the confidence to know he could stand up for himself.

What neither of them, discussing this solution in the early hours over a deck of cards, could have foreseen, was that lanky Liam would turn out to be a natural.

When he put on his gloves for the first time and stepped inside the ring to try out trading a few punches with the other boys, Father Darragh noticed a change in the skinny lad. He seemed to grow bigger behind those gloves. Pitched against boys his own age, Liam was taller, sharper and faster, with a stunning reach and a swift, powerful left-hand jab that always met its mark. Liam Neeson had found a place where he belonged – inside the boxing ring. If Father Darragh was not mistaken, young Liam had the makings of a very good boxer indeed.

And he was keen. Punctilious, well disciplined and ever ready to please, Liam Neeson was a guaranteed turn-out, never missing a training session. Every week, come rain or shine, he'd be at the All Saints, eager as ninepence, bang on time – even coming in early sometimes to get in a few extra hours of practice, to give him the edge on the competition. Soon, he had outclassed all the Ballymena boys at the All Saints. He was ready to be pitched at other opponents from other youth clubs. As he started boxing competitively, he grew in confidence. He was rarely beaten, never outclassed. He had, in fact, Father Darragh reported back to a pleased-as-punch Barney Neeson, the makings of a champion.

Pat McRory, president of the Ulster Amateur Boxing Association was soon alerted to this towering young blood who was catching the eye of boxing talent scouts.

'I remember him at first as a really shy lad, and I thought, that's good, that's the first step. A lot of boxers are shy when they first come into the game, but it gives you confidence in yourself.

'You could actually see this happening to Liam. You could chart his progress as he moved up through the ranks. He was painfully shy to begin with, but as he began to build up and to win, he came out of himself.

'We all knew it was his dad who pushed him into it in the beginning. Barney had felt it would help make a man of him. I always had the feeling that Liam was a reluctant recruit, certainly to begin with. He'd only got into it at first to keep his father happy. He wasn't one to say no to his da but then once he discovered he was winning, he got a taste for it.

'I'm convinced it gave him enough belief in himself to go on in life and treat it as a game of boxing: think about your strategy, focus on it with all you've got, bide your time, watch for an opening, make the right move at the exact right split second.

'When lads start boxing young like he did, you see their character being formed. They know where they're heading in life. Liam never would have got there if it hadn't been for boxing. Definitely not. He was a dreamer, he needed channelling, otherwise he might have just drifted all his life. There are a lot of guys like Liam who come into the game, because they're the sort of guys who always got picked on, bullied. Liam was one of them.'

The irony was, shy boys like Liam made the best boxers. You'd get the bullies coming into the game and all they wanted to do was hit people, but the timorous ones were going to get a bit of confidence in themselves. And they were dedicated. They'd nothing much else outside of boxing, they weren't hanging around on street corners, going to clubs, chasing skirts.

McRory concurs: 'Liam wasn't a one for the girls either, not at all. When the other lads were getting distracted by the pleasures of the flesh – that's when a lot of the promising ones fall by the wayside! – Liam was up at the All Saints, getting his hours in with the training.

'That was when I knew for sure he was going to make it. He was one of those one-track-minded guys. They've only got one thing in their lives – that's boxing – and they give it all they've got.'

Being a bit of a dreamer helped Liam too. He'd seen all the films about boxers. He fancied himself as a bit of a Rocky Marciano. Okay, so it was only a dream. But if you don't have a dream you might as well be dead. Liam had that and more; he had determination like they'd never seen.

For two hours at a stretch, four nights a week – and more at weekends – he would push himself to the limit in training. One of his many sparring partners was Tony McAvoy who recalls: 'Liam was different to the rest of us. His dream was to be a champ, nothing less. He lived for his boxing. It wasn't just in the ring or in the gym. At home, his bedroom walls were covered with posters of his heroes, Jack Dempsey, Joe Lewis, Sugar Ray Robinson. Liam could have been a great all-round athlete. He played hurling for the school. But boxing took him over. And he got very, very ambitious.'

Lots of shy boys are dreamers and go nowhere. The dream soon got knocked out of you unless you were good. And Liam was. Anyone could see that. Before long, he was boxing under the eagle eye of the much respected Northern Irish coach, Willie Agnew.

'Willie was a hard taskmaster,' remembers McRory, 'but Liam was a willing learner. He was avid for coaching. You'd see some of the boys buckle when they got a tearing-off, and you knew they didn't have the guts to make it. Some of the others would get the glint of steely determination in their eyes and you knew they were thinking, F. . . you, don't talk to me like that. And they would get reckless and not control their anger. And they wouldn't make the grade either.

'But Liam had what it took. He had motivation and patience and determination, in all the right proportions. He wanted to be the best he could possibly be. So if he got yelled at, he took it in his stride.'

His was absolutely the right temperament for it. You couldn't be arrogant or a bullshitter if you wanted to box well. Boxing makes you modest because you always know there's someone better than you. So you've got to push on, push yourself to the limit – and then beyond.

Tony McAvoy agrees: 'You've got to keep on trying to be better and better. You know you'll probably never be *the* best – and you respect people for their skills, but you keep on trying, keep on punching away until you get the very best you can be.'

That was how Liam was. They could all see it in him, driving him on. He wanted to fulfil his potential. He didn't want to kill people, he knew that wasn't what boxing was about. He didn't want to be champion of the whole world, he wasn't a megalomaniac. If he wanted to be a champion, it was to be the best, to satisfy himself.

So Liam adapted to the strict training regime that saw plenty of other potential boxers fall by the wayside. He didn't neglect his schoolwork, but he had always had plenty of time on his hands. Now he filled it with boxing. When he wasn't in the ring, he was thinking about it. Liam had always been a deep thinker; now he applied those thought processes to the sport that consumed him. When you're a boxer, you examine things very closely: why you lose and why you win, how this move gained you points and that move gave your game away. You take your game to pieces and see where you can improve all the time.

The pace was relentless, the pressure immense. Most of his teenage boxing mates slipped away one by one but Willie Agnew and Pat McRory stood by and cheered as Liam powered his way on, despite the bouts that left him sometimes bloodied, once with a broken nose, but never bowed nor cowed into submission.

'Being a boxer is a tough life, mentally and emotionally as well as physically,' says McRory. 'When you're beaten, you suffer psychologically as well as taking blows to your body. The discipline and training are so rigorous, you've got to put heart, body and soul into it. And your mind must be alert at all times, before, during and after a game, to see where you went right and where you went wrong.

'And of course, you're performing in front of a lot of people who are watching your every move and one minute they're criticising you, the next they're praising you. There's not many people are cut out to take that pressure. But it got Liam young and once you've taken that kind of pressure on board, you're equipped for anything life has to throw at you.

'It affects your whole outlook and your standing for ever. You roll with the punches when the going gets tough and at the same time, you know how to apply yourself and go for the ultimate goals.

'By the same token, you've also appreciated what's really hard in life. You've taken lots of knocks – not just physical ones, and it affects your sense of values. You learn about humility.

'Liam was a sound lad, he'd been brought up to show respect for his elders and his betters. Boxing honed that up. He learned to take his wins and not get big-headed about them. He'd had it drummed into him in his upbringing that there but for the grace of God, a decision might have gone against him and he could have lost.

'Boxing gave proof to that credo. So he learned how to take disappointments in his stride too.'

If McRory is right, these were truly the formative years when Liam learned the art of competition and of focusing single-mindedly on victory. Boxing is not just about playing the game, it's about winning. If you didn't have 'Play To Win Or Don't Play At All' engraved on your brain in boxing then forget it, you might as well be playing dominoes. It's not about taking part just for the sake of taking part.

As those around him witnessed, young Liam's concentrated boxing experiences throughout his teen years did indeed shape him as a young man. Embracing the paradox of a love of performing and the attendant adulation that went with it when you performed well, along with the art of humility, would form the touchstone of his developing personality. To be the best and still remember where you came from. To pitch yourself for the top, the prizes and plaudits, but never to forget what you learned along the way. And above all, the art of timing. Sidestep at the wrong moment and an unlucky blow could fell you for good. But equally, the right hit at precisely the right moment could win you the game.

It was all down to timing. Thinking it through and striking when the iron was hot. It was an art that he had learned through boxing, and which he would adopt as his philosophy in life. It would stand him in great stead.

There was another bonus in boxing that young Liam had not bargained for. What he had always seen as a lonely preoccupation in his childhood years now became a huge advantage. His predilection for distancing himself from the crowd, for pursuing his own individual path now came hugely into play.

Reveals McRory: 'When you channel your energies into something as physical as boxing, it's vital to know how to switch off and stand back. It's simply not a sport where you go in with all guns blazing. Liam always had a bit of coolness, of distance, of keeping himself to himself. Boxing brought that out even more. It's just you up there in the ring. You stand or fall by your own doing. It suits you to be a loner, like Liam.

'You're on your own. It's all resting on you. That's a heck of a responsibility and a weight on your shoulders. The pressure is immense – and solitary. In a team game you can play the best game of your life and still be on the losing side. Or you can play the worst game and still pick up the points.

'That's about as lonely as it gets. But of course, the pay-offs are out of this world. When you win, you've done it all on your own. Yours is the power and the glory. Yours alone. You stand there and you punch the air in victory and you're physically and mentally completely drained, but you did it. You won. The opposition's wiped out, the other guy's on the canvas. There's no feeling like it.'

Liam mostly stood victorious. Few opponents could fell him. Then he stood back, surveyed his progress, saw how he could better himself and pursued his ideal of attaining perfection.

The results were encouraging. As he grew and built muscle, he became a conquering Colossus. Still not quite hitting his optimum height of six feet four inches, at fourteen he had topped six feet and, weighing in at around eleven stone, he powered his way to becoming Ulster youth heavyweight champion for three successive years.

McRory, by then Secretary of the Ulster Amateur Boxing Association, had high hopes for this giant among lesser men, as did his colleagues. At the Amateur Boxing Association they were all of the firm opinion that Liam Neeson could certainly represent Northern Ireland in the Commonwealth Games – and probably even Ireland in the Olympics. He was that good.

'Throughout the game he'd got a name for himself as a big upright strong boxer with a good left hand. He could have done the business. We were all rooting for him. He had a lot of local support and a good reputation as a clean boxer with a good technique. Particularly at that time, when he outclassed all the competition, he could have ended up a professional boxer. It was as simple as that. He'd already put in the youth training and had a lot of experience and a lot of wins behind him. There was no doubt among us that Liam could have gone the distance, brought home Gold for Ireland and made a name for himself in the world – and not just the boxing world.'

But it wasn't going to happen. At least not in the boxing world. Liam Neeson was covering something else behind his gloves. Inwardly, he knew he had come to the end of the road. He had gone into this sport for his father, now he did not know how to get out. But he knew he wanted out, for sure. And the moment he knew it was after one vicious match when he stepped down from the ring, victorious but exhausted and, he remembers, 'My father handed me a towel and said, "Go and get changed." And I didn't know what he meant. My brain just went. It was very, very scary. It lasted for about two minutes, this complete blank and I thought, Fuck, if this is happening to me now . . .

'I didn't talk about it, I just thought to myself, That's it. Get out of it now.'

From that moment on, it took just one defeat to provide the excuse he needed to spit out his gumshield and the boxing game for ever.

McRory was among the ringside audience at that fateful match. 'It was the finals of the All Irish Championship, at the National Stadium in Dublin. It had been a long haul for Liam to reach it; he'd won the contest all the way from Ballymena to Dublin – by a very narrow margin, but he was still on good fighting form.

'He wanted that title real bad – we all did, because if he won, then the All Saints would have scooped the Lombard Murray trophy for best club too, thanks largely to his performance.

'But in the end, that was what got in his way. Because of the politics in the sport at that time, there were some judges who perhaps favoured one club above the others. I'm not pointing fingers but that club wasn't All Saints. It was our belief that a political decision could prevent the cup from going to the All Saints – which it would have done, had Liam won.

'He went into that fight and gave it all he'd got, as he always did. There was no knockout, it went to a points decision – and the judges awarded against Liam. He was totally gutted. I've never seen a man look that sick when they made the announcement. He picked up his towel and walked out of the ring. I put my hand on his shoulder and said "It wasn't down to you, son. You were robbed by that decision."

'But he was inconsolable. He looked me in the eye and said, "I'll never box again." And he didn't.'

Plenty of boxers react as vehemently after they've had a decision go against them. It wasn't always fair play in those days. But they usually pick themselves up, put a bad decision behind them and carry on, more determined than ever. Not Neeson.

'With Liam, you knew he always meant what he said. There was no back-tracking. When he made his mind up, that was it. He hung up his gloves that very day.'

McRory speaks for all his ABA colleagues who shared Liam's disappointment that day, though none of them was privy to the real reasons behind his decision to quit boxing for good. 'It was a shock to us all when he walked away from it, so sudden like that. We had seen such great things mapped out for him. We felt he could have had another go the following year and walked away with the title. But he walked away from the sport instead. It was a real sickener, not just for Liam, but for all of us. We felt we couldn't let it happen again. We'd not just lost Liam's title and the trophies, we'd lost a champion boxer from the sport for ever.

'The following year, we put through a motion to change the rules to avoid political bias. We used Liam Neeson's name and his example to campaign against the current rules of the Boxing Association. It didn't happen overnight, but a few years later, with our campaigning, the rules were changed to set up an unbiased, fair judging system.

'So perhaps Liam's defeat that night wasn't entirely in vain. He did make his mark in boxing history, but sadly not in the way he should have done.'

What was boxing's loss was the theatre's gain. Because, shaken by the realisation of the brutal revenge the sport could wreak on the battered human mind and body, disheartened and disgusted by the corruption he'd encountered, Liam Neeson immediately looked around for another activity to engage him. He needed an outlet that would satisfy his need for performing, something all-consuming, where he could still put down the quiet, self-contained lanky lad from Ballymena and transform himself into a conquering hero.

He found it in amateur dramatics, and Gerry McKeown.

3

The Acting's The Thing

'What was I doing in the sixties? They passed me by. All that free love 'n' stuff? Forget it.

'I was locked away in my bedroom, reading Hamlet, *I swear. Butter wouldn't have melted between my knees . . .'*

Actors were not the kind of people normally produced in a place like Ballymena, lacking in all cultured. As far as the Neeson family were concerned, well, acting was no kind of a job, not a proper job at all. Foppish sort of thing to be, an actor. Barney Neeson had not inveigled young Liam into boxing for him to renounce the toughness of a pugilist for some pursuit of a decidedly cissy nature like acting.

But just as Liam Neeson turned eleven, and made the transition from junior to secondary school, the tide turned. And one man rose to act as King Canute, standing up to be counted, stemming the flow of local ignorance when it came to culture and the arts. Ballymena, he had decided, would have theatre, even if it killed him in the process. As it happened, he would find such a tidal wave of enthusiasm among the small band of troubadours he recruited he would near enough be swept away by it.

A former alumni of Ballymena High School, Gerry McKeown was a man with a passion for literature and the performing arts, a man whose love of poetry and theatre had led him, not into directing plays, which was his heart's desire, but into the more prosaic field of teaching. Ballymenians must first and foremost earn a living. But as a qualified teacher, he believed, he could further his own passion – and even introduce it to his young charges.

In 1963, newly qualified and clutching his teacher's diploma, he took up his first work post as English teacher at St Patrick's High

School. To begin with, he was unsure of himself in this, his first teaching role. But he was sure of one thing. He wanted to introduce the notion of drama to his pupils.

Liam Neeson was among them. McKeown couldn't miss him. He was six inches taller than the rest of the class. And he always sat in the front row – the swot spot, as it was called. 'I can still see him sitting there to this day,' recalls McKeown, 'and although I couldn't recount the names of most of the class, I couldn't help but remember Liam. He was a diligent pupil, always trying to do his best.'

Young Liam, newly started at senior school, thrown into the world of the big boys, had his inherent insecurity reinforced. Everyone treats first years, fresh out of short trousers, still wet behind the ears, with derision.

Barney Neeson, sensing his son's lack of savoir faire, the difficulty he had in joining in, had already plucked him from the ranks of the potential bullying victims, and coaxed, cajoled or coerced him into boxing. Unbeknown to Barney, boxing filled Liam with trepidation, but at this stage he did it out of duty, as he did most things.

But here at school he found something that he enjoyed, something he would enter into entirely of his own volition – and the luck of the timing that had put him together with Gerry McKeown at this seminal point in his life.

The teacher wanted his pupils to act. It was not enough to learn about Irish literature. Read it, digest it parrot-fashion, spit it out on your exam paper and what's the benefit of that? In one ear and out the other. No real appreciation. But if the children were to act it out, put themselves into it rather than stand back and hear the teacher droning on about the merits of Synge and O'Casey and all the time wondering what was on the telly tonight and what would be for tea, then maybe some of them would take it on board as a living, breathing creation of beauty.

Rather than settle down into the humdrum obscurity and safety of a stolid teaching job, McKeown, fired with enthusiasm, was ready to push back the boundaries and the constraints of his position. It was a move guaranteed to get up the noses of old-style teachers who had been sitting, comfortably, boring pupils out of their brains for donkey's years. But it was a gamble he was willing to take.

In his very first, first-year class, he saw the opportunity. Fresh into secondary school, they had not yet been sullied by teachers looking for the easy option and the downhill slide into retirement with as little ruction as possible, if you please.

He scoured this class of innocents for signs of the potential he was looking for. He saw it, even at eleven, in Liam Neeson. 'I gave him the lead role in our very first class drama production, an Irish legend, *The Wooing of Emer*. It was a masterly role,' recalls McKeown. 'I wanted Liam to play the protective father, thwarting the suitors who relentlessly pursued his daughter. It was a very democratic play, everyone in the class got some kind of a part, so no one was left out. Why did I pick him for the lead? He was the obvious choice. He was bigger than the rest by a long shot, you couldn't fail to miss him, and he sat right in front of my nose. But what he also had was an air of someone older than his years, a quiet dignity that set him apart from the other boys.

'It wasn't just during a play he was like that, either. When the bell went and the other boys all ran out and were playing in the yard, Liam was not among them. He didn't join in.

'As a teacher, you soon get to know the gregarious lads. The gangs. Liam was never in them. He was the one wandering off quietly on his own.'

Liam Neeson saw something simpatico in his teacher, too, something that made him respond to McKeown's request to stand up and perform. Normally it was a situation that would have made him go weak at the knees. Drawing attention to himself was totally alien to his reticent nature. His natural instinct had always been to blend into the background. He was seated at the front, purely and simply because he was there to learn, to do what his parents had instilled in him was essential – study, pass the exams and get some qualifications for a decent job.

His father Barney, after all, was a school janitor. It was a job, but not one that commanded respect. It was Barney himself, Barney the man, who had earned the respect and affection of all who crossed his path. But his job rankled him. It was a demeaning position for a man of intelligence. He had determined that his only son would never suffer the same fate. Girls could marry, have babies, keep a nice home; careers were not as important for them. But Liam was earmarked for something special, Liam would achieve the hopes and dreams his father had never been able to realise. Barney Neeson was a dreamer too. Like father, like son. But Liam had also inherited the fierce determination and solid application of his mother Kitty . . .

Thus motivated by his mother's drive, and burdened with his father's unfulfilled ambitions for an education and a safe, respectable white-collar job, Liam undertook, at least, to work hard and be a diligent, exemplary pupil.

By preference, he would rather have been at the back of the class, where he could go unnoticed, unseen, a blurry little grey boy who wouldn't say boo to a goose. But the back rows were the domain of the would-be bad boys, the naughty kids who liked to make their statement: we're at the back because it's all the better to pass notes and flick ink pellets. Not that they'd get away with it, under the sharp eye of Gerry McKeown. Neeson was never cut out to be one of them.

The middle rows were inhabited by the couples, inseparable friends who preferred to sit together. Liam did not fit in there either. So he sat at the front like a good boy, hair neatly combed, uniform immaculate and perfectly pressed by his ma. Being at the front had the added advantage that he could not indulge in his favourite pastime – gazing out the window and dreaming.

What he hadn't figured on was that he was in pole position to be picked for any integrative class activities. He had absolutely no experience of drama or the theatre. The only acting he had ever seen was on the screen – on TV or at the State cinema. Now here he was, to his horror, being plucked by Mr McKeown to act in the very first class production. He couldn't even hide in the chorus line. McKeown wanted him for lead male.

But Liam came to life in the one-act plays that McKeown began to introduce regularly into his English classes. So much so that McKeown felt confident enough finally to cast him as the lead in the big production, the end-of-year class play.

Neeson, nervous enough about being singled out by his classmates for his enthusiastic performances, was at first unnerved. He asked his teacher if he was up to it. McKeown had no doubts. 'He'd been an ideal pupil, right from the start of the year. He was quietly determined to succeed. You always felt that Liam had a fixed point ahead that he was completely focused on. And when he undertook to do something, he was completely committed. He had that rarest of human qualities – you could depend on him. Liam was always there if he was needed. He was never off doing something else, like most boys of his age. Sure, he had his boxing, but there were no gang activities, like you normally find in young lads.

'And he was not an extrovert. They rarely make great actors. You have to be able to reach inside yourself to be a good actor and Liam always had that. You felt he kept most of himself locked away inside. He was quite definitely an introvert, until he stepped on a stage. Then he would lose himself in the character he was playing.

'With some of the other boys, you knew they wanted a big part so they could impress their peers. Liam was never like that. He didn't feel he had to compete, to brag or to show off. Frankly, he didn't seem to care what anyone else thought of him. It was as if there was a kind of *steel* within him.'

In fact, contrary to what McKeown had perceived in Liam, there were other areas where Neeson cared very much what other people thought. In boxing and in the school plays, he had developed an unquenchable thirst for applause. To be respected, fêted and cheered on was a hallowed role he had found himself in. He was very comfortable with that. It made him feel special and it would help goad him on to greater heights, drive him to higher goals.

It earned him the grudging respect of his colleagues, who previously found it so easy to ignore this gangling, soft-spoken outsider. By the same token, it also reinforced his role as just that – the outsider.

McKeown noticed that for all his steel within, paradoxically, Neeson was also incredibly willing to please – particularly those in authority. 'He was always willing endlessly to keep practising until he got it right. He did his homework, neatly and thoroughly. And later, when he started to do scripted drama, he worked tirelessly in his own time, too. That was obvious. Lines were never a problem with Liam. You felt he knew the whole play, line for line. He never missed a cue, never stumbled over his words. He was a workaholic when it came to getting it right.'

McKeown was not sure if talent was bursting out of Neeson at this stage, but the commitment and the desperation to please were. 'Talent? Well, if someone's going to be an outstanding pianist, they have to practise six, seven hours a day. It's the same with all the performing arts. Liam had the drive and the capacity to put in those hours. Most kids of his age didn't. They were too busy enjoying their teen years.

'Let's face it, talent alone doesn't take you to the top. You need constant application too. If I'm honest, I saw others with the latent talent that Liam had – not many, but some – but what set him apart was that, apart from his boxing, he had absolutely no outside interests, no friendships to distract him. There was nothing else alongside.

'It is so rare to come across that exemplary discipline and dedication in a child. You couldn't fault Liam for application. He was always first in the classroom, and bagged the seat right at the front. I can never forget the sight of him, squashed in to a little desk, all six foot of him near enough, his hand always in the air with the answer.'

McKeown felt confident enough in Neeson's consistent and infallible reliability to produce the goods, word perfect, then to cast him as the lead in Synge's *Riders to the Sea*. This would test his mettle. The play was in Irish.

Without a word of native Irish at his disposal, Liam was too embarrassed to confess he hadn't a clue what it was all about. He set about learning it, word for word, syllable for syllable. The memory of it would never leave him. Thirty years later he recalled: 'There was nothing else for it. I had to learn the whole script phonetically. I wasn't too enthusiastic, performing a play in a tongue I had never understood, never mind spoken. But Gerry was not the sort of man who took no for an answer. He coerced us into it.'

But to Liam's amazement, once he stood up there and began to speak in front of the whole school, once he let his fertile imagination embrace the role of the tragic son, his mother's last surviving child who goes in search of his drowned brother and ends up drowned himself, he found himself transported to another place. It wasn't just him, Liam, standing in front of his class and spouting parrot-fashion-learned lines. When he began to talk and move, something came over him. He *was* that son.

It was a revelation, just as much as it had been when he first put on the boxing gloves and found he was, indeed, Rocky Marciano. Now he was . . . well, anybody he wanted to be. The dawn of realisation that he could create his own dream life, in a performance, was a cataclysmic moment for Neeson. From then on, he would volunteer his services for all Gerry McKeown's school plays. He'd caught the acting bug.

McKeown, in turn, was rewarded by his pupil's enthusiasm. In particular, he watched Liam Neeson grow in stature as his first academic year merged into his second, and then his third. Alongside his growing performances in school plays, Liam's confidence was boosted by his boxing prowess as the silver cups and trophies began to line the mantelpiece of his parents' modest home. He was indeed, seeing his mammy and daddy proud.

By the time Liam completed his fourth and final year at St Patrick's, he was set to compete in the All Irish Championship. Reigning youth heavyweight champ of Ireland for this and the two previous years, he had his sights firmly set on winning the title.

Boxing was his main course, and performing in school plays came a long way second. But again, fate intervened when Liam lost the title he had his heart set on. And just at that point, Gerry McKeown decided to branch out from school plays into amateur dramatics proper. Ballymena would have an outlet for the creative talent he had nurtured – and for those locals who had long harboured a burning desire to act. He knew there were some, though none with the drive nor vision enough to launch and sustain a group themselves.

He would step into that breach. 'I guess it had taken me those four years to build up my own confidence in my abilities to produce and direct plays. It's not something you enter into lightly. You can't let people down. If you're not up to it, you can't just launch a venture and leave it hanging there. It was a full-time commitment.

'And by then I felt maybe I had a bit more gravitas as well as confidence. It's one thing getting schoolchildren to follow your directions when you're standing over them, the school figure of authority, but it's something else again, trying that with adults.'

Liam Neeson was not quite one of those adults, not yet. At seventeen he had made the move from St Patrick's to the local Ballymena Technical College, still in pursuit of those elusive academic qualifications that would enable him to pass muster in his parents' eyes.

There would be little time for anything other than study if he was to attain the A-level passes necessary for him to move on to college or university. Neeson was not a natural academic. But he was a slogger, getting consistently fair marks, and never plummetting below the midway line in the class.

No longer did he have the distraction of boxing; he still, shy and incredibly tall, had insufficient confidence to go in pursuit of girls. But an amateur dramatic society, both inspired and led by his former English teacher, gained his folks' approval. Couldn't come to any harm there, could he? Might even help with his English exams.

In fact, Liam had already, thanks partly to Gerry's enthusiastic teaching, and partly to his own propensity to lose himself in works of fiction, developed the habit of avid reading. 'It made me feel ignorant, being surrounded by these people who knew so much about plays and poetry. I wanted to learn, to be as knowledgeable as them.'

He would come to Gerry McKeown's newly established Slemish Players – so named after the local table-top Slemish Mountain – an enthusiastic recruit. 'That's truly where I got hooked,' he would later recall about the fortuitous way he fell into acting as a career, 'And where I got the training.'

As a bonus, it offered him escape from the person he was. As a double bonus, he had begun to grow into a good-looking young man, a force and a commanding presence on stage. Sure, there was the broken nose from his boxing days, but his stature and his soulful blue eyes were beginning to get him noticed by the girls. With his mother's dictum, 'Beauty's only skin deep, Liam, and don't forget that,' ringing in his ears, he took the precaution of adding courtesy, charm and good manners to this potent mix.

The first and last of those qualities were by now inherent in him, drummed in by his parents throughout his childhood and adolescence. The charm was his own invention. Liam was learning that being a great big hulk was fine in the boxing ring, a plus on stage, but in real life could get you marked down as a bruiser. He offset that possibility by developing himself into soft charm personified. Far better to be a gentle giant who wouldn't hurt a fly, than an aggressive bruiser whose presence threatened.

That charm itself would be shaped and altered into something else altogether: ultimately, it would rest this side of charming for the men, but when it was switched on in female company, it came up in a different guise – as unabashed, out-and-out, unrepentant flirting. He would get so good at it, it would become almost second nature. But in the beginning, at its inception, it was, as with everything else Liam Neeson undertook, a strategic game plan. And one that took all who knew him by complete surprise.

Gerry McKeown concurs, in somewhat milder vein: 'Liam was always hard to fathom. You never knew quite what was going on in there. But what I've always found particularly hard to comprehend about him is this purported sexual magnetism that I keep reading about him. You know, he's sitting there in the hotel reception and he lifts a quizzical eyebrow, then from a hundred metres away a waitress picks up the signals of his sexual allure and shoots over to be by his side. Excuse me?

'This is not the Liam Neeson I knew! Nor anyone else around

these parts. I think it's a myth. It's certainly not what he was born with. For donkey's years, Liam Neeson would walk down the High Street in Ballymena and no girl would bat an eyelid at him. He had all the allure of your average lamppost.

'But it's strange what money, success and publicity can do for you. Create a legend and everyone buys it. Wholesale. I think it's kind of sad, that. Either women are being too easily impressed or else Liam has perfected the art of sexual magnetism. In which case, he's a better actor than anyone ever game him credit for!'

Gerry McKeown has no reason for the waspish aside nor the bitter backward glance of a man who might resent what he himself could never achieve. While he doubtless precipitated Liam Neeson on the acting career that would take him to the heady heights of fame and fortune, McKeown himself ultimately opted out of the constrictions of teaching and built up a highly successful and lucrative factory farm business.

Perhaps he is disappointed with his protégé. More likely, he saw it coming all along.

'I was always aware that Liam took his acting very seriously indeed, which was unusual in an adolescent. He always treated it as a business. He knew it wasn't enough just to be oozing talent. You had to make it work for you. You had to concentrate on it, sell it, trade on it, do deals.

'He comes across as terribly laid back, disarmingly charming and easy going, but beneath that cosy exterior is a very astute business brain. After all he comes from Ballymena and Ballymena people are renowned for looking after themselves financially.

'Although Liam found himself drawn to the theatre in a place which did not actively condemn theatre, but certainly saw no point in it – I think he took a bit of that attitude to his acting career.'

Liam Neeson did not see stardom coming. But he wanted it. And what Liam wanted, Liam always made sure he got.

4

Sweet Sixteen And Never Been . . .

'I always got off on confession, up to a point. And that point was masturbation.

'I remember saying to this priest once that I had committed the sin of Onan and oh my God, I'll never forget it, he just tore strips off me.

'He said, "You'll have no confidence by the age of twenty-one! And no willpower!" I just shrivelled right up. I thought, Fuck, I've committed the big one now.

'I walked out from the confessional feeling about so-o big and people were gathered in the aisles for mass that evening. Walking down that aisle, past all these old biddies, it felt like it was six miles long. It was terrifying.

'So I vowed to myself, "That's it. I'm never touching my dick again. Ever."'

The only area in which Liam Neeson was a little lacking these days, was, as locals observe, with the girls. At seventeen, he had not yet developed the sexual allure that would one day be irresistible to women. He was too busy concentrating on the one thing he knew he truly was good at: acting. But he was beginning to try to practise his hand.

Where was it he succeeded in attracting girls' attention? Not walking up the streets of Ballymena, that was for sure. But on stage, in the spotlight, assuming the mantle of some other character, well, that was something else.

His motivation to act was not always altruistic. While at school he had put himself up for a particular part in one school play, not so he could impress his English teacher with his enthusiasm, but so he could get the attention of the leading lady. Years later, he would confess: 'I fancied her like mad. But the only way I could get a look-in was on stage, in a role opposite her.'

Out of character, in his school uniform, trousers flapping an inch above his ankles, shirt sleeves trying desperately to meet his bony wrists, the skinny six-footer knew he was not going to get so much as a backward glance from the gorgeous blonde lead girl.

But on stage, playing alongside her, perhaps she could be persuaded of his burgeoning charm? In this instance, the sexual allure fell short. Neeson got the part, but not the girl.

Throughout his teenage Ballymena years, Liam Neeson was a girl-free zone. Never dreaming that he would one day date some of the most stunning women in the world, he explored his own sexuality alone. But being a good Catholic boy, he would then take his guilt to the priest in the confessional. The resulting scenario was one of many that later led him to question his Roman Catholic faith.

To compensate for his lack of amorous and sexual success, Liam channelled his energies into acting. In 1969, when Gerry McKeown set up the Slemish Players, Liam was an eager recruit. Gerry remembers the pleasure with which he greeted the young tech college student.

'I hadn't really expected Liam to join, I felt he'd be out of my reach having just left school. All the other members were much older, adults in their twenties and thirties. But he was keen to join, despite being the youngest by a long way. He'd always been competent in the school plays, but it was in Slemish that he really came into his own and excelled.'

Other members of the Slemish Players were surprised by this lofty schoolboy who appeared from nowhere to swell their ranks. Alannah Boyle, who had been with the Players since its inception some weeks before, remembers the gauche youngster as he enrolled. 'Everybody round here knew the Neesons – Barney and Kitty, Auntie Peggy, the sisters, but Liam was new to us all. We'd never seen his face before, nor knew anything about him. He must have been in hiding all those years!

'They were a colourful family, the Neesons, but Liam was not like one of them at all.

'Barney's sister was Peggy, who was married to Jack McCann, a great colourful local character – Liam's uncle. He was a solicitor by trade, but he was also a broadcaster and raconteur – the only mark of showbusiness in the family. He founded the John Hewitt

Summer School, in memory of the poet, to keep his words alive and encourage the arts in Ballymena. But as he wasn't a blood relative, you could hardly say Liam inherited a taste for the performing arts through him. In fact, Liam was the least 'act-*ory*' person you'd ever seen.

'To look at him now, Liam Neeson, film star, well, you'd never have guessed he was the same lad we had in Slemish. He's changed so much physically, he's practically unrecognisable.

'In those days, he was always very reserved in his looks. It was the era of long hair, 1970, but Liam was very conservative. His hair was always neat and combed, a regular short back 'n' sides, often with a dab of something like hair gel on it to flatten it. Nobody under ninety-two wore Brylcream in those days, but to look at Liam with his hair slicked back with this gunk, you'd swear that was exactly what he put on it. He was terribly old-fashioned for one so young. Square, was the word you would have used then.

'I think he knew it would upset his mammy and daddy if he'd turned into a hairy type.'

The teenage Liam Neeson was never going to rebel and be a hippy. He was dead straight. Neither his hairstyle nor his clothes style were flattering. They were always untrendy, did nothing for him. He was never one to make much of his appearance. His clothes were safe: jeans and big woolly pullies, the kind of clothes you could hide in, remain anonymous in.

When they noticed him – which was only ever because of his height, not his pronouncements, for Liam Neeson said little that was not required of him – they noticed his clothes always looked like he'd slept in them. And they would wonder, if they could be bothered, whether it was because he could get so little to fit him that he just made do with the few things he had.

He was never grubby, more dishevelled. There was no way he was a snappy dresser or a follower of fashion, which was unusual. Most other lads of his age were into flower-power at that time, listening to acid music, going to parties and smoking dope. Not Liam.

Alannah Boyle observes: 'It was like he was stuck in a bit of a timewarp, rooted somewhere in the fifties, when he was still a wee boy, dressed by his mam. He was that for sure, very unsophisticated, completely unworldly wise, maybe a wee bit of a mammy's boy – but certainly a boy, as opposed to a man, even if he was turning eighteen.

'We used to call him Wee Liam – which was a standing joke, since he towered over the rest of us – because he was so much younger than us, in every way.

'As a woman, you'd look at him and think how, if he'd just smarten himself up, he'd be quite a handsome young lad. But he never made the most of himself. It was like the only time he bloomed was when he was on stage, in someone else's clothes.

'The rest of the time, he would melt away into the background. He never wanted to draw attention to himself. You got the feeling he might have had a wee bit of a complex, with his shyness and his drab appearance. Perhaps it was down to his height. He was certainly a good six inches ahead of the rest of us. And he did sometimes look a bit uncomfortable with that.

'He didn't apologise for his height, but he never used it to full effect. He was not one for the dramatic appearance in ordinary life. He never made a grand entrance, framed in a doorway, so all eyes would rest on him and you'd think, Who's that stunning young man?

'With Liam, it was more like you'd look over your shoulder and suddenly he would be hovering there, apologetically, and you'd think, Where the heck did he spring from?'

The other Players also noticed that Liam was a loner, with few, if any, close friends. Both shy and nervous, certainly for the first few months, he would never join them for a drink in the bar after rehearsals. Then, gradually, they noticed he would slip in quietly, trying not to draw attention to himself, or the fact that he had finally succumbed to the camaraderie. They'd all have had a few drinks by then and Liam would suddenly appear in the background. He would join them, but not join them – not quite, not yet. He was just there, watching, hovering. He'd not participate in the singing, even though there was always a singalong going by that time.

The Irish always sing in bars. Some people talk, some argue, some just sit there and stare into their drink – but the Irish sing. Then, for the Slemish Players in their cups, the favourite songs were those of the sixties – 'Summer time', 'House of the Rising Sun' – the hits of a few years previously, showing their age, of course. It took some time, but gradually Liam came forward and eventually he sang, too.

But there was only one song he sang, and that was a Simon and Garfunkel number: 'The Boxer'.

They watched him come out of his shell gradually, and saw how he yet preferred to sit back and observe. And listen. 'He loved to listen to things like "Me and Bobby McGee" and 'Tubular Bells', all that gentle, non-offensive music – none of the louder, crazier stuff of the time. He fitted in well with us. His taste was conservative, middle of the road. He could have been the same age as us. He was certainly not of his own generation, at least in terms of enjoying the trends of the day.'

So this was the loner who in his own time, and at his own pace, gradually let himself be drawn into the company of the amateur dramatists who were so much older than him. And yet he still stood apart, there but not there.

The same was true of his participation in the actual productions. Liam remained in a world of his own. They never saw him until the split second before he was due on stage. That was all down to Gerry's direction. He believed the minute you left the dressing room, you had to be the character. Liam adhered to that as if it was the word of God written in tablets of stone.

It was a dictat that the fledgling Slemish Player would adhere to ever after, preferring to keep his own company in the theatre before a performance and on a film set through production. Never gregarious at the best of times, he applied this philosophy down to the last letter. It gave him time and space to be on his own, to shut off, shut down and get into role.

His strict behaviour code again singled him out. 'There was sometimes a temptation for the rest of us to have a bit of a laugh while waiting in the wings,' recalls fellow Player Joe O'Neill. 'It was simply release of nervous tension. But you never, ever did it when Gerry was about. For him, the whole process was much more than just going out and saying your lines, acting a part. It was *being* the role, living it.

'And Liam believed that too. You could see it in him as he ascended towards the stage. He was oblivious to anything around him. He couldn't tell you the colours of the walls in the corridor leading to the stage. He was completely wrapped up in his part. More so than any of us.

'Of course, there were times when, especially to outsiders, this looked like Liam, keeping himself to himself, was being stand-offish.

He wasn't. He was simply being dedicated to his art. That's what it was to Liam. Acting, for him, was an art form.'

Alannah Boyle agrees: 'You always got the feeling with Liam that acting was close to Godliness. It transported him to another plane. And of course, it was as hard for him to put down afterwards as it was easy for him to slip into at the start. We'd all head off for the bar immediately after a production, always the same crowd of us. After a while, Liam began to join us, but it was never straight away. It took him some considerable time to come out of character.

'He really was a funny one. He didn't appear to be daunted about joining an adult drama group, and his performances were very confident, powerful. For all he was so quiet and withdrawn, some kind of incredible transformation came over him when he stepped on stage.'

Acting, as all the Slemish Players will tell you, is a very insecure profession, but they watched as Liam came to life when he was acting. 'It was as if all his insecurities and inferiority disappeared when he took on another role. It fed him.'

Despite his lack of experience compared to the other Players, Liam was given a part in the very first Slemish production, *Philadelphia, Here I Come*, by the Irish writer, Brian Friel. Gerry McKeown selected him for the role. 'I knew Liam had read Friel's work at school and was keen on it, so I gave him a part. It was a gamble, but he had never let me down before. I just backed a hunch.'

That part was the role of Gar O'Donnell, a disillusioned boy who finds the parochialism of his home too much to stomach. Liam would play his alter ego, the private Gar who reveals the secret, most intimate loves and longings of the public Gar.

It was inspired casting. Liam Neeson had spent his childhood and adolescence living two lives. The public perception was of a dutiful, diligent, shy boy. Inside his head, however, Liam Neeson was many things – but none of them those. There was a whole other world of fantasy, dreams and desires within him. That was what had brought him here, to the theatre. In a play, he could act them out. Liam Neeson knew Gar. He *was* Gar. He gave this, his first amateur dramatic role, everything he had. And Gerry McKeown shaped him, took his raw enthusiasm and energy and channelled it into the play with sharp precision.

The Slemish Players, in their very first production, took the play to the Ballymoney Festival where they were lauded for their high standard of production then nominated for the prestigious Larne Festival. This unprecedented success by a virgin company came as no great surprise to those in the Slemish Players who had been involved with other drama groups before.

Joe O'Neill recalls: 'Slemish was a great training ground. Gerry was a consummate professional who ran the company along totally professional lines. It was very disciplined, certainly not just a hobby or a social activity. If you wanted in on the Slemish Players, you had to take it very seriously indeed. There were very strict rules to be adhered to. You were always utterly punctual. Gerry wouldn't tolerate latecomers straggling in once we were under way.

'And the script got in the way. So far as Gerry was concerned, the sooner you got rid of it, the better. It wasn't enough to just go on stage and learn your lines. You had to have something to fall back on – something within yourself.

'It stunned all of us when it was actually young Liam who proved most able to do this. He had this knack of being able to pull something out of himself that you never in a million years would have suspected was there, not in one so young, so gauche. But in *Philadelphia*, as Gar, Liam came to life. He was mesmerising. He just appeared and the whole place stopped in its tracks.'

Kitty Neeson, in the audience that first night as she watched her son bring to life Friel's creation, was fit to burst with pride. Years later, when he was Oscar-nominated for his role in *Schindler's List*, she recalled, 'There were people in Ballymena felt Liam deserved an Oscar for his performance that night. They still like to talk of it, even to this day.'

When the play was performed to rapturous applause at the Larne Drama Festival in April 1970, the judges awarded him, if not the Oscar which Ballymenians believed he so richly deserved, then at least a trophy for Best Actor.

Competing against far more experienced amateur players, Slemish swept the board with two awards, the Regal and Nichol Jeffrey Cups. But it was Liam's best actor accolade that people remembered. It was a stunning debut for a novice amateur actor. And no one was more stunned at his success than Liam Neeson. Just turned seventeen, as he stood on stage at Larne with the applause of distinguished judges and a rapturous audience ringing in his ears, Liam Neeson would remember this night throughout the following two years as he struggled to make his way through college and university.

The reception he got for that first performance was so positive, there was no holding him back. He immediately volunteered for a role in the next production, also a Friel play, *Words Upon the Windowpane*.

In this one-act play he had a smaller role, as one of a group of people who visit a medium and hold a seance, hands linked around the table. It, too, got rave notices in the local press, and drew crowds expectant with the hope of seeing another skilfully produced play. They were not disappointed.

Increasingly, the other Players noticed too a growth in their youngest performer. 'Liam had suddenly developed a new maturity. He was focused. He had total commitment, maturity, even then.

'And he had developed into a generous actor. Despite the fact he had held starring roles, won awards, he was not at all precocious. He didn't think only of himself. Where some of us were chewing our nails, thinking only of our lines and our own part, Liam was always concerned about the performance as a whole. And he was precision-perfect when it came to his lines. He never, ever fluffed.'

Everyone, within the Players and without, was impressed by their young protégé. But as the play came to a close, and Slemish celebrated their first, hugely successful year, Liam Neeson finished his schooling at Ballymena Technical College. It was time to take his leave of the Slemish Players. The big world beckoned. Now he had to do his duty by his parents and go on to further education. It was a move he was positively dreading, even though he knew only too well he could take his passion for amateur acting no further for now.

'I never thought you could make a living at acting. I didn't even dare to think I could, because it wasn't a proper profession. You have to be a doctor or an engineer or a teacher.

'What I actually wanted to be was a naval architect. I remember filling in the UCCA forms after A-levels, and I thought, yes, naval architecture in Bristol, that would be good, to build ships there. It was all very romantic, in my head.

'I was good at engineering drawing and the mechanical stuff, but they were asking for incredibly high grades, like two As and a B, to get in to this course. And I didn't get them. So I went to Queens, to do maths and computer science. Some mistake.'

He had picked Queens University in Belfast, only twenty miles from home. It was not a big move for a young man beginning to build his future. But Belfast, big, sprawling and dangerous city with its history of conflict, escalating spates of bombing and revenge attacks, might as well have been a million miles away from peaceful, inward-looking, safe little Ballymena, so far as Liam Neeson was concerned.

It was his first venture away from the close-knit family. Like most freshers, he was desperately miserable at first, missing his mother's home cooking, the organised daily routine of set family meals, his washing, ironing and cleaning done for him. And the bustle of family life that was Home with the Neesons. Unlike the other students, however, Liam stayed miserable, unable to join in the freshers' activities, too shy to participate in the social events. He holed up in his rented room and felt utterly, desperately sorry for himself.

'I was like a catatonic zombie for that year, something was happening to my spirit. I switched off completely, didn't smoke or drink, didn't go out, didn't go to parties. I can still remember feeling so depressed, yet not knowing why. I just sat in my room feeling like a blob. Nothing was happening to me, below the waist or in the head.'

What made things worse was that no one even noticed. The world left Liam Neeson to get on with his own misery. 'I felt like I was on another planet. I wasn't part of the whole student scene, I was detached from it. And that was brought home to me one Monday morning as I was coming out of a tutorial. Suddenly, in front of me, there was this huge crowd advancing on me, yelling, "Scab! scab!"'

'I didn't know what had happened, what I'd done. It turned out there was a huge students' strike on that day because the day before was Bloody Sunday in Derry. Just a few miles up the road and I didn't even know about it.

'I felt terrible. I knew I had to get out, blow away the cobwebs.'

Was Neeson the only Irishman in Belfast, or possibly the world, who had let the events of Sunday, Bloody Sunday pass him by? The horrendous brutality was reported at length and in full gory detail by every TV channel, radio station and newspaper the length and breadth of the country. All Ireland was up in arms over the massacre.

What precipitated all this? Liam Neeson, Ballymena boy who had always had problems integrating with his peers, found himself in an academic world, the real world, the big world – and knew he did not fit in. He was scared, he was miserable, he was more lonely than he had ever thought possible. His family had been his safe, familiar crowd around him, with all their fussing and flapping, their giggling and chivying, his battalion of women; his mother and three sisters were what made Liam Neeson feel secure. Now he truly was on his own, alone for the first time. And he hated it.

He lasted two terms. Never an academic in the true sense of the word, he had scraped through school exams with adequate – though never brilliant – marks because he studied. He had the ability to assimilate facts, then regurgitate them for the examiners.

At university he could not get away with that. Though he was used to discipline, welcomed it because it gave structure and meaning, boundaries to his life, and within them he could let his imagination flow free, here in the halls of academia, he was lost.

He later claimed he was thrown out for cribbing, plagiarising another student's notes. Fact or fiction? The university has no record of this. Maybe he did, stretched by the demands of a more intellectual environment than he had ever encountered before. Or perhaps he had simply had enough and gave in to his own greater knowledge that this was not, was never going to be, his métier.

The undeniable fact was that now he dropped out of university life altogether and went home, where it was safe, where he knew who he was, where he belonged.

His parents' disappointment was palpable. But what was of paramount importance to them was their only son's happiness. He could try again next year, couldn't he? He could not.

A compromise was sought. Neeson agreed to have another try at student life, but in perhaps not such an academically strenuous field. He would go to Newcastle, to teacher training college.

Were it not for his parents' insistence that he attain career qualifications, Neeson might have stood back and said the idea of him teaching was risible. He should be a teacher, communicating with children? He knew where he communicated best – and that was the theatre.

He returned to the Slemish Players, where they welcomed him once more, with open arms. Though he had never voiced it to the Neesons, Gerry McKeown had always felt, in his heart of hearts, the lad had never been suited to further education. 'I don't think Liam ever intended to go away for long. He did it because he was bowing to pressure from his parents and didn't want to let them down.'

He had also discovered that in Belfast he was but a very small fish in a very big pool, even more of an outsider. He had never been noticeable in Ballymena – even those who knew the family, as Alannah Boyle pointed out, had never set eyes on Liam – but he had found a niche there, in amateur dramatics. Take him out of that environment and he was lost.

'My feeling with Liam was that he always thought, I'm going to stay here in Ballymena for as long as I can, because I have to until I can escape.'

Yes, he wanted to get away, like Gar, escape the confines of his parochial and narrow-minded prison, set free his dreams of being an actor, and not just an actor, but a star. A huge star, a megastar, a name that all Hollywood would sit up and notice. Just one problem. He didn't have the confidence to do it. And he didn't know where to start.

Acting was his escape from that loneliness. Acting made him feel good about himself. Acting made him feel he was someone. Better start back at the beginning then, back with Slemish Players. It was time to go home, time to find himself. Then, perhaps, he could start over. And this time, he would do it for himself.

5

Starting Over

'Sure, it would be colourful to imagine I had a rebellious, uproarious Irish background, a bit of Brendan Behan in my blood. But the facts were much greyer. Irish, yes. But all that nationalistic stuff, crying into your Guinness and singing rebel songs – that was never my scene.

'I was shy, studious and I boxed. I was dead boring, really I was.

'Then I discovered older women at eighteen and that . . . was a kind of deliverance.'

Returning to Ballymena was not the obvious move. Others might construe it as a personal failure, eating humble pie. But Neeson said, 'I came back to find my roots.'

His ambitious parents, though disappointed with Liam's dropping out of university, were happy to welcome him home. With one proviso: he got himself a job while he was sorting out his next move. It just wouldn't do for him to be sitting around at home all day long, reading books, watching films on television. No, he could find work.

He took on a variety of short-lived jobs, fork-lift operator in a brewery, truck driving, working as general factotum for a local architect. As Mary Mulholland, a close family friend and his erstwhile babysitter as a child, noted, none of them lasted very long. 'He was at them about as long as he was a student – not long at all.'

It was to his acting that he devoted his time and attention. He still harboured the fantasy of making it as an actor, but even then he felt it was just wishful thinking.

When he tentatively brought up the idea to McKeown, the fanciful notion was quickly quashed. 'He would often broach the subject of breaking into professional acting, but I used to sideline him. The main reason being, I for ever had this vision of Kitty, his mother, and Barney, his father, chasing me, saying, "This man McKeown led our son to hell and back, to rack and ruin." They were extremely ambitious for their son and so far as they were concerned, acting was no career, it wasn't even a proper job.

'So I certainly didn't encourage him. I was realistic. I would tell him, "Look, the acting world is full of talented people – how many of them do you think actually make a living at it? Not many."

'I was dismissive but it didn't put him off. He kept that wee flame of the idea burning away there. I still think it was the right thing to do. You point out the pitfalls and the stacked odds and if they still decide to carry on, then they have the right to. They've proved they have the dedication.

'It takes some stamina to survive the long period of lean times before a would-be actor even gets a taste of recognition – if he's lucky.'

Despite Gerry's phlegmatic reasoning, some of the other Slemish Players were beginning to believe Liam might just have that extra bit of determination that sorts out the wheat from the chaff when it comes to success. They were of the opinion that yes, there was lots of latent Irish talent around in clubs and parish halls up and down the land, but Liam had a bit more than that. 'He also had the courage to grab it and go for it. There was plenty of ability around, but few had the guts to take it further. Most of us, in the end, settle for a quiet life, a home and a happy family, and an outlet to take our frustrated talents – amateur acting.

'Liam had more. He was determined to get out, to free himself, to unchain the shackles he felt tied him down. He was a free spirit, he had never really fitted in. He wanted to fly. We were too mundane for him.

Others simply adopt the natural stance of the Irish, ready to heap praise on one of their own: 'Gentle big lamb, he had no malice in him, nor a bad bone in his body. If Liam Neeson were to play Jesus Christ, he'd convert the world.'

He was not yet ready to play *that* role – though it would wing its way to him soon enough, but he was ready for a new challenge. That Easter, after he had dropped out of university and a few months before he would try his hand at teacher training college, Liam found the Slemish Players had already cast their current production. There was no room at the inn but his luck was in.

At the eleventh hour another actor dropped out of the play through illness.

Recalls McKeown: 'It was a very small part, only a few lines, but Liam leapt at the chance. He learned his part and knew the scope of the play – it was a Tennessee Williams – in no time at all. That, of course, was where you could always count on Liam, in the hard graft department.

'And it paid off. Despite the size of the role, he certainly made an impact. There was a producer in the audience who was very well thought of in acting circles in Northern Ireland, a man called John Knipe, who had also worked with the likes of Colin Blakely, so he knew talent when he saw it. And after the play he came up to me and said, right out, "Tell me, who was the barman?"

'That was Liam. The main characters had huge parts, the whole thing hung on them. But the only person this producer wanted to know about was Liam. He'd been on stage for about a minute but the expert had spotted his potential in just that wee role.

'You had to give Liam all credit for that. He certainly had presence. And versatility. He stepped into that role at no notice at all, and carried it.'

Neither was he, for all his illusions of becoming an actor proper, the slightest bit of a prima donna. He did not covet the huge roles, he just wanted to act. And he knew that he could make a small role big. 'Liam had learnt that a small part doesn't necessarily mean a small actor or a small talent. You can still outshine the stars.'

Make an impact, make people sit up and notice. Then the rest follows naturally. He would not forget that. Shortly after this, Neeson set off for college in Newcastle. It was another episode he likes to draw a veil over. The bleak industrial northern city held no allure for an Irishman used to the rolling fields of home. Unemployment was rife, the dour northern attitudes hard to penetrate for an insecure Irishman never blessed with the gift of the gab, and the thick Newcastle accent, when crossed with his own brogue, made conversation tortuous. Once again, he had to admit defeat. He was home within the year.

But it was not all in vain. He had made use of his time in Newcastle to haunt the city's theatres, seeking out productions the like of which he was never likely to see in Ballymena. One such starred his fellow countryman, Colin Blakely.

On his inglorious return to the Slemish Players, he would recount the episode to the enthralled team. 'He told us this story about how he met Colin, who'd won considerable praise for his role as Christ in *The Son of Man*, on television. Blakely was playing with the National Theatre and they came to Newcastle while he was studying there. So Liam stood outside the theatre door for two days in the pouring rain and finally Blakely, out of pity, told the backstage staff to let him come in.

'And then he had talked to Blakely for around an hour about his performance on stage. He told us how enthralled he was by this. Now, that said a lot about Liam. It's not your usual sort of person who would persist in hanging around the stage door for that amount of time in all weathers. You can bet his fellow students weren't giving up their time to do that.

'And also, it struck us that Liam was so full of admiration for an Irishman who had actually turned his back on Ireland. It made you wonder if Liam, too, didn't want to transcend his roots, get away from his home, forget it was where he came from.'

This time around, Ballymena folk noticed a change in Liam Neeson. At twenty, with two failed student courses behind him, he did not have the air of a man defeated. He had the air of a man, first and foremost. He had grown up. He had a new kind of inner confidence that comes with the transition from innocence to knowledge.

In his freedom from home, away from the ever-vigilant eye of his mother and sisters, Liam Neeson had finally been able to lose his virginity. He is coy about the event. All he will say is: 'College was an education in one thing. That was where I learned about women.'

He would attempt to continue this education back home in Ballymena but the pursuit was made all the more hazardous by the strict Catholic rules by which he had to abide. Viz: girls only of the same faith, and naturally, given the sanctity of marriage, they must never have entered into that Holy Union before.

He fell down on both counts, according to a close friend, who will not be named for fear of the wrath of the Neesons – and the whole neighbourhood – being wreaked upon her. 'Yes, Liam had a serious girlfriend here after he came back from college. There was only the one that we knew of, but it's never spoken of. If you mention it, you're out with the family. They'd just stonewall you. Permanently.

'The reason being, the lady in question was that bit older than him by a fair few years, which was a sin in itself to Kitty Neeson, but worse, she had been married before. And in the eyes of the Catholic Church, that's forbidden territory.

'Liam, of course, kept it very quiet. If you saw them together, you'd never have known they were involved. They played it very cool. They would meet at her place and sometimes, the pair of them would have some of us back for supper. We knew what was going on, but no one ever dared breathe a word, for fear of Kitty getting to know about it.

'We all felt the same. It was a terrible shame. You knew it never was going to go anywhere, because the family would forbid it. And she was such a lovely girl, tall and blonde and a real good-looker, but not at all conceited about it. She was honest, open and friendly, very genuine, an awful lot like Liam, really, no side to her.

'It wasn't her fault the marriage had broken down, it wasn't as if she was a scarlet woman or anything like that. She was the one who'd been left hurting when her husband just upped and left her. And it wasn't like Liam had broken up the marriage. The husband had been gone off the scene for a good three years before Liam came along.

'We used to think how nice they were together as a couple, her and Liam. He was still that bit young in his ways. She put him right about things. She was more knowledgeable than he was, being that good bit older.

'But the family would have none of it. When it finally came out – remember this is a very small town where everyone knows everyone else – and their business – the word from the family was Liam was not to go with her. It was a very Catholic thing, frowned on. To be keeping the company of a woman who had been married was a sin.

'Liam, of course, did as he was told. He was never one to upset his parents. The girl had to go. They stayed friendly, though, even after Liam left, I know for sure. Liam didn't like to lose friends. He had never had that many, so he liked to hang on to those he made. He made an effort to stay in touch, even when he went to Dublin, then London. He wrote to her.

'She was a bit cut up about it, but when he left Ballymena, she accepted it a bit better. She knew, like we all did, he had always wanted to move on, better himself. She told me he was still her best friend, even when he was in London with Helen Mirren, a few years later. It was sad, though. That was how much he meant to her. And he knew it. In a way, it was a kind of torture for her, him keeping her hanging on like that, as just a friend. It might have been kinder just to cut off all the ties, then she could have picked up the pieces and gone on with her life. Instead, she had to see him going off with these other women.

'It's a good job Helen Mirren wasn't a jealous woman, too, because they stayed that close, and there was an intimacy between them that comes from having been lovers. You don't lose that when the affair turns into friendship.

'A few years later, we all went down to see him in a production at the Riverside Theatre, after he'd been living in London for a while, and this ex was with us. Helen was with him, but they greeted each other like old lovers – very warmly. That's a rare man who manages to hang on to ex-lovers like that – and even parade them in front of current lovers.'

But it would turn out to be a precursor for virtually all Liam Neeson's lovers. His pattern with women was beginning to evolve. Woo them, win them, walk away. . . but keep them hanging on.

Where did it come from, this predilection to dive deeply into passionate affairs, then pull away again with such apparent ease? Psychologists would argue that, being raised surrounded by women, a boy who found it hard to communicate with males but slipped readily into the company of females would find that environment hard to relinquish. This kind of male needs the intimacy of unconditional female love but, by the same token, knows he can extricate himself from it. So long as it's there, in some form or another. Hence the need to retain it in the more benign form of friendship.

Liam Neeson adored the female species that had enveloped him all his life. But his biggest love was acting and his quest was to further that ambition to act. It all worked out rather well, really, because in the theatre he found the perfect milieu for attracting women.

On the stage, he was beginning to evolve as a demi-god. Not just to backstage groupies, but to every woman in the audience. When Liam Neeson strode on stage, all eyes were upon him. Some would look on him with admiration, others with awe. But the women would look as with one glint in their eye. Liam Neeson was raw, soulful sex on mile-long legs. And now, he knew it.

His taste for love-'em-and-leave-'em-longing also served several purposes. Having ex-lovers still enraptured by the time they spent with you can only serve to bolster the fragile ego. And if you're in the public eye, such a reputation could only further enhance your standing as a lover of considerable stature. Which, in turn, attracts the interest of would-be lovers, curious to see, at first hand, the talents and allure of a man who can both attract and keep the attention of so many women. So it was come full circle. Liam Neeson, at twenty-one, had found the recipe for sexual success.

He now turned his increasingly adept hand to a new challenge with the Slemish Players: a play which many regard as his finest amateur acting hour, and of which they still like to talk in Ballymena today. In *Dark of the Moon*, in 1973, he played the part of Witch Boy. It was a demanding role, entailing his transformation from witch to human and back again.

The rest of the cast were so overawed at the adroit way in which Liam transformed himself, they would exit round the back of the stage and go frontstage to watch him. It was then that they knew they would not hold on to Liam Neeson for much longer. Not only had he set his sights on higher things, his talent was outgrowing a stage that was too small for him.

Praise was heaped on him for his role – rave notices in local papers lauded the award-winning actor from the Slemish Players. Neeson's response would be, when he finally parted from their ranks, to send back autographed photos of himself, years later, signed: Love from Liam – Witch Boy.

It was around this time, too, that he made his first foray into an entirely new medium – film. The word had gone out among the local groups that a film unit was casting around for players to perform in a religious epic. It was a Billy Graham-backed production of Bunyon's *Pilgrim's Progress*, destined to preach to the as-yet-unconverted at missionary halls throughout the Baptist world. But it was a start. And young Liam, with his height and his presence and his sticking-out ribs, was perfect for one part – that of Jesus Christ.

So it was that he found himself one misty morn on Carn Hill, just outside Belfast, being crucified. It was an other-worldly situation that he sometimes had to pinch himself to believe was really happening. There he was, slumped from the wooden cross where he was pinioned, nails driven through bloodied hand and foot, a crown of thorns piercing his forehead. Surrendering himself to God, he gazed, not on the crowd before him but beyond, into the distance. His eyes, unseeing, suddenly filled with light and a look of divine truth transformed his tortured face.

The director froze for a second before yelling a jubilant, 'Cut!' Neeson, he knew, had just captured the precise expression of the

ascent of His spirit to heaven. 'Perfect, Liam,' he praised the star
'At last the spirit is among us!'

Liam grinned. His inspiration came not from God, but from the
sight across the valley of a procession of little green men. They turned
out to be soldiers on manoeuvres.

For him, that moment had all the makings of a scene straight
out of a Fellini film. He loved the irony of it. He also loved
his first taste of acting for the camera, where every expression,
every nuance and gesture, no matter how slight, was both mag-
nified and frozen on celluloid for ever. This was timeless acting.
His appetite whetted, he knew then that he would be back for
more. Stage acting fed him, screen acting thrilled him. He knew,
even then, where his destiny lay.

But in the meantime, there was one more production that would
be graced by the talent of Liam Neeson; his one and only venture
into pantomime came that Christmas. It was a memorable event for
all involved. The panto was *Cinderella* and Liam landed the only
part that could possibly be allocated him, that of an Ugly Sister,
Tapioca.

This in itself presented a few problems of fairly gargantuan proportions. The costume girls found themselves with the devil's own
job trying to find size eleven high heels. But finally they did. And,
according to the convulsed group of Players, 'He walked in them
like he was born to it, wiggling his skinny bottom and sashaying
across the stage. If he hadn't been six foot eight in his stilettos, he'd
have made a great transvestite!'

The run-up to the panto was the only time the Players would
see Liam Neeson sitting in the wings enjoying a laugh. Panto was
fun, the atmosphere was lighter. This was not a dramatic role, it
was playtime. The agenda was not to impress the audience, nor to
mesmerise, it was simply to entertain.

And yet, they noted, Liam still took his role seriously enough when
he went out on stage. Comedy was not an area he was familiar with.
In himself, he was a serious, inward-looking man. He had a sense
of humour, but it was soft and seldom self-generated. Accordingly,
he took his role of Tapioca in deadly earnest. His brief, to make
the audience laugh, meant as soon as the curtain went up he was
working at just that. Because of his quiet, taciturn nature, the other
Players were not expecting Liam to be hell-bent on making the
audience guffaw. But he was.

A Portstewart friend, Niall McCabe, was in the audience that night and recalled: 'Liam took us all by surprise, he was superb. He had a natural gift for comedy. Of course, he had a head start – he looked so completely ridiculous. There he was, this enormous, angular fella all togged up in a flouncy frock, stocking, suspenders and stilettos. You just had to look at him and that set you off. He camped it up no end too, pouting and blowing kisses at the audience.

'But the Ugly Sister is an important part. You can't just stand there and say "Knickers!" and expect the audience to laugh. Liam knew that. He had perfect timing, perfect delivery, he both worked hard and enjoyed himself hugely.

'You knew he was working because he never made a single gaffe, and if someone else did, he'd come up with some spontaneous ad lib that had the audience falling about.

'We were all of a mind afterwards; we felt it would be a shame if he never pursued roles that would showcase his comic talent. There's not many actors have this rare gift for comedy, but Liam proved he did.'

It might be panto, but for Liam Neeson it was still a responsibility. This performance was all about getting bums on seats, and generating the funds that would allow the Slemish troupe to finance dramatic productions for the remainder of the year. In the three years since their inception, the troupe had gone from strength to strength, pulled together and held together in a close-knit group. There was none of the dissent, the petty resentments or the prima donna behaviour that can spark up and set fire to many a well-intentioned small town drama group.

And by now they ranked among their prize assets Liam Neeson. He was no longer Young Liam, nor Wee Liam. As Liam Neeson had grown in height, in confidence and in stature, he was ready to burst forth from the bonds of the amateur group that had so far contained him. They had long known of his dreams of moving on, becoming a professional but, like Gerry McKeown, they preferred to stay sceptical about his chances.

What they didn't know, as the panto drew to a close, was that Neeson had already made the first move.

He felt a particularly strong sense of responsibility in this panto because he knew he would never be in a Slemish production again. He had secured a job – a proper job, as he called it – with the Lyric Theatre in Belfast. Tapioca would be his last amateur dramatic role.

He planned to go out on a high. And he planned to tell them on the last night. Liam Neeson would be bowing out with a grand finale.

The Town Hall threw a reception for the Players, as a thank you for their performance in the Town Hall itself, packed to the gunnels as it had been.

Alannah Boyle had reason to remember the night well. Playing the role of Principal Boy, she had picked that night to announce her engagement to fellow Player Jimmy Boyle, who was starring in the role of the wicked Baron. There were cheers and tears that night. Congratulations for the happy couple, the first marriage to be made out of the Slemish Players, and commiserations all round, because they were losing Liam.

But none begrudged him his success in making it to the Lyric. 'By then Liam was extremely confident in his abilities. He wasn't nervous about making this leap at all. He believed in himself and in what he was doing. It was, above all, what he wanted to do with his life.

'And now his family had given their approval. It wasn't what they would have picked for him, but he had done well in amateur dramatics, won awards, gained lots of praise from respected judges. The whole town had seen him in one performance or another and felt the same. He was good, very good.

'Now he'd got a paying job in acting, they were right behind him, backing him all the way. The old disappointments over college were put behind him.'

And yet. . . He might never have escaped had it not been for one thing. It was not so much his talent, nor his determination that had facilitated his leap into professional acting, though no one who saw him perform and heard him talk could doubt that he had plenty of both. It was his old friends, luck and timing.

He had put in a call to the Lyric Theatre, asking about a job, any job. And his call had gone through to the director, Mary O'Malley. As it happened, she told him, she was casting around for a man to play Big Jim Larkin in their upcoming production of *The Risen*. How tall was he?

Six foot four, came the reply. Liam Neeson was in.

Gerry McKeown noted this curious circumstance with his inimitable wry humour. 'D'you know, the only thing Liam had going against him in amateur acting was his height. He dominated the cast – by a long way. You couldn't find leading ladies to play opposite him, he dwarfed them. He dwarfed the whole cast. Now

that's a serious problem in amateur theatre, where you're performing on a small stage with the audience only a few feet away
from you. There's no way you can hide that huge discrepancy
between one man and everyone else.

'But it was that very problem that Liam turned to his advantage.
Of course, height is an asset in professional theatre, which is played
in front of a much more impressive backdrop. If you're not dwarfed
by the set and the other acting talent, it's a bonus. Liam's stature
meant he wouldn't be. He just had to stand there and you'd notice
him. It gave him, quite literally, a head start.'

Liam Neeson, posted to join the respected Lyric Theatre in Belfast,
was starting head and shoulders above the other actors. And he
planned on keeping it that way.

6

In Dublin's Fair City
Where The Girls Are . . .

'Sure, my size won the day for me. I was twenty-three and far too young to be playing this Goliath of a man, but they offered me the part and I thought, Well, I'll have a stab at it.

'It was just so easy. I became an actor and my life changed, just like that. And I had friends so desperate to get an Equity card, they were stripping in the West End!

'I didn't know I was born.'

The luck of the Irish, as they say, was with Neeson from the start. Though no one who saw him act was in any doubt that this virgin performer at the Lyric had talent to spare.

Mary O'Malley, the director, took him on for the princely sum of £31.50 a week, '£1.50 more than I was getting in my last job as a repro assistant in an architect's office,' he bragged to friends. She knew she had found a winner as soon as she tested him out for his first six-month contract. 'Liam had a very commanding presence. You wanted to watch him, he was quite compelling.'

He was fresh and raw, but that very presence was enough to start him off. He soon found himself working alongside illustrious names: 'These incredible people I'd worshipped from afar like Joe McPartland and Stella McCusker and all these wonderful pillars of the Northern Ireland theatrical community. It was some learning curve.

'We were turning out plays every three to four weeks from Shakespeare through Synge and O'Casey to Tennessee Williams and Arthur Miller. I worked my way through the whole dramatic canon.

'And the theatre never closed. It was Belfast and there could be bombs outside the door but the show went on. If there was a bomb scare, we'd stop the play and join the audience outside till the all-clear. Then we'd all troop back in and start where we left off.'

That said, even from the early days, Neeson knew he would have to leave the Lyric to spread his wings. There was only so far you could go in Northern Irish theatre, even if it was in the capital. Whoever came to see you there? Belfast, bombed, beseiged, torn apart by the Troubles . . . was actually nothing like that at all.

Like any large city, anywhere in the world, it had its share of poverty, crime and drug abuse. It had areas, like the Falls and Shankill Road, you'd be well advised to steer clear of. But by and large, people lived in Belfast much as they did in countless other capital cities. There were smart shops, clubs, a university of renown, history, culture and good spirit among most of the residents.

Sure, for forty years they'd had a hard time of things, the sectarian conflict, the closure of the shipyards, the collapse of industry, the economic decline, but Belfast was not alone in that. And despite their problems – or perhaps because of them – most Belfast people strove to lead full and happy lives.

But that's not what the outside world perceived. The damage had been done by worldwide news reports and media coverage that concentrated exclusively on the bombings. The imagery fed to the outside world was one of buildings ablaze, bodies mutilated and murdered right in front of camera lenses. The propaganda was of chaos, carnage and a city rent asunder by sectarianism. It was a one-sided, biased and microcosmic view but it was what people outside Belfast embraced as the truth. Visitors stayed away in droves.

Those who came to watch the masterly productions at the Lyric were by and large Belfast folk. Directors, producers, agents were not among them. In Belfast theatre everyone knew everyone else. Through time, it became abundantly clear that Neeson was not going to be head-hunted here for some starring role, or even a fresh start. He had to take things into his own hands. He had to move on.

London, of course, was the place to be for anyone in the theatre world. But Neeson had friends who had gone before him and come to grief. He would be seriously disadvantaged, too, by his Irishness. Hindered by their peaty and sometimes impenetrable brogue, tagged with the Thick as an Irish Navvy label, he knew few of his fellow countrymen had ever broken through the ranks and gained acceptance in English theatre. The exceptions, such as Colin Blakely, had negated their Irish inheritance, adopted anonymous, English-derived accents and postures. Neeson knew he could not do that. Accents were not his strong point.

It was no use. Not yet. Unless you knew someone who knew the right people who could give you the breaks, there seemed little point in that kind of reckless move. He had not come this far to throw it all away.

So where does an Irishman go if he wants to enhance his standing in the theatre, without risk of losing it all and ending up busking on the streets? To Dublin, of course. Renowned for its literary connections, its beauty, its history, its culture and its laid back lifestyle, it was also a Mecca for producers, directors and assorted media types who wanted to combine getting away from it all with an all-expenses-paid scouting jamboree.

He left the Lyric in 1977 with no secure job to go to, but a few theatre contacts and an intuitive feeling he was making the right move at the right time. He had had those feelings before and they had not let him down. He might have to step back a bit, from the Lyric to the Dublin fringe theatres, but at least there he would be meeting people, making his presence known. He knew all too well the Irish tendency to deride those who try to come in at the top. Dubliners, in particular, held no truck with those who had paid their dues, but if you thought you could just walk in the front door and expect them to fall over themselves at the sight of you, well, you were wrong there.

It's worth noting, contrary to the legend he later built around himself that he transferred direct from the Lyric to the prestigious Dublin Abbey Theatre, that Liam Neeson actually started in fringe, first at the Gate Theatre, then the Project and the Peacock. It was some time before he was accepted at the Abbey. His was a much more modest start in Dublin, back playing fringe, hopping from play to play, existing on low and erratic wages, living hand to mouth. But then again, he had the grounding in that. He'd been raised in a home where every penny was carefully counted. He'd known no other way of life, apart from in his dreams . . .

He made his debut at the Gate Theatre in East Sussex Street, right in the heart of Dublin. It was a tiny venue, the epitome of fringe. A one-time music-hall, its facilities were the barest minimum. In order for the audience to reach their seats, they had to troop through the actors' dressing room.

Neeson could not have known it then, but some major names were to evolve from these days of the Gate Theatre. The artistic director, Jim Sheridan, with whom Neeson made friends, would later go on to direct *My Left Foot* and *In the Name of the Father*. Another of his contemporaries at this time was Gabriel Byrne.

Neeson began his stint at the Gate with the role of Big Chief in Sheridan's production of *One Flew Over the Cuckoo's Nest*. Virtually a mute role, it gave him plenty of scope for his full range of doleful, soulful and inspired expressions. It was all good practice for another deaf-mute role he would play many years later as a vagrant accused of murder, opposite Cher in *Suspect*.

For now, he was happy to be acting – anywhere in Dublin, happy to put himself around a bit, be seen in the local pubs, hang out with the right people, get himself noticed. Now you could hardly fail to notice him, big fella like that, could you?

Liam Neeson was noticed all right. First and foremost by women. As a new guy in town, he was of great interest to the small-knit theatre community. One woman who worked alongside him remembers his debut as the new local lustbucket with stunning clarity. 'Liam had a role in *Streamers* at the Project Theatre. I can still remember it to this day. It wasn't a huge role – but Liam had a huge part, as we were all to see. In one scene he had to run stark naked across the stage. Let me tell you, all these rumours are absolutely true.'

Despite the cool temperature in the theatre, after all it was a fringe venue and funds did not run to heating the place, the temperature among the audience was pretty hot. 'Usually, a naked man is the most ridiculous sight you can hope to see. This was not the case with Liam Neeson. Once the word got out, it was a full house every night. The girls were practically queueing round the block. Liam Neeson naked, what a lovely thought!

'He hadn't been in Dublin long before he had an effect on all us girls who moved in theatre circles. We roughly split into two well-defined camps – those who fancied Liam Neeson and those who fancied Gabriel Byrne. They were definitely the two leading lights in Dublin theatre at that time, the late seventies.

'Liam was huge, rugged and protective, Byrne was dark and pretty and much more playboyish. At a rate of about 2-1, Gabriel had the lead in the fanciable stakes. Most of the girls went for him, because he was simply better looking. But all those who came under Liam's spell, when he got them in a one-to-one, were swung over to him.

'You almost got the feeling it was a kind of crusade with Liam.

He was trying to prove he was gorgeous, and he most definitely didn't like the limelight being on Gabriel – especially not the female limelight. He knew his biggest voters were women.

'He was *never* a man's man. You couldn't name one of his really close male friends – he didn't have any. He had mates he would do laddish things with, like go down the pub and have a few jars, but he never hunted in a pack. And he never had a mate in tow. Liam hunted alone.

'The thing both Liam and Gabriel had in common was they were both talented, both incredibly hard-working and both going in the same direction. You always had the feeling that they knew their destiny. Liam's was unquestionably not Ballymena, nor even Ireland. He wanted to soar. And he wasn't going to be distracted from that, certainly not by love. He never entered into a single in-depth relationship in his years in Dublin, whereas Gabriel always had a girlfriend. He had Katie, then Anya, then Ellen, he skipped from one to another, like he had a female dependency problem.

'Liam was the antithesis of that. It was as if he had a problem even contemplating a close union with a woman. It was like, look, touch, then love me from afar.

'To this end, he always had some vague escape line about some love of his life back home in Northern Ireland. It was never quite clear whether it was Ballymena or Belfast or somewhere in between. Liam was very good at the vague idea, you could rarely get him to be specific on things. And he would never speak out of turn about anything. He was the least opinionated person you'd ever meet. It was all charm and inner pain and potential devotion, except that was reserved for this nebulous northern lover. She was just there, like some spectre, tugging away at his heart strings, which of course, was a doubly effective pull for other women. They wanted to believe that, firstly, Liam was the devout, devoted slave to love – and secondly, maybe they could win this overwhelming lover over to themselves. Quite a few of us were deluded into that one.'

Years later, Neeson himself would admit. 'I hate all this talk about relationships and stuff. I prefer to be vague. Yes, va-a-ague. It's better that way.'

But at that time, he was merely practising his art. And as he gradually began to feel more confident about his powers of attraction, he began to play around with them a bit, experiment, test them out on the budding actresses and theatre girls.

Janette was one. A stunning redhead with an hourglass figure, she had never been short of male admirers. But Liam, she says, was different. 'To tell you the truth, I was never really attracted to Liam until one night I found myself in company with him and a few others in a Dublin pub and I realised he was chatting me up – major league. The thing with Liam was, he never let you realise he was on the make until it crept up on you after you'd been chatting for ages.

'It would be general talk about this and that, the play, the production, the performance and suddenly you'd realise the way he was looking at you was well, kind of . . . "We could, if you wanted to . . ."'

'That sudden realisation came as a shock because he didn't put out those predatory vibes at all. He was so unassuming. For such a big man, he has such a soft voice. He was never pushy, you always got the feeling he was a bit unsure of himself.

'But that was exactly what he wanted you to think. It was all a bit of an act. He knew the girls fancied him and adored the softly softly approach. Compared to the me Tarzan, you Jane, let's fuck approach that was prevalent at the time – well, this was the seventies, the era of the pill and sexual freedom and pre-AIDS, after all – this quietly charming, "Will we, won't we?" line was at once old-fashioned, quaint and deeply alluring.

'Once you got to know Liam, you saw it in practice time and time again. He'd long since worked out that that was the best way to get a woman into bed, by not being threatening or overtly lustful.

'He had another little ruse up his sleeve. He would focus on you like you were the only important person in the world – and it was his world but he was welcoming you in. I can't tell you how special that made you feel. It was never just sex with Liam. He made a girl feel like he wanted her heart, body and soul.'

Ten years on, actor Tim Roth would verify Janette's perceptive observations. On the scale of male attractiveness, a fair ten-pointer himself, he found he was none the less washed up in the shallows when it came to competing with Neeson for a girl's attention. 'When you're with Liam,' he says, 'don't even think about being looked at by a woman. They go all glassy-eyed and it's, "Ooooh, he's so *sensitive!*"'

Todd Haines, artistic director of the New York Roundabout Theatre, who would later direct Neeson in *Anna Christie*, comments, 'The thing about Liam is, when he looks at you, you become aware of how rare it is that anyone actually *looks* at you. And when he listens, he really listens. Women just love that.'

The Dublin girls, more used to men gazing in earnest devotion at their drinks, and listening keenly only to male banter about the merits of football or fishing, were bowled over. Like Janette, they would revel in how, 'You could be at a wild party, the room heaving with people, and you'd have to strain to hear what he was saying, he spoke so softly, but that was his way, he lured you in, so it was just you and him. It was very, very effective.

'It worked on me and I saw it work on other girls, but the thing with Liam was, he was incredibly discreet. You never, ever saw him in a relationship with a girl, never necking, never in a compromising position. You never even saw him leave with anyone. And you certainly never saw him on a date.

'But you *would* see him closeted in a corner of a bar, or a party, with some girl hanging on his every word. He had a knack of making the most trivial thing sound like it was a poem. Seriously. He'd say, "Been a lovely day today," and you'd picture all these blue skies and dappled sunlight coming down through the trees and you and him walking hand in hand . . . Straight away you were in this romantic dream idyll with him. But it was actually your dream he had somehow managed to tap into, not his.

'I later discovered, through spending a fair amount of time in company with him, that Liam never actually had much to say, which is probably why he'd devised this way of investing trite nonsense with such feeling. Still, you can't knock him for it, because it worked.

'The bottom line with Liam was, he'd realised that when you're surrounded by intelligent, creative people who are able to intellectualise about things while you can't, it's best to say as little as possible, so you don't blow the gaffe. Liam had sussed that out a long time before. He became the master of deep-thinking soulful looks and few words. It didn't wash with men, but it was a positive wow with women.

'One of the girls, Ruth, had a big scene with him. We were all dying to know what he was like in bed, but she played it very coy afterwards, didn't give hardly a thing away. That was another thing that was different about Liam. Girls never came back and discussed the intimate details like you normally would after a fling.

'He invoked passion, loyalty and also a kind of sympathy in

women. He made them feel a lingering desire for him to look after them. Which was curious because he would never commit to a relationship, not ever. He kind of left you hanging there hoping that maybe, one day, if you remained friends, it might actually happen.

'Looking at it objectively, it was a very egoistic, manipulative thing to do. But of course, you could never be anything but completely subjective with Liam. He turned you inside out so that you looked at yourself and you were just a quaking mass of feelings and desire. All that effect via just a few well-chosen words on his part, and a look that you felt bored into your soul.

'He was a master actor when it came down to persuading you you were in love. But all he did really was simply be there, looking like a great big bear with a tender heart. Your own imagination and emotions did the rest.'

A few speculated that Neeson might be anally retentive. According to them, he manifested all the classic symptoms: nervous disposition, dependency on rules and self-discipline, wanting to possess, to hold on to women, while at the same time retaining his own distance and space.

He needed that, not only for himself, but also for his work. Though he had taken a huge risk in leaving the safe tenure of a contract at Belfast's Lyric for the insecure future of a freelance in Dublin, he had landed on his feet and found work in constant supply. After *Streamers* and *One Flew Over the Cuckoo's Nest* at the Gate, he joined the Abbey Company and appeared in a succession of notable plays: *I Do Not Like Thee, Dr Fell, The Death of Humpty Dumpty, Juno and the Paycock,* and most memorably, Brian Friel's *Translations,* which ultimately moved to the British National Theatre. It was both a rapid rise to local deification and a coup for the boy from Ballymena.

One actress who worked alongside him corroborated: 'Liam became very rated around Dublin, and he knew it. But he was never arrogant. He'd worked out that arrogance got you disliked and above all Liam wanted to be liked—adored, if possible.

'He wanted to win fans and friends. He had the most impact with women, so he concentrated on them. But although he wanted them to adore him, he wasn't willing to give himself in return. He just gave the illusion that he did. And we all fell for it.'

There are those, too, who believe that people normally afflicted by Neeson's painful condition are those who are constantly straining to achieve something, yet can't quite get to it. Some say this is classic Neeson style. Certainly in his Dublin days there was a general feeling that Liam was only there under sufferance, all the time waiting, wanting to move on to bigger things.

'There was always something terribly controlled about him. He seemed like he was more capable of letting go than any man you'd ever met. But he never actually did.'

One woman who felt the full blaze of the Neeson charisma said: 'You always got the feeling with Liam that he had his sights set on greater things, less provincial prizes. That feeling was endemic in all of us. Everyone knew he and Gabriel were going to make it. They had a different aura about them. They were quietly confident, very ambitious.

'But Liam went about it in a peculiar way. Everyone knew he was a potential starfucker. He loved to chat women up but we only ever knew of one he actually had sex with. It was like he was practising his technique with women, but would pull back at the very last minute, like he was saving himself for something better.

'And he invariably reserved his most meaningful advances for the same type—strong, successful blondes. Those were the ones he'd gravitate towards. He was just playing with the rest of us.

'Because at the end of the day, he slept alone. I think that was what perplexed us most. We all thought it odd. It was the seventies, everyone slept with everyone else. Free love and all that, every girl on the pill. And Liam was so gorgeous, he could have snapped his fingers and had any girl in Dublin he wanted—especially after the long, slow, chat-up against the wall routine. But he didn't.

'We did speculate at one point in the early days that he might be gay, even ran a book on it. But the way he turned on that slow, sexy charm left you in no doubt that he was attracted to women. We ended up thinking he maybe didn't know what to do with it. Girlish frustration, I guess. We'd all have jumped into bed with him at the drop of a hat.

'But whenever he felt he needed an escape route from any girl's over-obvious approach, he quietly let it be known he had—God, but it got tedious—this girl up north and was being faithful to her. None of us ever saw her and we heard enough about her to know better— but we bought it. It was another thing to add to the myth. He was even more desirable because he was loyal. What a bonus, what a guy.

'Of course, it never crossed our minds then that it was another way of making himself Dublin's most desirable man. When you got right down to it, Liam Neeson at that time was the male equivalent of the prick-tease. He was just the biggest flirt.'

The general consensus of opinion among those who worked with Neeson at that time was that he was not a particularly social animal, preferring to monopolise women in a one-to-one situation.

A well-respected Irish actress, who happens to be lesbian and who never succumbed to Neeson's charms, stood back and watched the long-limbed Ballymenian cut a swathe through the heterosexual women around the theatre scene then. She reveals: 'What personally intrigued me about Liam was that he stood back too. He lived alone and never threw parties, never invited anyone back to his place either. It was like he was embarrassed to be living in digs because he felt he should be living somewhere much nicer. Well, we all lived in fairly shabby accommodation, and we threw parties. What was there to be embarrassed about? We were all in the same boat, broke and struggling. But Liam had this terribly working-class attitude about needing to better himself, and expecting better for himself.

'He never actually went to parties that much, just the odd one. You'd mostly see him in the pub, which was also unusual. Dublin is an incredibly small social scene. Everyone knows everyone else, particularly the members of Equity.

'He always stood away from the rest of the gang. He wasn't coldly aloof, just a bit detached. You always knew he wasn't comfortable in crowd scenes. He was best in the intimate tête-à-tête, and *always* with a woman. So long as it didn't go too far and get too close . . .

'Liam actually created himself as the lover to be desired above all. Without actually putting it about. Clever, that. But the thing you've got to remember about actors is that sometimes they can't switch off. When you're acting out fantasy for a living, sometimes it can spill over into your life.

'Think about it; an accountant has a certain way of looking at money, whether he's sitting in the bank or sitting at home. He probably sees percentages and share indexes jumping in front of his eyes. You can bet he doesn't put his ideas about money on the back burner when he locks up the office and goes home. It's with him, in some form or another, all the time. It shapes his ideas and his life.

'It's no different with actors. We're so used to living out different characters that we sometimes create one for ourselves. It slips easily over our own skins and gradually it all merges into one and we can lose sight of who we really are.

'That's even more so if you make the transition to a land of pure dreams like Hollywood. That's Fantasy City. Liam knew he had to create the right kind of illusion in order to make his mark there. And I don't for one second doubt that he always had his sights set on that.

'He'd already done it, in one way. It was as big a leap being a lanky lad in amateur theatre in Ballymena for God's sake, of all the nowhere places to come from, to make it to Belfast and then the Dublin stage. He created a persona for himself there—the gorgeous, soft, big gentle giant that girls wanted to sweep them off their feet and protect and love and cherish them for ever more. It's a romantic pastiche—but it fitted Liam, all six feet four inches of him, like a glove. And the trouble with girls is, we're all too ready to believe in the illusion of love.

'Of course, since he's made it in Hollywood, he's revered in Ireland. We're all looking at him with rose-tinted spectacles. In England, if someone debunks to LA they've deserted ship. In Ireland it's "Hey, we'll drink to that, he's a son of the auld sod!"

'Well, frankly, we can find anything to drink a toast to—three weeks of wind and rain, the milkman delivering Gold Top. But Liam Neeson, now there's really a cause for celebration. It's because there's only two and a half million Irish in this wee country. So when one of us makes it, we're cheering him all the way.

'No wonder he loves to come back. He's not local hero any more, he's global hero. And after all, he's paid his dues. He's not like those lads in *The Commitments* that everyone, but *everyone* in Ireland hates. They got jumped up with their success, and believe me, it was overnight for them. And where are they now? Nowhere. Which is where they deserve to be, goes the Irish way of thinking.

'But Liam did his groundwork, he did his provincial theatre, his time in rep, he put in his dues to Ireland, then he decided to take his talent on a bigger journey, and good luck to him.'

The curious thing you find in Dublin, among his ex-peers, some of whom are still working away in theatre, others who have capitulated and gone on to lead 'normal' lives, teaching perhaps, or nursing or even working in the fashion world, is that no one begrudges Liam Neeson his success. Nor does anyone resent the fact that he, with one leap, left behind the chains that still bind them. The thing is, Liam Neeson, whether coolly, calculatingly, or simply by his own design, never offended anyone, nor trod on any toes. He was always Mr Universally Likeable. And he worked hard at it.

Janette is typical among those who remember him fondly. 'The other thing that was different about Liam was that he's very even-tempered. You never, ever saw him riled or upset, which is rare among thespians. They've usually got the artistic temperament, are prone to throwing the odd tantrum—usually for effect, of course, or a bit of pretentiousness. Not Liam.

'You'd always, always see him on an even keel, concentrating on the act in hand, whether it was polishing up his act on stage or polishing up his, look deep into my eyes and tell me you couldn't fall for me, routine.

'It doesn't matter that long before he was Liam Neeson megastar, he was just another Ballymena arsehole. Because he blinded you to the truth. He created this fantasy that he was the softest, warmest, most inviting man you'd ever met. You wanted him to do well. He deserved it. He wasn't a nasty, thrusting cut-throat shit determined to get to the top.

'But what he was, of course, was an actor, on stage and off. He perfected his art long before he took it to the film industry.

'He never played around. There was maybe the odd fling, but the girls involved kept absolutely schtum because they adored him. There was absolutely zilch dirt on him. And believe me, if he'd been having an affair on the quiet, we'd have known about it.

'But it was no surprise when we heard about Liam Neeson and the Famous Actress. You'd always, always known that Liam had an eye to the main chance. He'd worked out a great number on women, he's practised it, polished it, seen it score countless triumphs, but all the time he'd kept his nose clean, if you'll excuse the expression. Our theory was he'd been saving himself for the big one.'

And that was Helen Mirren.

7

The Double-Edged Sword

'It's a weird thing to do, to have to sell your looks and your reputation, but that's screen acting. You want to work in film, TV? Then that's your factory.

'I can manage it when the cameras are rolling, that's where the craft and technique and experience come in. But then when you're not filming you've got to be out there, selling yourself. It's a funny thing to do for a living. Especially if you're shy like me.'

When Neeson had first fetched up in Dublin, a self-conscious northerner looking to integrate into the more cosmopolitan southern theatre circles, he had initially felt overawed and out of place. Fazed at the thought of appearing on the same stage that had launched the plays of the Irish literary greats such as Yeats, Synge and O'Casey, he claimed he had felt massively inferior to some of the actors he worked with.

'I was young and raw, totally inexperienced compared to some of the talent I worked alongside. Theatrically, I felt like a hick. When I was onstage with some of these people, who were really, really good, I was thinking to myself, It's no use. There's no way I can match them. All I thought I had going for me was a lot of energy and enthusiasm.'

Luckily, it was just that raw, inexperienced enthusiasm which director John Boorman was looking for when he shipped up at the Abbey Theatre to watch Neeson in Ray McAnally's production of Steinbeck's *Of Mice and Men.*

Boorman was in Ireland to cast and shoot his epic movie, *Excalibur*, based on the legend of King Arthur and his Knights of the Round Table. This was a prestigious British film, backed by high finance, in the hands of a renowned director and starring well-respected actors: Nicol Williamson, Helen Mirren, Nicholas Clay, Cherie Lunghi. Every actor in the Emerald Isle had his heart set on a role in it.

Neeson of course knew the director was in town – Dublin is a small place, news travels fast – and also that Boorman was scouting for young talent. Epic adventures on an Arthurian scale need large casts. Neeson determined that he would be among them. This was what he had been waiting for since his days at the Lyric.

His wait had not been in vein. Boorman was impressed by Neeson's stage performance. He sent a message backstage asking Neeson to meet him.

'John told me he wanted to use as much Irish talent as possible, I met him after the play in a pub – the Flowing Tide – for a chat. It was kind of relaxed and casual which surprised me, because I was real nervous about it. He was very open and positive, said he'd liked my performance. There and then, he said he wanted me to be in the film. A couple of days later, he sent me the script. Believe me, I was thrilled.'

Things were moving fast. But Neeson was still somewhat naïve about the protocol in the film industry. The fact that Boorman had made a swift offer and supplied the script for his perusal did not actually mean Neeson could pick his own part. Neeson made a gaffe of fairly major proportions when he replied to Boorman's offer.

'Being maybe a bit gauche in the ways of the film industry, I assumed I was in and it was down to me to choose the right role. So I just rang John up and said, "Yeah, great, I love the script, it's really good. Can I have the part of Pendragon?"'

'And there was this silence at the end of the line for a moment, like a sharp intake of breath and then he said very calmly, "I'm afraid someone else is playing that part."'

'I still hadn't cottoned on that he wasn't actually asking for my opinion on the script or my preference for a particular part. "Oh," I said, "who?"'

'And he said, "Gabriel Byrne."'

In a double whammy, Neeson learned the first rule of film: the director calls the shots. And that no matter how good you are, there's always someone else above you. The fact that it was his old adversary, Gabriel Byrne, was a bit of a sickener, too.

He was not to be cast as Uther Pendragon, but he was allocated another sizeable role, that of the Good Knight, Sir Gawain. He was hugely pleased to be making the transition from stage to film proper, but the circumstances rankled.

From that point on, he made himself a silent vow to aim for top dog. He wanted to be in the position where he would be first choice for the plum roles. And beyond, the ultimate dream, to call the shots, pick his own scripts, have a role written round himself. Well, he could dream. He always had . . .

It was a quantum leap, but Neeson was not deterred. He had film experience, of course he had. Christ on the cross, no less. But he acknowledged his debt to Boorman.

'I owed John a lot. Not only is he a great film-maker, but he's an inspired teacher, too. I had a lot to learn. When you're from the theatre, you don't know one end of the camera from another. Thankfully, John was a true movie megalomaniac. He told us exactly what to do, in no uncertain terms. He gave me a great grounding in the technique of film-making. Few directors will take the time to tutor. I got lucky with John. I'll always be indebted to him for that.'

He also laid claim to John Boorman awakening in him 'a thirst for myths and legends. I loved doing the film, the sheer story of it. The Arthurian legends are all about the development of the Western world. And you don't get much bigger a story than that.

'I think that was why I got hooked. The film industry really got under my skin in a big way with this. Suddenly I was bursting with this wonderful new euphoria. Not because I was particularly great or anything but there was this *smell* to it. Making movies has a smell, a taste and a flavour all of its own. There's nothing quite like it. Maybe it was the subject of that particular film, the telling of Arthurian legends. As a child, I'd always loved mythology, but this restored my fascination for it.

'I believed then, and have ever since, that what films should be all about is basic story-telling. Us Celts love telling a tale. We're rightly famous for it, the gift of the blarney and all. There's this great oral tradition in Ireland for just rabbiting on. You never say A is B or B is A when, you see, A just might be B and the other way round or anything in between. And that's the truth. When you're brought up that way, fed on that stuff, you keep your imagination open to that way of thinking.'

Neeson had to keep his imagination open in this movie. He had landed a decidedly less than glamorous role. Virtually unrecognisable, Dublin's heart-throb made his movie debut sporting a profuse bush of whiskery facial hair (liberally smeared with pork dripping) and a greasy ponytail, throwing back flagons of mead at Round Table feasts and thundering into battle on what looked like ghostly primeval landscapes – but which was actually the backdrop to Boorman's home in County Wicklow. 'Real scenery,' Neeson called it, comparing it to the travesties Hollywood conjured out of wood and paint and attempted to call landscapes, 'not the stuff they try to recreate in the studio. The country round these parts is thousands of years old, with a Celtic-twilight feel to it. You have to be God to create that, not some movie mogul with a multi-million dollar input.'

When he hit Hollywood, he would not be quite so vociferous in his criticism, but now, still a novice at the movie game, he was holding on to his lofty ideals. And he was thrilled to be taking part in this fantasy creation of such elaborate scale. It tied up his love of a strong story with his homeland – and paid him handsomely for the privilege. Humble theatre paypackets paled into insignificance compared with the movie actor's salary.

Having been given a taste of movieland, Neeson had already made up his mind that was where his future lay. Most definitely. And luck was at hand – a two-hander, as it happened. This was not just great experience, and a nice starter to his film CV, it also taught Neeson the benefits of networking, a technique he would see so much in action when he went first to London and, later, Hollywood.

Budding film-maker Neil Jordan was making a documentary on the filming of *Excalibur*. Ultimately, he would end up a Hollywood director himself. Then, remembering Neeson from *Excalibur* days, watching his progress through the celluloid maze, he would cast him in his ghostly comedy, *High Spirits*. This reinforced in Neeson his own personal maxim: always be charming to those you meet on your way up, because one day they'll be nice to you in return.

And with the second stroke of good fortune, he met Helen Mirren.

He had always shown, as his Dublin fan club observed, a preference for older, strong, successful blondes. Helen Mirren was all of those, and then some. She was thirty-four to his twenty-seven, an actress of considerable renown, having starred on the English stage and in such redoubtable films as Lindsay Anderson's *O, Lucky Man* and *The Long Good Friday*, opposite Bob Hoskins. She was blonde, gorgeous, sexy, intelligent, and according to theatre legend, had a keen appetite for men. Resolutely single, she had, so showbiz rumour proclaimed, a predilection for younger men. Neeson knew of her reputation. It served merely to entice him. With all his practice in Dublin's theatreland, he was feeling fairly confident in his pulling ability. But this was a new challenge. Helen Mirren, they miaowed, chewed up ingénus for breakfast. And spat them out.

'Of course, I'd heard she had this name as a bit of a ball-breaker. But I also heard that when she wanted a man, she did a curious thing. She intimated she was interested by mimicking him, taking off his posture or his walk. That way, she alerted the guy that she was up for it, without actually having to lay it on the line.

'So when I saw her on set one day and she was taking these great big strides – just the way I do – I knew what she was after.'

She got it. As it turned out, they would walk together a long way. First, Helen Mirren would hold his hand while he made the giant stride from Dublin to London. Then they would stay together in a relationship that meandered between passion and friendship for nearly four years.

Having been involved in a frightfully theatrical world, peopled by 'luvvies' for so long, Mirren was captivated by what appeared to be Neeson's straightforward 'Irishness'. She referred to it as 'very family-orientated, with a feeling of gentleness, civility, graciousness and an immense sense of discipline'. For her, he was a breath of fresh air, a return to basics, a welcome retreat back to simple values after so many years drowning in the pretention, obsequiousness and pushiness of the English media.

Neeson recognised this need in Mirren and took her home to show her his roots. There was no need to be embarrassed about his humble beginnings. Mirren positively relished them, though she was astounded by the diminutive terraced home in which he'd been brought up. 'It was so tiny,' she exclaimed to friends, 'absolutely minute. You just couldn't imagine a family fitting in there, let alone a family of six.'

For all her sophisticated tastes, generated by a decade of moving in celebrated and moneyed theatrical circles, Mirren was cheered by this evidence that Neeson was a solid, down-to-earth, hardworking provincial Irish lad at heart. She was as cultivated and accomplished as Neeson was gauche and awkward, but no one who knew Helen was surprised by her choice.

'At first,' says one of her colleagues, 'it was, "Oh, who's Helen's new toyboy?" I'm afraid no one took Liam very seriously. We never gave him as much staying power as he turned out to have. He was just this amiable gentle giant. But he was around for a long time.'

No one who knew them in London was in any doubt who was pulling the strings in this relationship. Helen had always been the dominant partner, stating her case, making men dance to her tune. This time, observers noted, the balance of power seemed to have shifted. Not that you were ever aware of Neeson showing his strength. Charming, affable and apparently malleable as ever, he quietly made his presence felt. Having invited him to share her London home with her, Mirren did not move on from him. During their four years together she would introduce him to a different strata of society to any in which he had moved before. She would teach him the skills of etiquette, wining, dining and networking. In turn, he offered her something she had not found in a relationship before. She discovered in him that rare gift of a quiet inner strength, the backbone (or was it heart?) of steel that Gerry McKeown had noted. No matter what was thrown at him, Neeson remained calm and resilient. He was a rare find among that most histrionic of professions, acting. In fact, as his Dublin circle could have told her, Neeson had always manifested the subtle capacity to exert his own quiet power. And strong, successful feisty actresses were as susceptible to it as anyone else.

Mirren's London agent, Maggie Parker, was also won over by Neeson's apparent naïveté and charm. She came down firmly in favour of Helen's latest choice too. 'Helen believed in Liam immediately – and immensely. She wanted to do things for him, open doors. She took him around, introduced him to people. She wanted to promote him.'

And so she did, quite successfully. By introducing him to the London theatrical scene, she opened doors to a whole new dramatic world. Mirren was not just respected and well known in London, but also in Paris and throughout the European theatre. By appearing at social events on Neeson's arm, she guaranteed he would be noticed in the inner sanctum of English theatrical circles. Neeson, in his soft and charming way, made sure that he would be not only noticed, but remembered.

He began to land new parts: there were small roles in several BBC productions. But the postman was not ringing twice – or even at all – with film offers. He had followed Mirren to England with his eye still to the main chance – ultimately, film fame. But, he had discovered, her contacts were largely the stage. So it was the stage he found himself on, culminating in his last, award-winning, *he was 34*

theatre appearance at the Royal Exchange in Manchester in 1984, in O'Casey's *The Plough and the Stars*. It was not where he wanted to be. The stage was too small for him, too restrictive, the audiences too partisan and again, too small.

Neeson was not happy. Television and film parts for Irish actors were few and far between and competition was intense. Even in the lucrative – but terribly infra dig for classical theatre actors – field of advertising, he found doors stayed resolutely shut. It was not, however, his Irishness that stood in the way here, as might have been expected. As a general rule of thumb, the advertising industry held it improbable that the British public might succumb in droves to the selling power of the Irish accent, unless it was flogging potatoes.

In Neeson's case, it was not his voice, but a certain part of his anatomy let him down. He had not imagined he would be driven to tout for work in downmarket telly ads, but here he was, with the wolf at the door, hands in pocket and only loose change jangling there. It was just a pity he took his hands *out* of his pockets . . .

He confessed, 'I used to bite my nails, not just to the quick, but right to the stumps. That had to stop in this game. I went for an ad, to get some extra money; it was a carpets ad and I had to be the salesman displaying the carpets. Well, the camera panned down on to my hand pointing at the carpets in the foreground and there were these chewed, ragged stumps. Looked like a bunch of half-eaten bananas. I didn't get the job. But I stopped chewing my nails.'

Advertising, TV, theatre, he still had not found a niche he could successfully exploit and move in. He was still playing second fiddle – by a long shot – to Mirren. Her light shone far brighter than his. Her salary dwarfed his erratic income. He was not making noises about it, that was not his style, but it was not a situation he was comfortable with. He decided, early in the relationship, to break away, assert his independence, as had always been his pattern. Keen to regain his personal space and his equilibrium, he moved first to a tiny flat in Parsons Green, west London, then, when that became too bourgeois for his taste, swiftly on to another flat in less than salubrious Stockwell, south London.

'It was lovely to begin with, there in my wee flat in Parsons Green, just down the Fulham Road, nice working-class feel to the place. I felt quite at home there. But overnight, it seemed, it became like this last bastion of the British Empire, full of frightfully naice types with their Golf GTIs. I couldn't bear it, had to get out.'

You could see where he felt uncomfortable, too, with some of the frightfully naice types who also moved in theatrical circles. They were not Neeson's style. He found it hard to mix and mingle with them, never knowing quite what to say without betraying his working-class roots.

None the less, he had begun to get some press exposure and now felt confident enough to grant interviews to publicise his latest ventures. In this, at least, he felt at home. He discovered, as had happened in Dublin, that when in a one-to-one situation with a woman, whether actress, reporter, barmaid or bus conductress, he could wind her round his little finger with just the right look. Hardened hacks would come away from interviews with this gorgeous Irishman and breathily agree he could charm the birds from the trees. The parts might not be coming in as thick and fast as he would like, but those that did were guaranteed maximum exposure in the press. Like TV and the theatre, the media was a small world, vicariously feeding on itself. Writers read each other's features, primed themselves on previous cuttings prior to interviews, saw that little-known Neeson was eminently lustable-after. They came, they saw, they lusted. He flirted and enjoyed himself enormously, then delighted in reading, in print, what he had long known to be true – he was irresistible to women.

The truth was, however, that Neeson, in interviews, actually said very little. He divulged no details about his private life. When asked questions about Mirren, he would deftly bat them away, claiming he had to keep a bit of his private life to himself. As a marketing ploy, it worked superbly. The female interviewers did not really want to pursue the notion of Liam Neeson actually involved with and, perish the thought, in bed with someone else.

He was quickly learning the rules of self-promotion. Keep 'em intrigued, say as little as possible and they'll fill in the spaces in between, usually with superlatives proclaiming this six foot four inch Ballymena export to be the tastiest thing to come out of the Emerald Isle since Baileys Irish Cream. And of course, so much smoother . . .

But for Neeson it was above all a time of frustration. With *Excalibur* the hoped-for transition to the big screen had taken place. He had moved to London, made himself available for more. But nothing much had happened other than bit parts and mini-series although he was prudent enough not to criticise *them*. After all, it was these which generated the publicity that had thus far made his name appear in print. Never knock the knock-on effect. Make enough noise and one day, the right producer or director might say, 'Oh yeah, I've read about this guy. He's supposed to be good. Let's try him out.'

He worked on four major oeuvres of the genre so derided by theatre actors: author Barbara Taylor Bradford's *A Woman of Substance* and its sequel, *Hold the Dream*. And later, *Ellis Island* and *If Tomorrow Comes*, based on Sydney Sheldon's bestselling blockbuster, and in which, playing the role of French detective André Trinault, he adopted a peculiar hybrid French-Irish accent. Directed by Gerry London, filming took place in Amsterdam, America and on the *Orient Express*. But Neeson, concerned about his accent, spent an additional two weeks in Paris, trying to capture the nuance and cadence of French speech. He confided to friends, 'The character doesn't present any problems, but the accent does. I have to adopt a French accent and actually speak some lines in French.' Whatever else the mini-series were, they offered massive public exposure, experience in front of the camera, travel and a sizeable fillip for the bank balance.

He knew his more classically trained peers would never deign to appear in any such TV pulp, and he felt the need to justify himself thus: 'They're fantastic learning grounds for any actor. You've got to think fast, act fast. In minutes of film time a day, with a feature film you might do two. A mini-series will shoot several times that. You've got to think on your feet. There's not much room for the Method kind of acting.'

Such self-justification in the face of his erstwhile colleagues' approbation some interpreted as wince-making. Why couldn't he just admit he was in it for the money? Or as one step up the ladder to blockbuster movies? Anyone who had ever known him, worked with him, had logged into the fact that this was Liam's ultimate ambition. But he felt the need to apologise for what he knew others would perceive as selling out.

Not for the first, nor certainly the last time, would he go public about his sorrow over the truly great actors whose great work would go unseen and unappreciated by the world at large: 'Ireland has some wonderful actors working away in rep – and no one who doesn't go to the Irish theatre will ever see the fruits of their labour and their talents. I worked with these people for ten years.'

It's the rider that gives the game away. Neeson wanted the world to know that there, but for the grace of God, went he. He had paid his dues. He was a classical actor too. But he was currently just filling in the spaces between the to-die-for roles. It was a long way from the truth. He had eschewed the challenge of acting in an intellectual milieu. The rewards were insufficient. Neeson wanted more – more fame, more fortune, more fans. But he still wanted to retain his kudos as an Actor Propre. He was determined to combine the esoteric background with the far greater rewards of life in the fast film lane.

Few who met him were perspicacious enough to see the single-minded motivation behind the apparent easy-going charm. But those who had seen Wee Liam evolve into Big Liam, Wannabe Movie Star, saw the reality behind the art and artifice.

As his erstwhile mentor, Gerry McKeown put it: 'So why did he pick film acting? If Liam was truly interested in the arts, as he always purports to be, he would have picked directing, but no. He wanted to be up there on stage and screen, to be fêted and applauded and hear that applause ringing in his ears. He wanted the glamour.

'Well, you can't claim to be an actor and want to hide your light under a bushel, be shy and self-effacing and inward-looking. That's what Liam tries to sell about himself. That's not just an anomaly, it's a contradiction in terms!

'He's always saying it's such a shame, there's so much talent back home in Ireland on the stage that's never going to get real recognition, but what's he talking about? They have the rewards they want, otherwise they wouldn't still be doing it. They'd have done what he did. The truth is, they didn't want it.

'Because what Liam did was trade that for something that's unreal. It's fantasy. And when you're living in that kind of fantasy, you can apply it to anything you see and do. So you paint pictures of your quaint Irish roots and that's not real.'

Liam Neeson had not swallowed his own fantasy. He knew exactly what he was doing and where he was heading: Hollywood, the big time. With lots and lots of acclaim and even more zeros after the first figure on his paycheck. His acting was vital because by using it, he could persuade people he was utterly ingenuous, charming, sweet and gorgeous. They would swallow the fantasy wholesale. And that would help him on his way.

8

Man With A Mission

'I never went to drama school. I did apply once, but I didn't go. It didn't matter, in the end. There's nothing like getting up and doing it, to study it. Well, acting is about performing, and performing requires an audience, and that is what I did.

'I dabbled a bit in the study side. I did some courses, two-week seminars in the summertime, a bit of Stanislavsky, bits of this, bits of that. But just working with people is the most effective way to learn. It worked for me, anyway. A lot rubs off on you along the way, and all the time you're working, earning.

'That's the main thing.'

Excalibur proved to be a gigantic and mesmerising slice of sorcery but it failed to cast a spell over Neeson's film career. Not for the faint-hearted, the movie alternated between being pictorially ravishing and an overdose of blood and gore.

Although it failed to set the box office on fire, it had fuelled Neeson's ambition to pursue more film work. It seemed to be a long time coming, though. He continued to work mostly on stage. For three years, between 1981 and 1984, there had been a few bit parts in TV drama and several mini-series, but film work continued to elude him, with one less than notable exception. In 1983, he landed a minor role in Peter Yates's *Krull*, a sword and sorcery sci-fi film which vituperative critics renamed *Krudd*. Although it had a strong cast, including Alun Armstrong, Francesca Annis and Lysette Anthony, the end product appealed largely to an audience with a mean age of four. Peter Yates was so impressed with Neeson, however, that he would later hold out, against heavy studio pressure for the Irishman to play the lead in one of his later, infinitely more successful, Hollywood films, *Suspect*.

But now, there were long periods out of work. After *A Woman of Substance*, Neeson found himself, for the first time, in the unenviable position most actors are familiar with at some point in their careers – of 'resting'. For five seemingly interminable months, the phone did not ring.

He recalls: 'I was going to spend some time learning French and Italian, jogging, putting that space to good use. But all I did was sit by the phone worrying, and drinking a lot of Guinness.

'That was when I realised that success puts you in a different bracket. You get a taste for it. You're no longer a jobbing actor. But you become very vulnerable. After five months with no work, you become convinced you're no good.'

Neeson may have been disheartened by his halting progress in the medium he wanted so badly to work in, but finally, in 1984, he landed a role in the remake of the 1962 epic, *Mutiny on the Bounty*. Originally, this classic tale of mutiny and betrayal was to have marked revered director David Lean's return to film after well over a decade in semi-retirement. But some way into filming, he left the project.

Meantime, New Zealand director Roger Donaldson was brought on board to sweep up the debris and put together a competent yarn. *The Bounty*, starring Anthony Hopkins as Cap'n Bligh, and Mel Gibson as Fletcher Christian had an impressive cast that also included Laurence Olivier, Edward Fox, Daniel Day Lewis and Bernard Hill. Neeson's role as rebellious sailor Charlie Churchill, who ends up with a flogging, had been played in the 1962 version by his fellow countryman, Richard Harris. It was a tough act to follow. Many said it was madness to try to better what was already a classic screen epic. Neeson defended the remake, saying, 'This is a much truer picture of what life was really like on the *Bounty*. It's not the sanitised version.'

In truth, he didn't enjoy making the film. As well as shooting in London film studios, he'd been given the Golden Fleece of travel opportunities – location shooting was based in Tahiti and New Zealand. But once cast and crew were ensconced in these most exotic of locations, Neeson discovered the reality of movie-making abroad was somewhat different to his previous home-based experiences in *Excalibur* and *Krull*.

'Glamorous, it wasn't,' he said. 'For the first two weeks, while you're still taking in the scenery and the tropical weather, it's paradise. But after that, you think, so what else am I going to do while I'm here?' Not that he was ungrateful, but he had now discovered that, even in some of the world's most exquisite far-flung places, when you're filming, there's all the hanging about. 'I'd been primed. I knew there would be lots of sitting around. I couldn't take off and coral dive. You're just sitting there, hour on hour, day after day, waiting for the call to do your bit. So I took some books with me and read them. Like *War and Peace . . .*'

Still, he never derided the other opportunities *The Bounty* offered him. Making contact with people like Anthony Hopkins was a decided bonus. He was much more at home working with Hopkins than star Mel Gibson. The two had little in common and did not form a bonding friendship. In fact, according to crew members, they gave each other a wide berth.

It was something Neeson was not to forget in the next few years as he plotted and made his move to Hollywood. Mel Gibson's name would always be above his on the billing. His trailer, his star and his salary would always be bigger than Neeson's. It was a fact that stuck in his craw. Though he acknowledged Mel's acting talent, he never could get round how a star like Mel was unapproachable, while an actor who had been around for much longer, like Anthony Hopkins, was immediately accessible – and a great crack.

He was held in thrall by the Welshman's performance. Watching him, it harkened back to those days on the Dublin stage where he recalled feeling inferior to some of the actors he performed alongside. He was soon to discover, however, that it was horses for courses.

The film opened in the US in May 1984, but was held over in Britain until Christmas. Meanwhile Neeson, kicking his heels, paid a visit home. He was fêted by locals and even made a piece in the *Ballymena Guardian*. BOUNTY BOY TIES UP AT HOME, ran the headline. But not for long. He only stepped ashore to visit his mam and dad and sip a few pints of Guinness at his local pub, the Globe, just up the road from his council house home in Corlea Gardens. The regulars were enthralled to hear how their own local hero was now the glittering star of the silver screen. *A Woman of Substance* had just been shown on television and well, if they hadn't known it was their Liam in the role of Blackie, they'd have never guessed . . . a reflection on the efficacy of prosthetic make-up. In the series, he'd had to age from twenty to eighty-four and sometimes, he told them, 'after wearing that stuff for hours on end, I actually felt eighty-four!'

Then there was *Ellis Island*, a CBS-TV drama which starred Richard Burton and Faye Dunaway. Appearing alongside such illustrious names was what hooked him, he admitted . . . along with the money. Though, to his immense disappointment, he never got to appear with them on screen. They were in different scenes altogether. It was another lesson learned about movie-making. Films and TV were like a knitting pattern. You shot all these separate scenes then they got knitted together into the end product.

But Neeson had not been deterred by the fact that he would not be working alongside Burton and Dunaway. He had wanted to meet them and so he did. Not for nothing was he that lad who had waited days in the pouring rain to meet Colin Blakely. He revealed, 'I was kind of like a fan standing outside the stage door, desperate to see these great stars. I didn't feel like an actor alongside them. I was really impressed. To my mind, they had some kind of aura around them that separated them from the rest of us. They were real stars.'

But here, he was still Ballymena Boy. It helped to keep his feet on the ground. But of course, there were still those dreams. Meeting Burton, particularly, fired his old fantasies. 'I was thinking, Yes, I wouldn't mind a slice of that particular cake.'

At the same time, he was hedging his bets by keeping an eye out for theatre parts. To this end, he pursued his fellow countryman, Colin Blakely, asking him for tips and tip-offs. The actor had never forgotten the tenacious amateur dramatic hopeful. Briefed by a package of cuttings about himself, proving Neeson had successfully made the move from amateur to professional, he agreed to meet.

'He was the most charming, marvellous man,' enthused Neeson, no doubt building up a wannabe profile of how *he* might be in the future, when luck and perseverance had won through, 'Thanks to him, I got the chance to do a TV play with him. Fantastic.'

In 1985, he was cast in *The Innocent*, a beautiful and evocative slice of English life in Yorkshire during the Great Depression of the 1930s. Sadly, it was so depressing that nobody bothered to go and see it. But great success loomed that same year in *Lamb*, the Colin Gregg film of Bernard MacLaverty's novel in which he gave a performance that really made people sit up and take note of the name Neeson.

The role was so right for him, it was practically an act of divine providence. After all, who better than a good Irish Catholic to play the part of a priest? Neeson had the perfect CV. Ex-choirboy, steeped in his religion, surrounded all his life by priests and prayer. Neeson could scarcely believe his luck. It was another of those peculiar twists of fate and coincidence that have woven the fabric of his life. 'It's ironic,' he admitted, 'how I ended up in this playing the part of a priest because I truly, seriously thought about joining the priesthood when I was a boy, I was that devout.'

Lamb is gripping drama and playing the lead was a tough, demanding and ultimately draining role for Neeson. There is scarcely a scene without him in it.

Troubled monk Father Michael Lamb is a teacher at a harsh Irish detention centre, isolated in remote and barren countryside, a kind of Badlands where 'boys beyond hope' are dumped for correction and reformation in the dubious care of the God-fearing brothers.

Father Lamb stands out among his decidedly un-Christian brothers in that he does actually care about the boys in his flock, subjected as they are to a regime of deprivation, victimisation and unwarranted cruelty. One waif-like victim evokes in him more pity than the other stronger, tougher inmates. A fragile bond is struck up between him and the boy. An epileptic ten-year-old with an alcoholic mother, the child has never known love until Lamb rescues the lad from his life of hell by abducting him and fleeing to London.

On the run, they're free to explore their curious symbiotic relationship and Lamb questions the big issues in life – his faith, morality, and sexuality. In a tragic and inevitable ending, Lamb gives the boy his ultimate freedom: death. He drowns the boy he loves in order to free him from his hopeless predicament, thereby condemning himself to his own private hell.

It is testimony to Neeson's skill that audiences come away from the film both shattered and deeply affected by the performance and the issues raised.

Neeson loved the film, 'It was a very personal film for me to make on several levels. I'd read the book myself, years earlier. I was really moved by it and I thought if it was ever filmed, I'd love to play that part.'

He was not perturbed by the prospect of going against the old W.C. Fields maxim of never working with children or animals. Although Hugh O'Connor, who played the boy, gave Neeson a run for his money in the acting stakes, Neeson managed to counterbalance the child's winning performance with his own sensitively tuned delivery.

In fact, off screen, Neeson was touched by the child's genuine innocence and, during shooting, the two became friends. They would not meet up again until 1990, in Hollywood at the Golden Globe Awards. The memories of his favourite film came flooding back and Neeson was shocked to see how time had moved on and left its mark on O'Connor. 'He'd changed – well, he would have, wouldn't he? He'd grown up and lost that wonderful innocence he had. But that's what life's all about.' He might have added, 'And especially life in Hollywood.'

Neeson had never forgotten the beauty of that winning innocence and how people responded to it. Life took its toll and gradually eroded it, but who was to say it couldn't be recaptured? And who better to do that than an actor? He had invested the character of Lamb himself with a powerful innocence. It was valuable, it affected people, it won trust. He had recourse to recapturing it himself on many occasions. Neither life nor Hollywood was going to take that away from him.

But he was ultimately to be disappointed in the film's reception. Though it was critically acclaimed in the UK, it was too esoteric for the public's taste and America was not interested at all, rejecting it on the basis of its tragic dénouement. If the Americans can't have a happy ending, Neeson discovered, you can forget it. Despite that, or perhaps because of it, Neeson continued to hold the film dear, as one of his favourites.

Years later, he'd still be putting in a word here and there, wherever he could, in the hope that people wouldn't forget it and perhaps the US would reconsider and release it, 'I think the producers are hoping I'll get famous. Maybe that would help,' he commented wryly at the time. Sadly, he is still waiting for his favourite work to be resuscitated in the US.

He would never forget that the vagaries of the movie industry were such that you could create a brilliant product, and yet it would end up going nowhere because the powers that be decided not to back it. Better to pitch for becoming a bit of the power yourself, then.

Increasingly, with Neeson's continuing involvement in film and TV, the stage began to appear a less attractive option. Neeson had played his first lead role in a film. Going back to sixth billing in a production that entailed slogging your guts out night after night, week after week wouldn't be an easy step to take. Neeson believed it would be a step backwards. But he was not yet confident enough

Liam Neeson. Open, honest, the kind of face you can trust

Kitty Neeson

The enigmatic smile
hinted at, even at
seventeen

As Michael Lamb, with
Hugh O'Conor, in
Lumb

As Danny Scoular, *The
Big Man*

No, you can't come in. I'm a private kinda guy

Liam alone: that inimitable look of the soul in torment

With Helen Mirren

With Natasha
Richardson. 'If
anyone's got what it
takes, Natasha has'

No, I'm not giving up –
they're such a great prop for
these moody introspective
shots

With *Nell*, Jodie Foster

As Oskar Schindler. 'I'm going to give you an entrance in a movie that no one's ever had before'

to close the stage door completely. What if the film roles dried up?

Observers noted Neeson's work was progressively concentrating on screen acting but when questioned about his move away from the theatre, he became very defensive. 'I still yearn to tread the boards. I'd like to go on stage at least once a year to keep in touch with the stage. It's where an actor should do his real work. His spiritual work.'

But it would be ten years before Neeson got near a theatre dressing room again. It wasn't for the lack of offers. In late 1984 he was approached by the Royal Shakespeare Company to consider a role in their much acclaimed revival of Arthur Miller's *The Crucible*. To appear with the RSC was the paeon of acting, every true thespian's dream. Here they were, the world's most revered acting company, actually knocking on Neeson's door and offering him a watertight six-month contract. From that point on, the world of theatre would be his oyster.

He turned them down. Why? Tricky question. He played it absolutely straight. No point in beating around the bush now. 'I was very flattered they should offer me that chance. It was a play I'd always wanted to do. I almost realised a great ambition there.' But 'right now I want to concentrate on films. That's the media that interests me the most.'

Helen Mirren, having introduced him to the leading lights of English theatre, respected his brave, some would have said foolhardy, decision. To turn down an RSC role that most actors would have given their eye-teeth and forelocks for?

But Neeson now firmly believed in the old adage: fortune favours the brave. He had seen it work for himself. He had done it time and again, walking away from university and college, safe jobs at the Lyric and the Abbey. Risk was not just his game, he had made it his business, and it had never failed him thus far.

Now he was taking another one. He was walking away from not just the RSC but also from Helen. The relationship that had freed him from the trap of the Irish stage, that had opened the doors to English theatre, TV and now the film work he had always aspired to, had run its course. It was over. People would soon find out and people would talk. Some might see him as a user, manipulating his redoubtable sexual charms to further his career ends. He had to head them off at the pass, then.

It would not serve his purpose well if he were portrayed as cool, calculating, exploitative. Especially not exploitative of women, in these, the aspiring to be equal eighties. Not that anyone who knew her could conjecture that Helen Mirren was easy prey for manipulation. Helen, by and large, danced to her own tune. But who knew, in lust and love, what blind alleys the emotions were capable of leading you up?

Neeson had never let any intrusive prying into his private life sidetrack him into comment before. As always, he had kept completely schtum over his four-year relationship with Helen even though there had been persistent enquiries. Outsiders, even friends and colleagues, had long been intrigued by the match, mystified by the secrecy shrouding it, astonished at the longevity, particularly when you looked at their track records.

Thus far, Neeson had successfully parried all questions with a charming but final: 'No comment, really. I can't say anything.' The only thing he had ever conceded was that there had unequivocally never been any chance of marriage on the cards. By now the deck was played out, the cards were frayed round the edges. The romance was dead and the relationship over. But Neeson still had one trump up his sleeve.

He would extricate himself from this relationship and still come up smelling of roses. He just had to feed the press the right lines. And he knew *exactly* how to do that. He would adopt his favourite stance – by saying so little, he would actually say so much, especially when accompanied by one of those mournful but resigned looks he had perfected over the years.

Neeson then went on record vowing how he had never, would never reveal anything about their relationship, other than to say that 'Helen was, and always will be one of my dearest friends. She taught me so much about life and love. She showed me so much, from the joys of older women to the techniques of eating sushi. I owe her so much.' Anything else, of course, was private. As love should be. The perfect line: Leave 'em guessing and your name will stay on their lips. And with such integrity. Let's face it, everyone hates a kiss 'n' tell merchant.

Mirren was slightly more forthcoming. She revealed she was phlegmatic about the separation, having long regarded it as ultimately inevitable. She was also concerned to put the record straight about just how *much* she had done for the fledgling actor. It was, after all, she who had taught him to fly. And now he had soared off into the great blue beyond. Such is life.

'Liam,' she said, 'was living in my house. All of our friends were my friends. It was time for him to look beyond. Yes, it was painful but there was no going back. We both recognised the need for it. It was time for him to gain his independence.'

Mirren did not let herself hurt for long. Almost immediately, she found herself another, more permanent partner in the director Taylor Hackford.

The truth was, it had for a long time been a relationship of some convenience to Neeson. Living a separate life in his own flat, he had time and space to call his own and a woman to call his, when the occasion befitted it. It was the perfect let-out clause. He could flirt and charm till the cows came home and still not have to pay the ferryman. Those women, whether they were casting agents, TV producers, press or simply the girl standing next to him in the pub, could succumb to his flattering attentions, but know, for now at least, he could not be theirs. He was already spoken for.

The fact remained that Liam Neeson was now, as ever, his very own man, answerable to no woman. He had been as true as his word when he said Mirren was 'a dear friend'. Let the world believe they were in love, if it wanted to. No such statement of commitment had ever been elicited from him.

Thus officially freed from his cage, Neeson could be seen to spread his wings. He would not touch down in another relationship for a long time, preferring to flit from one romance to another – although the women in question had no inkling of the flightiness of the hulking great Irishman who loped into their lives.

Neeson was free, just the way he liked it, and he was indeed flying. His film career was definitely on the up 'n' up. *Lamb* was no sooner in the can than he took off for his next role in *The Mission* playing . . . another priest. He shrugged what was beginning to look like typecasting as 'just coincidence. It's just a cough and spit part, anyway. I'm not in the horns of some dilemma, considering what I'm doing with my life, or rethinking my career. It's just the way it's panned out.'

Observers, however, got the feeling that someone, somewhere just might be looking after this man. Perhaps all those early prayers were now paying off. In fact, it was to be on *The Mission* that Neeson would actually claim to re-embrace the faith he had put on the back burner for some years.

Filming meant spending three months in the Colombian jungle. But the company was good. Ray McAnally, playing third lead as Altamirano, was a mate from days in Irish rep. The pair went back a long way and the bonds of this friendship were particularly strong. It was in McAnally's production of *Of Mice and Men* that John Boorman spotted Neeson and plucked him for *Excalibur*. They had worked together, played together and were mutually supportive. Neeson did not know it then, but this experience of working together in South America would be especially precious to him. McAnally died just three years later. Neeson was devastated. He would recall: 'Ray was a guru to me. We acted together, socialised together. He directed me in so many ways, not just on the stage.

'I once got a call from him on my answerphone. I can still hear his voice to this day. He said, "It's Ray. I'm in Birmingham. England, not Alabama!'

'I kept that message on my machine for months because I didn't want to lose his voice. Then I found a photo of him from *The Mission*. As usual, with his mouth open, talking. God rest his soul. It took me a very long time to accept he was dead.'

Their time together on *The Mission* was further enhanced by Jeremy Irons, whose work Neeson knew from his time on the London stage. Then, of course, there was Robert De Niro. It was going to be some learning curve this, to be working with one of the all-time great Hollywood legends, and Neeson knew it. He was not disappointed.

'De Niro was a revelation. He came on set absolutely stripped naked. His canvas was white and the frightening thing was, he waited for you to throw the colours on. There was none of this, "Right, I say this and then you . . ." stuff, no direction from him. When you looked at him, you looked right into his soul. Now that was daunting.'

It was also invaluable experience. 'I learned the value of commitment and preparation from De Niro. Preparation is all. But once you start, you have to put it down. You don't tie it on the character. You just rely on the fact that you've absorbed it, you're ready and it's there. It's going to come out when it's ready to.'

There were more lessons to be learned from Jesuit activist Daniel Berrigan, who was an adviser on the film. At this point, Neeson had long since questioned his religious faith and had subsequently let his Catholicism lapse. Berrigan brought with him the fire and the passion that had led him to his frontline position in religious politics. The pair sparked off each other and would often sit down together at the end of the day's shoot, thrashing out their opinions on religious politics.

Says Neeson: 'Dan had been over to Ireland when Bobby Sands and the other hunger strikers were dying. He had stood in the rain for days outside the prison in vigil. He cared passionately about these problems and had used everything in his power to work on them.'

Inspired by Berrigan's faith, Neeson adopted him as a kind of religious mentor. They fasted together and when Berrigan invited Neeson to help him conduct mass on a makeshift table in a jungle clearing, Neeson readily accepted. A crew or cast member would read the lesson and Berrigan would then interrupt the proceedings to quiz the congregation on what exactly the epistle meant to them. It was wholly interactive and, especially to Neeson, inspirational.

De Niro, too, was absorbed by the religious process. Playing the role of a Jesuit missionary who had converted from his previous life as a ruthless Conquistador, he had delved, as was typical of his Method-style preparation for the role, into the spiritual teachings of Jesuit founder Ignatius Loyola. When Berrigan quizzed him, he was able to pluck, as if from the air, an erudite and well-researched reply.

Neeson, closeted away in the middle of the jungle with these two zealots, was motivated to look deep within himself. He brought this new depth to the role he played, but he also brought it to himself. He said: 'We were so lucky, we had the luxury of time. It was a long shoot, so we were able to live the essence of these people in the jungle, in the real environment along with the natives. You could immerse yourself in the whole change, live it.

'You can't act that. I didn't. I didn't want any part of my character to touch the twentieth century. To be able to do that produces great screen acting. It's the process, it's what everyone aims for. It can last moments, or just seconds, but you are completely consumed. I saw it happen a lot with De Niro and with Ray. It was bliss.'

His own research into how best to play a committed Jesuit priest had led him to an interesting discovery. 'I discovered that the founder of Method acting, Stanislavsky, had been inspired by Loyola's spiritual exercises – and adapted them as the basis for all his teachings.'

This was perfect synchronicity, timing down to a fine art. 'It was the dawn of a revelation. In the middle of that jungle, the two great forces in my life – acting and religion – came together hand in glove.' Like that moment on Carn Hill. But this time, there were no little green men, no fireworks, nor even pink elephants. The epiphany this time was real. The conclusion was inevitable. 'I took up my faith again.'

From that point on, Neeson firmly believed in his destiny. What would be would be. But he could use this re-embraced faith in other ways too. It enhanced his performance in *The Mission* and he would later be able to call on it for other roles, like the part of an IRA assassin, which he played alongside Mickey Rourke in *A Prayer for the Dying*. 'I was able to look deep inside me and see where that faith could lead people to put it before everything. Even to the point where they would murder in the name of it.'

He could never have anticipated the strength of it, but *The Mission* proved to be a cataclysmic film for him personally, affecting him deeply on both spiritual and personal levels.

Professionally, it was a fair career-enhancer too. Unlike *Lamb*, *The Mission* had a widespread release and also won huge critical success, walking off with the coveted Palme D'Or award at the Cannes Film Festival.

It was also a lesson in humility. Neeson had come a long way in terms of acting success and ability, but *The Mission* made him feel like an ingénu. 'I felt like an acting student, frankly, working with three very different schools of acting, taken out of their environment and literally planted in the middle of nowhere in a jungle in Colombia. It was fascinating to watch. All that play and interplay and some very subtle mind-games going on. And of course, some incredible acting, too. I felt like a bit of a voyeur. It really opened my eyes to what film acting could be all about.'

The location shoot, originally estimated as three months, stretched into four before Neeson returned to his Stockwell flat. Although fastidiously tidy by nature, this was a typical bachelor pad and Neeson's hasty departure for South America, straight after putting *Lamb* to bed, meant he'd left it in a state of comparative disarray. The first thing he saw when he walked in the door was the mouldering, congealed cup of tea he had left hurriedly on the table just prior to his haring out of the door for his flight. The sight of it had a curious and unexpected effect on him. He burst into tears. 'It felt like I was in a timewarp,' he recalled, 'strange, misplaced. I knew a whole lot of experiences had bombarded me during those months and it would take some time to sift through them. I just sat down and cried.'

It was, he knew, going to be incredibly tough for him to settle back into the routine, the rut, of going back on stage. In that instant, he made up his mind not to do it any more. It was over. That part of his life was gone. There was no going back. There could only be moving forward from now on.

He took stock of his career so far. *The Mission* had made him realise that although he was a mite overawed by the talent of De Niro, his own potential was immense. It was only a matter of keeping moving, keeping learning, and he could be up there too. He'd never really questioned he was doing the right thing, ever since the day he quit college and came home to the Slemish Players, in pursuing acting as a career. But *Excalibur*, *Krull*, *The Innocent*, *The Bounty*, *Lamb* and especially *The Mission* had fuelled him with a passion and an ambition more intense than he'd ever known before.

'Right then I felt a new intensity about acting. There sometimes comes a point in your life where you wonder if you're doing the right thing. I've never doubted it in myself, but sometimes you wonder, when you're faced with parts that you feel aren't taking you in the direction you want to go. That's when you question, not what you're doing, but where you're going.'

He wanted to hold on to this intensity, this drive, this ambition. He looked at the opposite end of the spectrum – the mini-series he'd done. Working with some of the US actors employed on them had had the opposite effect. Compared to them, he had quickly realised how good he really was. He had emerged from them feeling the equivalent of a big fish in an ocean of plankton. Well, no point in false modesty, was there? American actors were not renowned for underselling themselves or their talents, no matter how slender.

'Some of the Americans I worked alongside – for instance those who specialise in mini-series, were truly terrible. Yet they always managed to land the big fat chunky lead roles. They couldn't carry it alone, so British actors would be brought in – in little breadcrumb parts – to bolster up the saggy acting. That struck me as a pretty sad state of affairs.'

And one, he vowed, that wouldn't happen to him for much longer. Not if he could help it. He was sharp enough to realise that if he stayed in England, he'd be more breadcrumbs for the birds. He wanted the whole loaf. There was only one way to do it. Go to the bakers.

9

Hello, Hollywood

'All I had was The Mission *and* Duet For One *lined up. I went on the back of them. That was it. But I got lucky. I did a* Miami Vice *which they used as the opener of their new series and twenty million people watch this fucking thing.*

'There was just one problem. We're set to shoot and they had me decked in these great clothes, Armani suits and all that stuff. Great gear. But they couldn't find one with long enough legs for me. So they shot me from the waist up in my polka dot underpants.

'There I am in my underwear, trying to act this cool dude for twenty million viewers. Some introduction . . .'

It was January 1987. New Year, new beginnings. Neeson packed a solitary bag and did exactly what his intuition had suggested and he had long known he would do . . . hit Hollywood. He'd had a taste of it with his forays into US mini-series, but this time he was throwing in his lot to make the move permanent. It wasn't a tough step. He wasn't looking back.

'I always felt that if you love what you do, you find a way to develop. If you want to work in films, which I did, you had to live in LA. There were simply no two ways about it. Otherwise you stay in London thinking, God, I want to be in the movies, but the Royal Shakespeare Company has offered me eighteen months in this amazing production and . . . suddenly your life's gone and you haven't done the dream.

'You take the RSC contract because it's a huge accolade and also, let's not forget, actors have to act. But the other dream disappears.

'Well, I was thirty-four, I'd done ten years on the stage and

films. I'd done the groundwork. I didn't want to be forty-four
and sitting in London saying, "I wish I'd done it years ago." And
knowing I'd never do it now.

'In my heart of hearts, it had always been a dream to combine
the two, but after I did *Excalibur* I caught the film bug. It gets in
your system, at least, it did mine.'

Nor could he put it down, not like he could most other things.
At thirty-four he was that rarest of things – a gorgeous, desirable,
eminently eligible single man with no ties and no responsibilities.
You don't get to be in that position at that age without a lot of
concerted effort in keeping things that way. Mirren had been an
advantage to him in so many ways, not least in lending credence
to the line: 'I can't. I've got a regular girlfriend.'

Not any more he didn't. He acknowledged what he claimed was
his new-found freedom. In fact, as he knew, he had always been free
to pursue his own choices. That hadn't changed.

'I had no responsibilities. I wasn't married. I'd accumulated some
money. Enough, I reckoned, to last six weeks in LA. If I didn't find
work in that time, I still had choices. In many ways, it really wasn't
as difficult a move as it had been from Ireland to London.

'There's a strong Irish-American affiliation in the States that's not
in evidence in London. So I didn't feel intimidated by the distance
or the move.'

What might have been more intimidating was the knowledge that
the Hollywood movie machine devoured hopefuls, robbed them of
their money, their hopes and their dreams, left them desolate and
broke – in every way. Neeson was unperturbed. 'I knew what the
industry could do to kids. It chewed them up and spat them out
in bits. But I was thirty-four. I'd seen a bit of life, knew what I
was going for, had my moral code and my sense of values already
sorted. I wasn't likely to be cannon fodder.'

Director David Leland, who became close to Neeson two years
later when they worked together on his film *The Big Man*, believes
Neeson made not just a smart move, but the only move that was
really open to him, given his thrusting ambition. 'Liam had no
choice. If he didn't go to America, he was going to end up in
the TV graveyard. He'd seen it happen to all the sixties stars.
They ended up, not as movie stars, but flogging themselves in
Agatha Christie TV specials.'

As a hiding to nothing, Neeson knew that couldn't be beaten.
Far better to gamble on a one-way ticket. So long as he had his

return fare safe in his back pocket – and he had; those canny Irish ways had made sure there was always some spare cash in the piggy bank – then it was simply exploring another option. He knew the RSC would always be there. He had turned them down once, there might be a minor fit of pique to contend with if he decided to walk back that way, but he had charm and persuasion enough to sort that out, if it came down to it.

He had another string to his bow, contends Leland, that made the Hollywood move the smart move. He respected and admired movie acting. He preferred it to stage acting. Leland explains: 'Liam is a technician. He's always had an American approach to screen acting. It's very different to the rather snobbish British attitude. By and large, British actors tend to think the finest acting shines out of the theatre's arse. And screen acting, at its best, is just theatre acting, but smaller.

'Liam does not think that way. He picked up the American attitude that screen acting is actually the peak of the craft. And he respects the medium. He's a perfectionist. He wants to know all about the machinery of the process, the mechanics of how a film works. And it's for one reason – so he can work out how best to respond to the camera.

'That's why he was always going to make it. He was destined to reach the top.'

Destined? Maybe. Determined, certainly. He headed, first, for New York. And right on top of his list of 'Must Do's was: make it happen.

He was ready. One thing he had not forgotten to pack was his confidence. Or his positivity. 'I felt physically and mentally as tight as a drum. If some director had said to me, "I want you to play King Lear", I'd have said, fine. Give me a week. You'll have it.'

He had reason enough to feel bullish. He wasn't diving in at the deep end in Hollywood, jobless, homeless with nothing but high hopes to sustain him. He had done his homework. On the dismal, sleet-driven winter day he'd decided to leave London, he'd done more than simply tot up his finances and his chances.

He recalled, 'It had been one of those December days when it gets dark by two in the afternoon and I'd said to myself, "I'm going to visit the bank manager and see how much I've got." Then I put in a call to my US agent and said, "Howard, I'm coming over.

And I'm not going to sit in a hotel room for six weeks. I want to see *everybody*. Get on to it.'"

And for good measure, he was stopping off first in New York where he would stay with a friend. That friend might be of some use in putting work his way. It was Robert De Niro. He had not even shrugged off his jetlag before De Niro pointed him in the right direction – his own casting agent, Bonnie Timmerman.

Timmerman can still recall Neeson's arrival in New York, and his immaculate timing. 'He was no sooner here than a script for *Miami Vice* landed on my desk with a part in it for a 'big Irish guy'. I thought, Yes, I know just the man for this job. He couldn't have been fresher in my mind. He'd practically just walked out of the office.'

He walked the part, too. *Miami Vice* was his ticket to Los Angeles. He rented a home, hired a car, invested in a street map and headed out on the 101 Freeway, putting his face around town. Well within his trial period, Neeson was established in Hollywood with a part behind him, other possibles lined up, a Green Card and a big smile on his face. 'It was,' he recalls, 'a great learning curve.'

Curves, after all, were what Hollywood was all about. And Neeson's first lesson was that Tinseltown was the Mecca for the body beautiful. For any budding actor, physical perfection had to come top of your list of attributes, otherwise you don't get past the doorman, buddy. Forget methodology. You could save the Stanislavsky school of acting for New York. Here in LA, it wasn't so much what you projected as the packaging it came in.

He knew that he had slackened off after relinquishing boxing. In *Lamb*, he had piled on a few pounds. His weakness for a pint or two of Guinness began to show in his rounded facial features. Now he was in LA he had to take stock. Luckily, Neeson had a lot of good things going for him, bodywise. His boxing past had stood him in good stead. It would only require regular gym sessions to get back into shape. He booked up at a local gym and began daily workouts with a vengeance.

Leland witnessed Neeson's addiction to rigorous fitness sessions. He knew that in this area, as with everything else he set his mind on, Neeson would not quit until he was in perfect shape. 'A major part of how successful you're going to be as an actor in Hollywood rests on how you look when you're stripped to the waist. You can actually hear studio executives saying, "He took his shirt off and blew it."'

Neeson had no intention of being blown away for lack of pecs appeal. Unlike many of his British counterparts, who felt it undignified to bare all for their art, he was absolutely up for it. Like his Celtic forebear Sean Connery, if a part called for him to strip off and flex, he would, gladly. But he liked to make out that he was not personally in favour of the demented physical perfection credo dictated by Hollywood. Being dictated to over the way you looked and behaved went against the grain of his free spirit.

'In LA you're made incredibly aware of your body. The media constantly bombard you with messages about how you've got to look. But I don't think Dan Ackroyd would have been as funny if he were built like a marathon runner. I still find it refreshing that people like him could let their bodies go to seed.

'Gérard Depardieu is the same thing – a great big hulk – yet he shows it all. And he's still a real sexy guy and a great actor. Personally, I'm tired of seeing actors whip off their tee-shirts at the drop of a hat to show they've done their press-ups.'

But he kept doing it all the same. 'I keep in shape because my body is my instrument. It's what I act with and pay my bills with – and a few other people's bills as well. My driving force is to keep in as good a shape as possible without people thinking I'm showing off. I'm just dreading the time when a director says, "Look, I need you to go to seed a bit." And yet I know, sure I do, that one day, it's going to happen . . .'

When it eventually did happen, that director was Steven Spielberg – not a man normally to be trifled with. And the part was that of Oskar Schindler. Now, when Spielberg says, 'I want you to gain ten pounds for the biggest role in your acting career, starring in a guaranteed multi-million global blockbuster,' most actors would be throwing back quadruple cheeseburgers and chips with double mayo before you could say 'Pass the ketchup.' After all, his old mate De Niro did it, gaining forty-two pounds for *Raging Bull*.

Neeson refused.

Of course, his refusal would be delivered with aplomb and plausible charm, and it would be Spielberg who backed down. So Schindler would be transformed from overweight roue to a man at the peak of his physical strength and stamina. A man, in other words, just like Neeson.

There are some things worth sacrificing for your art. Relationships, marriage, maybe. The body beautiful he had spent over two decades lavishing time and attention on? No chance.

It paid off. When he stripped down to bare essentials for his role as Diane Keaton's lover in *The Good Mother*, his performance gained rave reviews. From the public. Women everywhere went apoplectic about his 'great buns'.

He had long since learned that his looks opened doors to him. Now he stood framed in the doorway and heads were turning. There was just one tricky incident, early on in his time in Hollywood, where his looks proved to be a problem. But that was before he learned how to project them properly. Looking like the foreigner in town, with his usual slightly shambolic appearance, he was not sufficiently au fait with LA custom to know that no one walks anywhere. That's inviting trouble.

Out one day, strolling along, the way the Irish do, taking in the sights and sounds of Beverly Hills, he was stopped in his tracks when a police car roared to a halt beside him. Out jumped two LA cops, waving batons. They backed him up against a wall, spreadeagled him, turned out his pockets and searched him. They'd immediately assumed he was dangerous. Who else but vagrants, muggers and would-be burglars casing joints wandered the streets of Beverly Hills? All the evidence the cops required was written all over Neeson. Jeans, scruffy trainers, broken nose, and that most un-Hollywood of all things – irregular, uncapped teeth.

Neeson was released without charge. The whole incident, he later laughed, was farcical. Others might have found it terrifying. But he had always been confident in his ability to take on all comers. He also had a healthy respect for authority. Especially when it packed a pistol and had a baton sticking between your ribs.

It was a one-off however. By and large, his build worked very much in his favour. His acting mentor back in Ballymena had always known that Neeson's sheer physical size, such a disadvantage on the tiny stages of amateur dramatic productions and fringe theatre, would have maximum impact in the film world.

'Of course height is positively an asset in film. When it comes to filling bill roles, for big characters, then if you're six feet four inches and built like a brick outhouse, you're already in the frame. And of course, it means casting directors never forget you.

'It has its downside, too. It can lead to being typecast in the role of heavies – which Liam was for a bit.'

But, as film insiders observed, Neeson saw that one coming. He did not intend to be stuck with the broken-nosed-thug label all his acting life. Or any of it, come to that. And the only way round it, with his looks and stature, was to be the antithesis of the way he looked. That would intrigue them, wouldn't it? The brute with the soft centre. The romantic, the sensitive soul, trapped inside this towering bulk. Well, it had always worked on women. Why not on Hollywood moguls?

'Liam was canny enough to realise that if he played on this soft, vulnerable side to him, he would add another dimension to the roles he was offered.'

Again it was purely fortuitous timing that as Neeson was flexing himself to make his mark in film, the power-hungry, yuppie-driven, money-mad and macho eighties were drawing to a close. The days of the big male ego were numbered. The me generation were about to go down with Black Monday. The backlash had already begun in Hollywood, the quest was on to find – or create – a new breed of star: new man. He who had soul, sensitivity, compassion and care, an inner core of sensuality inextricably intertwined with a high moral code. But let's not make him foppish, hey guys? Let's give him some male credibility by marrying all that lot to a hulking great physique, then we'll get the men's vote as well as the women's.

Enter Liam Neeson, just the soulful ticket. Along with that other great big bear, Gérard Depardieu, Neeson heralded the way forward for Hollywood. Between them, they broke the mould. Before them, and still today, most of the top grossing box-office actors had a tendency towards being short. The Tom Cruises, Mel Gibsons, Dustin Hoffmans and Robert Redfords had a mean height of – let's be charitable here – somewhere around five feet six inches.

There was no danger of a repeat of the Alan Ladd syndrome with Liam Neeson. Ladd had to carry his own box to stand on for the love scenes, so he could rise to the kissing height of his leading ladies. Put Liam in a love scene and even the most robust of actresses, the Kathleen Turners or the Geena Davises, could melt into his arms like a delicate slip of a thing.

There was no doubt about it, in LA, Neeson felt he had finally come home. He might have virtually no previous track record of US movies, but that in itself was not disadvantageous. He was new, he was fresh, he was quite literally a giant among men in this town. It suited him. He liked the transient nature of the place, being a man of few possessions. Living out of a suitcase suited him. There was nothing to tie him down. Unencumbered, he could pursue his quest with relentless zeal. Work was both his motivation and his raison d'être.

Back home, such driven ambition was treated with suspicion or even derision. The British resent go-getters, the ruthlessly ambitious and the ultra-successful. They like to stay at home and play with their toys a while. There are other, more important priorities in life than work, like friends, family, long expense-account lunch breaks. Here in LA, work was the be-all and end-all and lunch was just another low-cal business meet. Yes, Liam Neeson fitted in fine here.

There would be no one poking accusatory fingers at him here, decrying him for his single-track mind. No one wondering how come a nice handsome fella like him wasn't settled down and married. He was finally free to be himself. Yet he was realistic about the fate of so many jobbing – or worse, jobless – actors here in Celluloid City. 'It's not an easy town to live in if you're not employed. You can't loiter on the streets the way you can in British cities, like London or Glasgow. It's a town I wouldn't like to be out of work in for too long.'

There was no fear of that. Word was out by now that there was new talent in town. For all its big noise and self-publicity, LA is different to any other Smalltown, USA, where everyone knows everyone else, says Gabrielle Donelly, author and doyenne of showbiz writers who, although Irish herself, has lived in Hollywood for fifteen years. 'If someone new and good appears, he's going to be hot news. Gossip in this town spreads like wildfire.'

It's not just producers and directors who keep their ear to the ground for new bodies: other stars keep an eye open too. There are some huge and fragile egos up there in Star Heaven. They don't want to be overshadowed by some big name playing opposite them. 'So they like new talent, so long as it knows its place.'

Neeson did. He had just the right kind of looks for leading Hollywood ladies to be seen with on his arm, yet he wasn't threatening enough to steal their thunder. And he was, by way of a bonus, just so damned attractive. And available. At least physically. . . Liam Neeson would soon prove to be one of the most prized catches in Hollywood for women in search of the ultimate bit of beefcake.

But all this was hovering on the horizon. First, there was work to be done. He knew he would have to sift among the rubbish for a bit, but that was okay, it would be a start. Consequently he jumped feet first into a disastrous movie – *Satisfaction* – from which he personally derived none at all. In it, he played a faded, ageing rock star. Even now, he would like to ignore it in the hope that it will go away. He is so embarrassed by this turkey that all he will say of it is: 'Unsatisfactory. I have no intention of ever seeing it.'

But it was not a wholly unprofitable experience. His co-star was the then unknown but ascending actress, Julia Roberts. The chemistry between them was explosive. The director, Joan Freeman, was a first-hand witness to the frisson between the pair which lent the only spark to an otherwise turgid film. She recalled how, 'Doing the film wasn't a pleasant experience for Liam. He felt it was creatively stifling – and Liam very much needs to be creative. There were people, too, who were not happy with him. The end result was he probably felt quite under-appreciated. But there was one bonus: he met Julia through it.'

For two hungry, ambitious actors, it was a precipitous meeting. Within weeks, they had moved in together. In fact, contrary to reports that the pair lived together for over a year, it was a brief relationship lasting only a few months, but one of such fiery intensity and passion that it left its mark on both of them. It set the pattern for a series of relationships that Neeson would fall into – and out of – with alacrity during his years in Hollywood.

But this one, the first, was different. Neeson and Roberts were both head-over-heels. A friend recalls: 'They were absolutely nuts about each other. They couldn't keep their hands off each other. It was incredible to watch. Liam is so cool but he was very, very responsive with Julia. In complete contrast, she's a very tactile person. She seemed to spark him off and they would be crawling all over one another. They didn't seem to notice who saw them – or if they did, they certainly didn't seem to care.'

Roberts's star was then very much in the ascendant, however – more so than Neeson's. After filming *Satisfaction*, and right in the middle of their passionate love affair, she leapt at the offer of a part in *Steel Magnolias* . . . and promptly repeated her pattern of falling for her co-star, in this case, Dylan McDermott. She abruptly traded Neeson in for this younger model.

According to his long-term Hollywood colleague and voice coach, Tod Todoroff, Neeson was devastated by her betrayal. 'Liam got very sick over that. He was hurting big-time.' But, according to other sources, the boot was soon on the other foot. Later, on the rebound from McDermott, Julia Roberts tried to win back the Irishman she had pledged her heart to in their passionate short fling. Neeson was having none of it.

Devastated, Roberts then took up with Brat Pack actor Keifer Sutherland, and the pair soon announced their engagement. He told a friend that, contrary to the rumours, even when they first met, Julia was obsessed with Neeson. 'She hankered after him, major league. Really painfully. She made a big thing of chasing him, phone calls, letters, the works, but he wasn't having any of it. And the more she tried, the more frustrated she got and the more she wanted him. But he just walked away. Maybe it was a kind of revenge thing. She'd hurt him, now he was getting his own back.'

Others speculated from the way he rapidly picked himself up after Roberts's shock betrayal, that Neeson had this curious ability to stonewall his emotions. He felt pain, sure, recognised the rare power of love, but he also knew how to switch it off. A bit like acting a role. You live it, breathe it, feel it, then you put it down. It's over. He seemed able, they perceived, to do this very successfully with other intense, short-term relationships that would follow in the years ahead.

And then there is the school of thought that believes Neeson was once so wounded he vowed never to let himself become so vulnerable in love again. Whatever his reasons, Neeson then threw himself back into work with a vengeance. It was much more than a distraction, it was his raison d'être. He would take anything that came his way over the next months. The only thing he promised himself was not to fall for his leading lady.

But you can't keep a good man down. His next role, in the film of the successful stage play – but sadly weak movie – *Duet For One*, was that of a Cockney rag and bone man, Totter, who becomes the toyboy of a famous violinist, cruelly stricken by multiple sclerosis. You'd have thought there was absolutely zilch chance of much sexual chemistry between the ex-choirboy playing a rag 'n' bone man, and his crippled much older lover – played by erstwhile *Mary Poppins* star, Julie Andrews.

But no. From somewhere deep within himself, Neeson found what was required of him. He was uncharacteristically flip about this film. 'It was nice,' he said, 'to get out of the cassock and have an affair with Julie Andrews. In fact, she's really very sexy . . .' Chivalrous? No, he meant it. Let's face it, the man who finds Mary Poppins sexy is a man to reckon with. But after all, Liam Neeson had always expressed a penchant for older women. And that wasn't about to change.

10

Who's Dying?

'We're all ostriches to any misfortune, any disease, but especially sexual disease.

'Not the Americans. They're very open about all that. You know, if you meet someone and get off with them or are very attracted to them and you think, Yes, well there might be a chance here . . . then you're out of luck. They just won't do it.

'But the stuff about AIDS comes out and then you talk about it. If you don't mention it, they sure will.

'It's not very romantic, but let's face it, it's practical . . .'

Rumour had it around Hollywood that director Blake Edwards tried to buy up every print of *Duet For One* following its 1987 release, so no one would ever see it – or his wife, Julie Andrews, in it – again. It wasn't that bad. But it wasn't good either. Things got better – though not much – for Neeson, in what critics later lambasted as Mickey Rourke's 'risible' IRA movie, *A Prayer for the Dying*, based on Jack Higgins's book of the same name. Starring the already notorious Hollywood hell-raiser, Neeson had landed the supporting role of Rourke's IRA sidekick. Rourke, power-hungry and unpredictable, the kind of guy who held no truck with anyone, had assumed the role of script rewriter. The whole movie was fraught with problems by the time Neeson arrived to add his bit.

Two weeks before the scheduled start of filming the omnipotent US distributor, Sam Goldwyn Jnr, decided the whole package was bilge. With one megalomaniacal stroke, he sacked the director, replaced him with Mike Hodges and insisted on a total script rewrite. Rourke took this blow to his screenwriting talents with considerably bad grace. Calling Goldwyn a scumbag, he vowed to be as truculent as possible until he got his own way.

Neeson, always one for the quiet, contemplative life, had walked right into a shooting match. He had never previously met Rourke, though his reputation as the baddest boy in town preceded him. When they met, it was an eventful occasion.

During those two weeks in pre-production they got together, not on set, but in a late-night drinking club. Rourke, with his open sympathies towards the IRA, was in explosive form. The outcome was inevitable. The only thing to do in the fiasco this film was turning into, he declared unequivocally to Neeson, was to drink themselves into oblivion. Which they did. Rourke was impressed by Neeson's capacity to consume gallons of Guinness, followed by Powers whiskey chasers. This consumption naturally, in the company of someone like Rourke, precipitated a session of dancing on tabletops and culminated in some critical damage to the bar chairs and tables.

It was not atypical behaviour for Rourke, but it was a scene seldom encountered by the likes of Liam Neeson. Luckily, he could remember little about it the next day.

So it came as some surprise when, a few days later, Neeson discovered that Rourke had written a Belfast bar scene into the script, based on their carousing. 'From this one wee incident that night, he'd evolved a whole scenario. It was a bit like Butch Cassidy and Sundance hitting a Belfast dance-hall and erupting.' Sadly, no one else was to be privy to the outpourings of Rourke's imagination. Goldwyn held his own and the scene ended up on the cutting room floor. But there were other memorable moments from the making of this movie.

Director Mike Hodges recalled one particular scene which called for a confrontation between Neeson and Rourke, with whom he was pleading to return to the arms of the IRA. Rourke had adamantly refused to rehearse throughout filming, so it fell to Neeson to improvise as Rourke set the tone of the scene, which called for lengthy sessions of retakes, but this time, the rapport was spot-on, the words flowed like wine, the scene went smoothly. And then Rourke suddenly went berserk.

Recalled Hodges: 'In this particular scene, the actress who played Liam's IRA girlfriend was supposed to be hiding behind a tree watching the two men having this conversation. Mickey suddenly turned on his heel and ran off into the woods! Liam was left standing there, wondering that the heck was going on. This definitely wasn't in the script.'

It later transpired that an abashed Rourke had confessed to a phobia about being assassinated by a woman. In this scene, his deepest darkest fear had crossed the line from fantasy to virtual reality because . . . 'this behind-the-tree stuff was making the hairs on the back of his neck stand on end. Every time we tried to shoot the scene it was the same. He got to a point where something suddenly snapped and he freaked out and took off again!'

Neeson, of course, took the star's continuing erratic behaviour with his customary good grace. In fact, he was observing the balance of power very carefully. He noticed an equation forming. How there came a certain point in the trajectory of a star to fame where the star was so much in ascendance that he could take greater charge of the vehicle he was working on. This movie was Rourke's brainchild. He had initiated it, was tampering with the screenplay, was calling the shots. Rourke had clout. Neeson wanted some of that.

He said at the time, in a tone that was more determined than wistful: 'I'd love to read a good book or play set in Ireland and think, Yes, this is screaming to be made into a movie, then get on the phone to some LA producer and get the thing into production in a couple of years.

'We've all read a book and thought, God, this would make a great film, but actually to be able to do something about it, get the ball rolling, that takes an actor with power. I've seen it work in Hollywood and I'm getting a taste for it.'

He didn't add that the flipside was if you're not up to it, or if some Bigger Brother upstairs doesn't like your ideas, the rug can still be pulled from under you. Rourke ultimately would disown his baby, this movie, after it was totally recut by the producer.

But then, Neeson didn't think that way. He was targeting success first, power second and he was canny enough to know that a few rejections along the way – on *his* part – would suit his purpose.

And so it came about that when he was offered the lead in a well-known American soap, playing the role of a reprobate sexual athlete, he saw his chance. He turned the part down. 'It was,' he justified, 'a part that required the character to screw everything into the ground.' It could be rejected, then, on moral grounds, thereby proclaiming Liam Neeson to be a man with an unimpeachable moral code. He could also use this opportunity to pitch home another message: 'The money they were offering was obscene.'

And so the puritan strikes back. Neither gratuitous sex nor gargantuan cash were a lure for this man. His values were the real values in life. Well, you could tell that just by looking into his eyes, couldn't you? But hold. There's more. Lest we underestimate the strength of his feeling he added: 'Actually, earning that kind of money for an inverse proportion of work frightens me. I just don't feel it's right.' In one fell swoop, Liam Neeson had become Ethics Man.

Having established his altruistic motives with a whisper in the right direction, and knowing that both in Hollywood and in the media that whisper would gather momentum and voice and eventually become laid down in tablets of stone – Liam Neeson is a good guy – he was then free to turn his attentions back to making money and making progress.

He knew his next US film could only be better than the last three. It was. *Suspect*, starring Cher as a simpatico lawyer defending a deaf-mute vagrant charged with murder – played by Neeson – was a box-office success. But Neeson nearly missed out on the role altogether. Casting a relatively inexperienced and virtually unknown – by Hollywood standards – Irishman as a leading character in an all-American mainstream film was a bold move by director Peter Yates. Studio heads and backers were against his choice, but Yates fought his corner. He had worked with Neeson on *Krull* and knew he would do the role justice.

Neeson recalled with gratitude: 'It wasn't a matter of accent, obviously. The character didn't speak. But the studios still wanted an American actor for it. Peter really hung in there and finally got his own way.'

Actor and director had a good rapport that helped flesh out Neeson's mute character even further. He also got on well with Cher. 'She's got street-cred, so far as I'm concerned. What she projects in public is this incredibly glam side. Well, that's her ticket to the bank. She looks sensational and the public lap it up. But when you get right down to it and spend a bit of time with her privately, she puts all that down. For all her overt and aggressive public sexuality, she's really one of the lads.'

Cher, it appeared, was one of the few females around who had not succumbed to the apparently irresistible Neeson allure. But then he did spend the greater part of the movie hidden beneath a straggly hedgerow barnet, bedraggled ZZ Top-style beard and the tattered rags of a Skid Row derelict. Hard to put *that* down, even if you know it's only acting.

Neeson admitted: 'We became friends but we didn't hang out too much together. She's a very committed lady in every area of her life. When she takes something on, she's completely dedicated to it, receptive and open. She's very focused.' Of course, there was another reason Cher was not playing ball. 'And right then, she had another guy in her life . . .'

Right then, Neeson had other things on his mind. His two previously released US films, *Duet* and *Prayer*, had neither set the box office alight nor gained him much credence. At best, they had put his name on celluloid. He had higher hopes for *Suspect*, and he already had his next venture, *High Spirits*, lined up. But they were all so much candy-floss. Time, perhaps, to look at tackling something with a little more substance. He found it in the script of a putative BBC play, *Sweet As You Are*.

It wasn't often in an actor's life that a part came along like that of Martin Perry in this controversial and emotive play, one of the much-acclaimed BBC Screen Two series. It wasn't treading the boards, but it was acting, capital A. With nous attached. Polytechnic lecturer Perry, ostensibly the epitome of new man, baby-minding, nappy-changing, equal with his wife in all things, makes just one self-indulgent mistake in his life. It will – literally – prove to be the death of him. Following a fling with one of his final-year students, he contracts the AIDS virus.

It was never going to make a global blockbuster, but because of the timely and sensitive nature of the theme, the play was guaranteed massive media coverage. Neeson admitted he was 'desperate to play the part'.

Although it was not pioneering a path through people's preconceptions about homosexuality and AIDS, he insisted it would still be a valuable contribution to publicising the dilemma. 'Films like that help change people's sexual mores. If the subject is treated openly and honestly, people pick up on that. There's a whole young generation who now feel confident about questioning prospective partners about their sexual history. They can discuss risks without shame or fear.'

All worthy stuff, even if not necessarily true. If Neeson had done his homework before espousing such lofty pronouncements, he would have discovered that the young generation in question were actually the most recalcitrant about demanding a sexual CV from those they were about to hop between the sheets with.

But this was one subject on which Neeson was keen to be heard – and his passion believed. 'There's no need for guilt to be attached to testing for AIDS, no hidden shame about wanting to know if someone else has. So far as I'm concerned, when you're attracted to somebody, that's a healthy attitude to have.

'It's valid because it means people take a little longer before jumping in, they have to talk things through and work at a relationship.

'Now there's a whole movement back to being monogamous and faithful, which is fine, great. The challenge is in finding someone to be monogamous and faithful with.'

Neeson was even moved to admit to having tested for the killer disease himself. Twice. Now that was really putting himself on the line. Or not, as it transpired, because of course neither of them was instigated by sexual reasons.

He submitted to a test prior to *Sweet As You Are* purely for professional reasons, to experience what it felt like to visit the clinic and go through the whole process. The second was part of a broad spectrum routine blood test after intestinal problems. Both tests turned up negative.

Sceptics might wonder callously whether this admission was perhaps cashing in on a high-profile issue? Neeson knew he might come up against just this attitude. So he pre-empted it. He was willing to take his confession session further, admitting that yes, he personally had been AIDS-conscious for years – and for a reason.

'You go through a phase when you're a bit reckless with women. Sure, I did.' But lest there be any women out there worrying themselves silly from this point on, he steps back into the domain of the responsible, conscientious, caring person we all know he is. 'But I became very conservative about all that some time ago, before AIDS became a major red alert with a massive public awareness campaign to heighten consciousness.

'You owe it to yourself to be cautious – and to everyone else you come in contact with. Personally, I've never been very promiscuous, even though this profession is renowned for changing relationships at a rapid pace,' he euphemises.

Despite the fact he had become comfortable with the fat acting salaries of Hollywood, Neeson was now willing to take a nose-dive into the relative pauperdom of the BBC wage-packet.

Money or ratings? No contest. 'The minute that script landed in my lap I thought, Yes, I have to do this. The sheer quality shone through. I was filming in South Carolina at the time. The temp was 120 degrees in the shade and I'm sitting there reading this with, I swear, a cold shiver up and down my spine. And I'm saying to myself, "Oh fuck, they're going to have a lot of class acts after this part. I just hope I can get it." '

Hope? Faith? And a salary that resembled charity. A BBC editor confided the competition was searingly hot, with much bigger British stars in the running, including one hallowed actor who was renowned for cornering the market in 'sensitive' souls. Still, Neeson landed it.

Luck or timing? A bit of both, he conceded. The fact that Neeson had not been seen on British screens for some time, had departed for Hollywood just as his British acting career had peaked at 'interesting' and 'one to watch' did him no disfavour. Few here had seen his American film work because of the inevitable timelag between films being released in America and much later in the UK.

In return, Neeson fulfilled the faith that had been placed in him. Viewers could not fail to be moved by his skilful portrayal of a man caught in the death-trap of his own reflected betrayal. But he had tough competition in the mesmerising stakes. Playing the part of his wife, Miranda Richardson was so compelling, the unanimous opinion was that players of lesser talent than Neeson 'would have been blown away'.

Neeson held his own with the full panoply of soul-searching, tortured looks that had become his forte. He was, critics noted, at his most eloquent when silent. That old Neeson body language was talking in tongues again.

None was affected by his delivery more than the Emmy and Bafta Award-winning writer William Nicholson who, tuned into Neeson's range, was inspired to strip the character bare so Neeson could express himself with fewer and fewer lines. And Neeson pared it down even further.

The director Angela Pope was fascinated by this process. Neeson was not one of those docile, subservient actors who bowed to the greater knowledge of writer and director. He might have been at one time, but he had been LA'd in the interim. Now he firmly believed in speaking his turn, bringing his own authority and weight to the production.

'Liam kept saying: "Can't we drop that line? Can't we do it with a look? Doesn't my body say it without having to utter the words?"'

'He really had his finger on the pulse. He conveyed tenderness, warmth and frustration which was the central core of the character – with immense subtlety. That's the trademark of a great screen actor.'

Neeson was bringing the confidence and authority of his two years in Hollywood to the British silver screen. But he was still leaning heavily on his old self too. He had always been a man of few words and a massive repertoire of telling looks. Now he had honed it to perfection. Best of all, now it was being recognised, even in Hollywood where the bigger, the bolder, the brasher the statement, was inevitably the better. Neeson had undercut all that to be among the first to deliver with subtlety – a rare and still undervalued gift in the land of everything mega. But its worth was rising, and Neeson's performances were helping.

He was all too aware of the folly of Hollywood. 'Suddenly I've become "interesting". That's the word they use, and the way they use it is with inverted commas around it. They're a bit scared of it yet. It's an unknown quantity. They're not sure how it will sell. But they're . . . interested.'

He knew, with unfailing certainty, that the price on his head was rising. 'Now I can walk into a room in Hollywood and people know who I am. That's a good place to be. It's not the be-all and end-all. I know that. There's one side of me that doesn't care because I know this whole "star" trip is phony. But there's another side of me which does care. Well, I look at Kevin Costner and I think to myself. Fuck, I can do that!'

Shades of Yosser Hughes, but Neeson knew he wasn't banging his head against a brick wall here. He knew, from experience, that if he kept banging, there would be a door in the wall that was going to open wide for him. It was already ajar a crack, and he had a size eleven foot inside. 'So I've got to try.'

Suspect was in the can and ready for distribution. *High Spirits* came next. No matter how debatable to the movie moguls was the value of his 'interesting' projection, the bottom line was, no one could now ignore the towering Irishman who had successively played opposite such diverse stars as Julia Roberts, Julie Andrews, Mickey Rourke, Cher, Dennis Quaid and Darryl Hannah in the short space of two years.

His agents, spotting a good selling point, would flog his versatility. Neeson let them. That was their job. But his own gut instinct was to promote the 'sensitive soul' aspect that wreaked every last ounce of emotion from the audience. And which, happily, few of the current supernova actors had successfully managed to harness.

But of course, he wasn't calling the shots yet. He would still hearken to the words of wisdom from the experts, the long-term players who had been around for a while, knew the people, knew the score. He was confident, but not *that* confident.

'I always keep my psychological baggage sort of half packed,' he confessed, thereby wringing from those who were listening a conviction that here was a man with the looks of a Celtic god, yet who still somehow retained the even more deeply attractive qualities of humility and self-doubt. Well, maybe . . .

'Some mornings you wake up and think, Gee, I look handsome today. Other days you think, What am I doing in movies? I wanna go home to Ireland and drive a forklift.'

There again, there were some lines that even the most convincing actor could not invest with the resonance of truth . . .

11

All Down To Good Mothering

'I arrive in Hollywood in January 1987 and do eight films in two years. It's either feast or famine here so I've been at a banquet till now. But I'm not holding my breath for the dessert to come along. I keep thinking I'm going to get found out.

'It's like suddenly you're woken up with your mother saying, "Come on, get up, you're late for school." Bang, the dream's gone and the reality is all about maths homework and exams.

'You know, I still wake up sometimes with that old exam anxiety in my head. I think it's going to be with me till the day I die.

'But that's what real life's about, isn't it?'

There was one vital element missing from Neeson's rapidly accruing film CV. He had dipped into an eclectic variety of roles, from priest to psychopath, taking in rebel and derelict along the way, but he had never yet played a romantic lead. For a would-be heart-throb, that was vital. Once people recognise you in that guise, the world is your oyster.

He'd had a taste of it when he played Julie Andrews's sexy and sensitive toyboy in *Duet For One* but it was a small part. Now he was ready for the big one. He found it in *The Good Mother*. Derived from Sue Miller's bestselling book, the film was intended to be a simmering vat of romance, sex and morality, with a bitter twist to its tale. Sadly, it didn't turn out quite like that.

The story hinged on single mum Anna, played by Diane Keaton, whose ex-husband is indignant over the open way she parades her passionate affair with her sculptor lover, Leo (played by Neeson) in front of their four-year-old daughter. Her ex tackles her head-on in a bitter custody battle. But this was to be no heart-tugging, box-of-tissues-at-the-ready *Kramer vs Kramer*. *The Good Mother*'s central issue was the single mother's love life and how this affects her children. There were sexually explicit scenes where the child was confronted with her mother's – and lover's – sexuality, including a scene where the lover allows the child to investigate his penis after she sees him naked in the bath. The couple also make love while the child is asleep in bed with them.

Although the book explored the single mother's dilemma to great effect, making a movie around this theme was going to have to be skilfully handled. As the lover, Neeson's was a particularly tricky part. How would audiences react to the sight of a small child examining a grown man's genitalia? Who could condone a man who had sex with a woman while her sleeping child lay next to him?

Adding this role to his track record, however, meant a certain pattern was emerging. Neeson, it would appear, had a penchant for difficult roles. He was shaping up nicely then, as a thinking actor, a man of some intellect, and steering away from the Himbo stereotype that often companies his kind of build and looks. Couldn't be bad.

Another thing was guaranteed: this was a film that would be talked about. As male lead, he would be talked about too. Controversy was only another form of publicity, after all. He started talking. He defended his choice of role by claiming it was a breakthrough in the way Hollywood looked at social mores. It was a line he had used before – referring to the BBC AIDS drama, *Sweet As You Are* – to great effect. It had gained him plus points, made people sit up and take notice.

Now it was America's turn. 'For the movie industry to tackle a subject as delicate as this, to focus on complicated adult re-lationships and the way children fit into them, to me seems a positive step in the right direction.

'I think women respond to the theme of the film – it opens up a real can of worms. It focuses on the fact that we have man-made laws, man-made rules and man-made jurisdiction. Where are the women in all this?

'What right does society have to stand on antiquated rules dreamt up by men?

'And the film asks this question, the big question: what right is there, fundamentally, for a man to tell a woman how to live her life?'

Sapient statements indeed, thereby neatly ensuring the vote of the feminist brigade alongside the vote of the lusting fans who would wipe their sweated brows at the sight of Liam Neeson – sharp intake of breath – naked. Such opinions were certainly going to stand against any accusations of Neeson being gorgeous-but-dumb. Liam Neeson the thinking woman's beefcake was rapidly taking shape.

'If the subject is going to make people stop, think and question preconceived and perhaps ill-judged ideas, then that's okay by me. It's not just relevant to me, it's relevant to society.

'If they're done with integrity and honesty, films can break down all kinds of social barriers.'

Films can. This one didn't. Sadly, among the cognoscenti, it earned itself the epithet: Good Mother. Bad Movie. Prior to its release, Neeson had high hopes: 'People tell me it's like this year's *Fatal Attraction* in terms of its controversy and thought-provokingness [*sic*] although it doesn't have the thriller aspect of *Fatal Attraction*, it certainly brings issues into the limelight that should be there.'

He also took the precaution of adding the mandatory plug for the film company funding his star salary on this one: 'I think it's great that a major studio like Touchstone Pictures, which is the adult bit under the umbrella of Disney, should be putting money into films like this.'

But Neeson was sorely disappointed with the end version when he viewed it at a private research screening just prior to its release. Time, then, to distance himself a little from the product. 'I felt let down. They had cut so much out, it had become sanitised, a nice, safe Sunday movie. I couldn't forgive the director and producers for that. I thought, bastards, they've put ten million dollars into this and suddenly they're scared of the issues involved. That's my reading of what happened, anyway. They really had a chance of doing something, of going out on a limb, but they chickened out, they really did.'

Why had it happened? The general consensus of opinion was that perhaps the director – actor Leonard Nimoy, taking a break from Star Trekking adventures as Mr Spock – was not the most apposite choice for the movie. In his previous directing capacity, he had turned in *Three Men and a Baby*. And some episodes of *Star Trek*.

Neeson's confidence was growing. He was not afraid to stick his neck out and criticise Nimoy – sometimes a dangerous step for an actor to take, but, well, he could still come out of all this okay, if it was made clear it wasn't *his* fault he'd picked another so-so-film.

'Leonard did an incredible amount of research on the film. He went to women's group meetings, held discussions on the book. He cared unbelievably about it. He was highly respected by the cast and crew.

'And yet, though I liked the guy a lot and learned from him, we had no real relationship with him. We never rehearsed or sat down and talked about what the film was about.

'Afterwards, I thought about this and I felt I didn't know the guy. He'd just directed me, he'd seen me naked – literally – and I didn't know who the hell this guy was. He's a very bright guy, a very able and competent director, but I don't think he's a film maker.'

Badmouthing the director can lead an actor into all sorts of bother, especially in an inward-looking place like Hollywood where one wrong word and you don't eat lunch in this town again, Buster. Neeson was unrepentant. All the sanctimonious stuff he had spouted before the film was in the can now fell down badly. He had to retrieve something of himself from this.

At least his own and Keaton's performances were blistering, even if the movie wasn't. No one could miss the palpable sexual charge between the pair on screen. That could be an appropriate selling point for someone looking to carve a niche as a hot romantic lead.

But Neeson had always genuinely deplored vainglory. Braggadocio did not rest easy on those mile-wide shoulders. He had always found the soft, self-effacing approach so much more effective. And you could still use it to make a point. 'I'm playing something here I've never seen myself as before – a woman's man, a bit sexy.' Disingenuous or what? Could it really be that even now Neeson still had no sense of his powerful sexual and emotional allure for women? Maybe he really, truly didn't, but it was hard to believe. Perhaps his sense of being a skinny outsider as a child, his determined quest to be someone through acting and his lack of prowess with women up to the age of eighteen had left their mark.

Then again, he knew how people respond to wide-eyed innocence. It touches them. Especially when it comes tucked away inside a muscle-bound six-foot-four-inch package. 'It's easy to turn on the violent stuff, the wild-eyed mania or the cold-eyed ruthlessness that doesn't really convey anything beyond that. I know I have a gentle quality and I like using it because it's something I don't think you see enough of in films.' Forget the pheromones, the hormones, even the primeval urge to procreate. Neeson was negating his sexual chemistry as simply pure professionalism.

'I was fairly staggered to get the part in the first place, truly. I believed it would go to someone like Dennis Quaid. The eternal pessimist, I said to myself, no way is this going to come my way. It was my agent who was positive, she was so insistent I was right for this. So I went and met Leonard Nimoy for the part and nothing was happening. It was just a little interview, "Hey Liam, tell me about this character, Leo." When directors do that, it's like an oral exam just to prove you've read the script so I went home, back to my house and thought, That's it, then.

'But behind my back my agent was talking to the associate producer and he was saying, "Look, if Liam and Diane could just meet, I know something would happen." He then phones me a couple of weeks later and says, "Okay, they're going to see you in New York, you've got to pay your own way, but you've got to go." And I'm real nervous, I've got a feeling in my gut, "Jesus, God, it's not going to happen," and he says, "Just go," so I went.

'I thought, Fuck, just get into it, will you? and then the second I walked in the room, there was this immediate rapport.' But when the cameras stopped rolling he was adamant the chemistry came right off the Bunsen burner. 'That's as close at it got,' says Neeson. 'We became real good buddies. Because of that, there was no sexual thing off screen.

'When you explore someone within the bounds of intimacy as a friend, you're safe. Yet at the same time, we could be quite daring with our feelings for each other. It was a good relationship, healthy.'

And it proved another point. In the States, when push came to shove, it was the push and shove that took you places. If his agent hadn't kept banging on, maybe no one would have considered him as a sexy, romantic leading man. This philosophy stood very much at odds with the self-deprecating, laid back, laissez-faire attitude he had worked so hard at projecting. Maybe it was time for a bit of a volte face? It was.

'That's the thing I really like about America. That you can make things happen by being persistent and knocking on doors. Back home you'll often find the door stays shut and the barricades go up. People think, Pushy so-and-so. Let him wait. Maybe next time. But more likely not . . .

'In America, they respond to it. "Hey, like your spirit. Great enthusiasm." "Wants the job real bad, let's give him a try-out." I had to learn that because basically I'm very, very shy. But if it's something I really believe in, I'll walk through hellfire to get it.'

Inconsistency can be so intriguing. But Neeson was learning, simply, how to adapt to Hollywood where the code of conduct was diametrically opposed to that of England and Ireland. There, diffidence and sangfroid were the order of the day. Hollywood was gimme, gimme, want it now.

But how to do both simultaneously? How about adding some appealing insecurity into the mix? Should go down a treat, especially in a place like LA, where everyone has their own shrink and a mandatory several-year stretch in intensive therapy.

Such a good talking point, sharing your explored deepest-seated insecurities. Then again, how would that sit with the caring, capable, shoulder-to-lean-on image? Not easy. But there was one other thing everyone could identify with. The insecurity of the *place* they all found themselves in and how *that* induced the inner turmoil. So it's not actually your *stuff*, as the therapists say, it's a condition of the environment you find yourself in, a necessary evil.

Smart thinking, Batman . . .

'Hollywood is not a secure place to be. Okay, so real security only comes from within yourself, but I recognise the nature of this beast that is the film industry in Hollywood.

'I've been lucky. I've never stopped working. But I know it can all disappear overnight. You have to be realistic. I bumped into Anthony Hopkins and said, "How ya doin'?" He replied, "Well, I haven't been found out yet, boyo!" That's the right attitude.

'It's the way this place operates. You never really lose the fear that it could all be gone tomorrow. Inside, every time I take on a new part, I'm still this quivering fifteen-year-old. Will I do it right? Will it pan out? Will I screw up?

'It's a bit scary because that's something you can't act. You have to just be yourself and hope it works. That your natural charm – or whatever it is, this indefinable quality that made the director say, "Let's cast this guy" – comes through.

'Even though it's something you may not be aware of yourself.'

Methinks the lad protesteth too much . . .

'I don't want to sound flash but I'm a realist. I know I'm getting a certain name in the profession now. Then again, I know it's all

about being in the right place at the right time. And having people
on your team who believe in you.

'I'm hardly your Mel Gibson. The big romantic leads are not
winging my way. They're headed straight for Mel, Harrison Ford,
Kevin Costner. When one does land on my doorstep, I always assume
it's because those guys have turned them down.

'And I'm not chasing them. I'm pacing myself. Truth be told, if it
was down to me I'd be happy lying around in bed, or sitting round
reading books. Compared to most American actors, I'm very laid
back.

'I don't much care for that fevered kind of ruthless ambition.
Relentless pursuit of a role just isn't my style. My pace is kind
of slow. Deathly slow, actually. If it was all down to me, I'd be
moribund. I've always had this kind of faith in *que sera*, whatever
will be, will be. If it's right for you and you're ready to greet it, the
opportunities will come your way. It's just a case of opening the
door when you're standing outside it.'

He might change his tune more often than he changed his socks
– or his roles – but one thing was unequivocal: Neeson was not a
Mel or a Harrison or a Kevin, but he was very much a rising new
name. He might be taking virtually everything that was coming his
way, but at least they *were* coming his way.

He knew the dangers of being labelled and how that could lead
to work drying up. 'I'd hate ever to be pigeonholed into a defined
area, whether it's "He's the thinking woman's actor" or "He can only
do these big bruiser roles". That limits you. Eventually, you start to
close off. You have to keep your options open, it can only do you
good to change roles. It keeps you on your toes, testing and flexing
different muscles and that's stimulating. Ultimately, it's what keeps
you alive.'

Equally, he knew the value of an image that would stay in casting
directors' heads, and make them think automatically of Liam Neeson
when just the right parts came up.

There was time for that image definition yet. Right now his policy
had to be, keep moving. And keep talking about these moves. Make
them considered moves, make some kind of sequence out of the
mêlée that was his CV so far.

'I love the historical notion of the actor: he's a bit of a rogue
and a vagabond, living off his wits. I love the whole tradition
of acting. How you can switch from playing a king one day to

a tramp the next. And never thinking, This goes against my image.'

However, being linked with big names with strongly identifiable images was certainly a helping hand until he found and promoted his own. And they didn't come much bigger than Clint Eastwood. Neeson had been in Hollywood less than two years when he got the call to play opposite Clint Eastwood in the fifth Dirty Harry film, *The Dead Pool*. Playing the role of a deviant serial killer director of video nasties, some said, was a serious bit of miscasting for Neeson, but it was bound to be a box-office hit.

There was another problem: how to avoid towering over Clint, who was still Hollywood's favourite macho man. With half an inch head start on the maestro, Neeson had to do his damnedest to look smaller than the big screen giant. The solution was simple. In front of camera, Neeson had to stand in dips and walk in hollows so he wouldn't overshadow the hero.

Inspector 'Dirty' Harry Callaghan was the monosyllabic macho cop who always got the baddies – even if it was in the back. In this, the fifth and weakest Dirty Harry film, Neeson played a foil who insisted in calling the dirtiest cop in the West, 'Love'.

Despite finding himself somewhat verbally challenged trying to get his Irish brogue around what ended up as a Midwestern-cockney hybrid accent, the film did not overly stretch his acting talent. He knew it. In movies like this, 'You learn the lines and don't bump into the furniture. It's a thriller. All you have to do is tell the story.'

And it's all money in the bank and a higher profile. Neeson was not knocking the valuable experience, either, of working with one of Hollywood's major megastars. Tying his name to Clint's could come in very handy. Eastwood, after all, in his sixties, had to be pensioned off soon from the rough tough all-action hero throne. Neeson did a timely bit of genuflection. 'I really respect the man. He's been a personal hero for a long time, even though I wasn't particularly wild about Dirty Harry. To me, where Clint excelled was on horseback in a cowboy hat. Somehow, he didn't fit with a suit and tie, not for me.'

Time to let the age difference show. Just how old was Clint? Why, most of us could remember him in the saddle when we were still in nappies. Certainly, Neeson could.

'I grew up raised on *Rawhide*. It was my Saturday TV treat. If I'd been a good Catholic boy all week, my reward was staying up late to watch *Rawhide*.

'So working with him was such a kick. I really enjoyed it. He's nothing like any character I've ever seen him play. He can just switch them on and off. You don't even notice the join.

'He's a direct descendant of the old Errol Flynn, Clark Gable school – big name, big personality actors. If you're in that mould, you hang on to your screen persona because that's what the audience pay to see and want to believe in.

'The real Clint is a good man, a quiet man and shy. I think his basic concern for people led him to stand for Mayor of Carmel. He's genuinely keen to help people.'

Obsequiousness being the order of the day, it came as some surprise when he later changed his tune about his 'hero'. In 1992, he was emboldened enough to admit, 'People are always asking me, "Wasn't it great to work with Clint Eastwood?" And I would go, "Yeah, it was great, sure."

'But afterwards I thought, Let's be honest here. It wasn't great. What did I learn? It was like clocking into a fucking factory. He was in the dubbing studio in his head. It was like conveyor belt stuff: "Okay, say your lines. Let's get this wrapped up." We probably said five words to each other the whole shoot.'

Ever the astute politician, he had felt it more appropriate at the time to hook his wagon to Clint's. Working his way up, still too new and too timorous to say anything adverse about anyone else, especially not one of the Hollywood greats. Nimoy, you could just about get away with, but Clint? No chance.

But his about-face four years later proved that Neeson had done what he set out to do. Shot his star higher than Clint's. To be able to do so, he had found the perfect compromise. Tough guy meets sensitive soul. Then he could cover the entire spectrum of big guy roles. After all, it was only the persona he had so successfully projected in his own life, vis-à-vis his screen life, for so long.

'Stripping yourself bare is the essence of good screen acting. You have to be your own spirit. You don't add on to what's already there.

'Strong and vulnerable at the same time? Yes, why not? That's real enough. We've been fed so much of this macho crap for so long people have actually come to believe in it.

'That's not real life. Men are vulnerable, weak, real human beings. It's just that you don't see too much of that represented on screen.'

Not until he came along, at least. In the intervening four years he had learned how to play the game, grab some of the power, while all the time making people think he was this charming, polite, eager-to-please innocent abroad. Whereas in fact, he was just waiting for the moment he could actually speak his mind, stand his own ground, call the shots. That time was coming.

'If some director or producer asks me for a meeting to discuss the possibility of me playing a particular role, sometimes I ask them, "Why do you think I'm right for this part?"

'The answer is always the same – a variation along a theme of "Well, you've got this special quality. You're vulnerable." Then they'll bounce it back to me and say, "What d'you think of the script?"

'And I hear myself saying, "Well, I liked it. There's this special vulnerable quality to the guy . . ."

'Let's face it, the bills have to be paid. Everybody does it . . .'

But few do it so well. Convincing all comers of his sentient being, his pliability, his versatility, goddammit, his very vulnerability, and all the while plotting. Just wait till my time comes. Then I'll show you who's boss.

But he revealed those inner machinations to no one. And few were observant enough to pick it up. Certainly no one in Hollywood saw through it or behind it.

But the Brits being more canny by far, a few friends had come close enough to Liam Neeson for long enough to know what really made him tick. One long-time friend, the English actor Richard Graham, was never fooled. He revealed, 'Liam was always extremely ambitious. He enjoys the success, but he still has the objectivity along with it. He plots his goals and can still sift out the bullshit.'

He knew how to spread it too. And mighty fine fertiliser it made.

12

Intimations Of Mortality

'I think a bit of dirt is good for you, it's no use living like a nun or a priest. Life's too short.

'I was really fit once and really proud of my stomach muscles. Then suddenly I'm in hospital and I wake up with this stapled scar running from left to right across me and it's gone, this perfect stomach, bisected. I thought, Okay, there's a lesson to be learned here.

'Like that classic statement they always make: here's something to make you appreciate what it's really all about.

'From then on, I took it strictly day to day. The problem with that, of course, is it's hard to reconcile with wanting something permanent . . .'

1988?

Liam Neeson lived alone. Like Garbo, he preferred it that way. He was thirty-six, a bachelor and time alone meant time to plan his career. Single and single-minded.

He was not motivated purely by the fame and the fortune. The ego and the bank balance had been healthy for a long time. Acting was in fact a bit like boxing. You plan your moves, weave and duck and bob about a bit, keep your eye on the target and when you're completely fixed on it – bang! You're home. The victor. And the crowd who've watched you win, backed you all the way, are elated. You take them with you on your transport of triumph. You all end up feeling good.

He'd discovered that power, that victory and that elation in boxing, back in his childhood. He'd dreamt of being a champ and done it. Was acting really so different? Here he was in Hollywood after all; he'd got that far on dreams and drive.

Neeson still spent most of his free time on his own. In his house near Venice Beach, he sat on his sundeck where the view was a never-ending blue, ocean met sky and the sight of it made his spirit soar. This was a place to dream. The sky was the limit. He didn't like bringing people back here. You could call him a loner, call him antisocial, call him anything you liked. Just don't call on him. He liked his routine and his space, the good Catholic boy who ate prunes for breakfast, the free spirit who rode a Harley Davidson.

He'd tell you, 'I have all I need right now. The Pacific Ocean right the other side of my window. Nobody looking down on me, nobody bothering me. I'm on my own with my shoes off, feet up in the Californian sunshine and a great book. I'm in heaven.

'I like to spend a lot of time on my own. Within my own four walls. I don't need to go outside for too much. I read books, an awful lot of books.'

It didn't bother him that he had few close friends. Those he had were those that mattered. 'At best we have maybe four or five friends in life that you would give your life for – but when you have that kind of friendship, they take you for who you are and what you are.

'I don't believe it has to be a tight thing, that kind of relationship. Not binding like when you feel, "God, I haven't written to so-and-so for ages." True friendships are like you've never been apart.

'I have a friend, Ciaran Hines, who's an actor and he joined Peter Brook's *Mahabharata* tour, took off round the world with it. I didn't see him for two years and then I get this card from China that starts off, "So, Big Lad . . ." like he was just taking up where we left off the last time I saw him, "Now what were you saying . . .?"

'I'm real grateful for the friends I have. When I was taken ill and had to go right into hospital, I was thinking, Who have I got I can call? And right away I thought of one friend, Louise, but I didn't know if she could make it. She said, "I'll be there in ten minutes." And she was. There aren't many people in life who'll be there for you like that . . .'

He'd always been a fairly solitary soul, preferring his own company. Even workmates rarely transcended the boundary between the profession and friendship. Being an actor is an isolating business, it sets you apart from the rest of the human race. They pay to watch you. You're different to them. This can give rise to friendships, bonds formed between the privileged few who share this exalted position.

Neeson worked with stars, but he didn't necessarily befriend them. 'Actors are guys I've worked with is all. They're part of the fabric of my working life, not my own life. So I work with them, so what? Fuck it, I've got my own life to lead.'

He was always at pains to denigrate the quest for fame, dismissing it as shallow and facile. The acting's the thing, fame is fleeting, transitory and ultimately worthless. When one hapless interviewer, during a terse and unproductive talk with Neeson, had the temerity to suggest he was now famous, he dismissed the notion with a derisory, 'Yeah, famous in Ballymena.'

But it was undeniable. His name was up there in lights. Diane Keaton had been tipped for an Oscar for her performance opposite him in *The Good Mother*. *The Dead Pool* went global, grossing $30 million within its first month of release. The name of Neeson was all over it. He'd just signed up for *Next of Kin*, a movie cross between *Deliverance* and *The Godfather*, in which he'd star opposite *Dirty Dancing* flavour of the month, Patrick Swayze. And he'd just wrapped up *High Spirits* which, sadly, had not had the same effect on him.

Irish director Neil Jordan, whom Neeson had first met nearly ten years before during the making of *Excalibur*, had found the transition to Hollywood movie-making fraught with problems: 'What happens is you slowly go insane and at the end of it, all you get is this vast, noisy and unfunny movie.'

A sad indictment, but a true one, that largely blighted Neeson's comedy debut. In it, he played an eighteenth-century ghost who murders his wife, played by Darryl Hannah, another Hollywood hot name, fresh from her huge successes in *Wall Street*, *Roxanne* and the witty comic fantasy *Splash*, in which she played a mermaid in love with Tom Hanks. Meant to be a rib-tickler, *High Spirits* was unfortunately more of a belly-flopper. The jokes, it was noted, were even more transparent than the ghosts. Neeson shrugged it off as a fairly minor disaster. 'At least it was fun to do.'

However, it added another dimension to his repertoire. With a comedy part – even in a joke of a film – he'd now run the gamut of theatrical roles. What can Hollywood say about Liam Neeson other than you could never stick him in a filing cabinet under P for Predictable?

Epics, thrillers, romance, comedy, controversy – he'd done them all in just two short years in Hollywood. But a continuous thread was emerging. Since his days as Big Chief in the Dublin stage production of *Cuckoo's Nest*, through to the mute vagrant in *Suspect*, he'd played more silent parts than Buster Keaton. But he always projected as strong, no matter how few, if any, lines he had to utter, or mutter. And to each of those roles, however disparate, he'd brought this consistent undertone of vulnerability.

The only star they could align him with in Hollywood was Gary Cooper, the strong, silent, chivalrous gentle giant. And when they did, he knew he was on the winning straight.

'I got a sniff of [success] with *The Good Mother* when it opened in America. People started responding to me personally. Of course, they want to create an identity for you, linking you up with someone else. People are comfortable with comparisons and mine is Gary Cooper.

'But I've essentially been trying to put across my own personality. When I'm off screen, I'm not putting on a false nose or a false beard or wearing a character. I'm just being me, and people have just started to respect that. It's kind of novel.'

Neeson had another gift – the happy knack of being able to look like whoever he wants. He could be benign or malevolent, lover or death wish, repugnant or swoon-worthy in the blink of an eye. He claimed he preferred being unattractive. It was better for the career.

'I prefer being ugly, there's so much more scope in it. Take a real good-looking guy like Mel Gibson, not just great-looking but a great guy and a really fine actor. But how many parts is he going to get off the back of that?

'Not the meaty roles, at least, not a variety of them. He'll never get Captain Bligh, he'll never get Quasimodo roles. Because he's blighted, cursed with this extraordinary good-looking face. It can be a blessing, having looks like that but it's a curse, too. It totally restricts you.

'I always get the feeling from Mel that deep inside him there's a real actor bursting to get out, an ugly fucking actor. But he's trapped inside those looks. Luckily, I don't have that problem.'

Though countless of us would disagree.

Neeson knew, however, that his acting skills could instantly transform him from gorgeous to gorgon. But that was nothing to do with looks, it was a process that happened within. 'It's a bit like plant life. You absorb something and you produce something else at the end of it. The acting process should be a bit like osmosis. You're transformed by it. Hopefully, what comes out at the other end is the spirit of the character you're portraying. It does happen. It can actually change you physically. You assume a different persona and a different look that goes with it.

'Magically, it happens in those few seconds after someone says, "Action!" That's on a good day, for me. But I've seen it happen to other guys. It's incredible to watch. There's De Niro, he's a guy for it. And Anthony Hopkins. They just transform. Boom. You're looking at De Niro and suddenly it's not him, it's someone else completely. Anthony Hopkins – boom! It's not Tony Hopkins any more. Fucking amazing to see.'

Neeson could transform himself too. He had already recreated himself countless times. From Ballymena college dropout into Irish actor. From stage actor to screen actor. From jobbing actor to star, although he was still working on that final transformation.

'I've got to a place where I don't have to audition. That's a rare place. There are only a very few who have that status: Mel, Costner, Harrison Ford, those sort of top guys.

'I'm kind of getting in there. I've been sent a couple of scripts for me to consider. Me. To consider. Thank you. Turns out Mel and Harrison turned them down first, but it's a start.

'It's like these producers and casting directors are sitting round saying "Okay, so the Big Boys don't want to know. Who else is there? What about this Irish guy . . .?" I can live with that.'

But not for long. The slice has got bigger. How about having the whole cake?

The thing about Neeson, as his Ballymena, Belfast and Dublin peers all testify, is that he is, one: driven, and two: has his eye firmly, unshakeably fixed on the goal ahead.

The laid back demeanour does disappear sometimes. Neeson is beginning to let the odd glimmer of a ferocious Irish will show through occasionally. He won't suffer fools gladly and if needs be, he can be a hard taskmaster.

Part of the accoutrements of stardom are the retinue of retainers who plug away at making the star not just a star, but a saleable package. The agent, the casting agent, the publicist – right down to the therapist, the masseur and the manicurist. The star is paying their wages. In return, they must feed the star's ego. The star, inevitably, can become a prima donna with so many people at their beck and call.

Neeson was never of that ilk, but he retained the Roman Catholic work ethic instilled in him from childhood and he wanted to see it reflected in those around him. If he had to shovel shit, he wanted them to do it too. 'Agents, for instance, take ten per cent of your earnings. I want to see them work for that. Well, I have to. And I'm quite capable of unleashing a lot of venom on them if I don't think they're working fast enough on a project I'm interested in. That's their job. I'm not going to be chasing it myself. That's what I'm paying them for.'

You wouldn't, therefore, find him schlepping round the high-profile, paparazzi-haunted watering holes of Hollywood. Firstly, he hates empty socialising. Secondly, he hates talking. After all, he pays people to promote his name, get his picture in the papers, so why should he have to do it himself?

'If I'm out somewhere and a director or producer of some project I'm keen on was there too, you wouldn't find me approaching them. In fact, I'd avoid them.

'You know, maybe you're expected to go to some party venue and photographers are around, snapping pix of who's with who and who's talking to who, well, I wouldn't want to be seen with this producer or that director in case they think I'm vying for their attention. Not for one second.

'That's partly the reason why I don't go to many parties. I hate that schmoozing. Parties to me should be just that, people having fun, enjoying themselves. Parties in America are serious business, though, gatherings within the industry to talk shop, trade information, set up deals. I pay people to do that for me. I'm not interested.'

He'd never been the type to offend, but he had some scathing comments to make about those who succumbed to their own publicity. 'I've seen all those Hollywood brats in restaurants, wearing their sunglasses in the middle of the night and sending their food back just for the sake of it. All that, "You'd better notice me, I'm famous," stuff. Really? Well, they're not, but they're trying desperately hard to be. And that's just exactly what it is – desperate. Who the hell do they think they are?

'Now, your *real* actors like Robert De Niro, now he's a class act. And he's a buddy. There's no pulling rank with him. I've walked down the street with him, sat in restaurants with him and he's the most unassuming, anonymous guy. I respect that. That's the way I'd like to be.'

He was getting there already. At this point, he'd made a jump from B-team name up a notch to potential A. 'When I got home to LA recently after a trip away, there were two scripts waiting for me. Stuck on the front of one of them was this note: "To Mr Liam Neeson. For Your Consideration, the Role of . . ."

'That's the best thing that's happened to me in LA so far. They're asking *me*! I was so made up, I actually took that note and framed it! It's on my wall at home right now. Gives me a buzz every time I look at it. It's what I used to dream about for so long. And finally it happened . . .'

Sadly, this was Hollywood, and Neeson had been here long enough to know there was usually a sting in the tail. 'The script was a heap of rubbish . . .'

The next script he tackled, however, was not. *Next of Kin* reflected Neeson's scope as he moved swiftly from the comedy débâcle of *High Spirits* to 'a real narrow-minded feudin' fightin' Bible-thumpin' hillbilly' playing Patrick Swayze's brother, keen to wreak revenge on their younger brother's murderer.

Again, there was a curious timing to his life. This hillbilly revenge story made him examine just who he was and what he was doing in America – and with his life. Filmed in Kentucky, the wide open spaces and Irish ancestry of the local inhabitants struck a chord in him that had lain dormant for a long while. He felt homesick.

'We were filming in this tiny community in south-east Kentucky. I went down three weeks before filming started because I wanted to get the feel of the place, take it in to me, observe the townspeople, see how they lived, all that stuff. I met some of the local people and it turns out all their ancestors were Irish or Scots. So there's this all-pervading sense of home, filtered into American life.

'I found myself reverting more and more to a rural Irish accent and I started to miss the Auld Country. It pulled on some strings I didn't expect, kind of crept up on me and took me unawares. And they were strong feelings. Those people reminded me of home so much. They had the same rhythms, the same attitude to life, a good attitude.'

But it wasn't one that took you to too many places. It was a *Home with the Waltons* outlook that made you content to be where you were, doing just what you were doing. And one that was the antithesis of the American credo which, as Sigmund Freud observed, was obsessed with 'becoming' rather then 'being'. It was an Irish, not an American attitude and it was devoid of ambition.

Neeson had successfully adapted to America, climbed the ladder of success, but right there in hillbilly territory in deepest Kentucky, he went back to basics, examined his roots, saw where he came from. These third- and fourth-generation Irish-Scots-Americans were exactly as the folk he'd left back home. They'd moved a continent, then never moved on. In stark contrast, he had moved apace. He was still moving. His lot was not to settle down, just to be. He was becoming. Was he becoming obsessed with it?

Certainly he had that slow 'n' easy Irish attitude tucked away inside him, with a facility that helped him reach peace when it was necessary. When the pace and the pressure got too frenetic and too much, then he could retreat into himself, access it, find the space and the peace and close himself off from the outside to be alone with it. Switch off. Just be. But alongside, he had this brighter light burning, a drive to move on and ever up, seek out new horizons, conquer them.

It was why he fitted in happily to both places, and such disparate places as the lazy, hazy Irish shores and the rapid quickfire of LA life. He was truly the consummate actor, the chameleon.

It was an anomaly that did not pass him by. He reflected: 'There's such an immense contrast between life in Ireland and life in the US. You can't encompass just how vast the divide is. In America, sometimes I think I'm too laid back, too easy-going. But when I go home, I'm ten times speedier than anyone else. My family are saying, "Take it easy, Liam!" And I think I'm already dead slow and stop!

'There's this amazing sense of peace in the Irish countryside too. You just breathe in the scenery and you're at one with it all. I love the scenery round LA, too. It's one of the things I like most about the place. You just step outside the city and up the coast there's Steinbeck country, and San Francisco and New Mexico. Santa Fe's down the road there. That's all big scenery, amazing places.

'But sometimes I get a real strong feeling for the little green field with a dry stone wall running along it, the kind of scenery you can just put your arms around, Irish scenery.'

It was time to go home, recharge the batteries, take a break and take stock. En route, he stopped off in London, where he had lunch with the blonde and beautiful Jo Fairley, a friend of one of his US girlfriends. When he turned up, Jo noted that he was dressed in even more shambolic style than usual. The jeans and crumpled shirt were topped off with a woolly cardigan of Val Doonican design. It was, she mused, as if he was acting out the part of a shambling, middle-aged Irishman, a considered million miles from the sartorial elegance demanded by Hollywood and the film industry.

Neeson confirmed the cardie was a rare event. 'It's just so rare you get the call for a nice woolly pullie in California,' he told her wistfully, 'you don't get much occasion for it in California.'

Even at home, he had to act a role. He'd picked the venue for their meet, a Polish restaurant called Wodka, famed for its vast array of different vodkas. She had braced herself for one of Liam's drinking sessions. But he was in reflective, not refuelling mood. He settled instead for a pot of tea, explaining he had 'given up the drink a while back. It was easier than I thought. I never really missed it. But the acid test came when I was back in Ballymena the other week. I'd be in the pub asking for a cup of coffee and you could hear all the regulars under their breath muttering, "Fucking pansy. If this is what living in Los Angeles does for you, you can stuff it!"'

The fact was, he needed to live a more temperate lifestyle right now. While filming *High Spirits*, he'd been rushed into hospital suffering from diverticulitis. There followed a major op during which surgeons removed 'three feet of my intestines'.

'I didn't know anything about it. I collapsed on set and that was it, the rest was darkness. I came to, in hospital, and this doctor is standing over my bed saying I'm lucky to be alive.

'I'm thinking, Wh-a-at? But he's looking me straight in the eye and he's serious. I've never had a day's illness, I work out six days a week, I've always eaten well – and sensibly – lots of fruit and veg. I'm practically vegetarian. So why me?'

What he wasn't revealing to anyone – apart from his doctor and surgeon, was that for nearly twenty years he'd been plagued by intestinal problems. He'd grown accustomed to the lifestyle his painful condition dictated, the clues were there for all to see. His kitchen cupboards, full of intestine-loosening foodstuffs: bran flakes, prunes, wheatgerm, muesli by the bagload. In the freezer, even more: bran bread, bran muffins, bran scones, and all things easily expellable, just in case. Cautious by nature, he always shipped in extra supplies to prevent the unthinkable – that one night, back late from a location shoot, stressed out, wound up, stomach in knots, he should go to the cupboard and find it bare. The mere thought was enough to induce dyspeptic tension.

Such an overdose of precautionary measures might be a clue as to why Neeson was so afflicted, and so young. Certainly digestive problems stand at odds with the person who's truly easy-going and able to get things out of his system. One glimpse in Neeson's kitchen and it didn't take a Sherlock Holmes to work out that this was a man with a few knots in his psyche. Or somewhere.

Whatever the speculation, this eruption of his intestinal problems had a dramatic and sobering effect on the erstwhile Guinness-quaffer. 'I said, "That's it, clean living from now on," although I'm still sometimes seduced by a tandoori chicken. I think I'll settle for a compromise. I'm trying to give up the bad habits, but it's no good living like a priest.'

He was more perturbed that the once-body-beautiful he had worked so hard on was now bisected by a Hermann Munster-like scar. 'Thank God I've had no problems since. Just a neat wee fifteen-thousand-dollar scar. It'll fade but it's always going to be there.'

Instead of recuperating in a leisurely fashion, he threw himself back into a rigorous fitness regime, training just as hard – and adding jogging to his daily workout. But it made him reappraise his priorities in life. 'The main thing my condition did for me – and I'm aware it's a cliché but it's the way I feel – is that it made me appreciate life more. Maybe once I was guilty of running a wee bit ahead of myself. But now I take it day to day.'

A favourite story doing the rounds of film crews centred on Neeson on the operating table. When, they said, he was asked through a pain-filled haze for his next of kin, he responded, 'Call my agent.'

Just another of those apocryphal Hollywood rumours? This one grew so big, it even got back to Neeson himself. He decided to not quite deny it. Keep your options open and at least you keep people talking about you. 'Swear to God it's blarney. But it just might be true. That's the fun of blarney, you have to keep guessing.'

Neeson had now taken to proclaiming that in accordance with his new, even stricter health regime, 'I've given up the drink, I've never smoked and I no longer eat red meat.'

Back in the pubs of his homeland, Neeson was rarely seen without a pint in hand, chainsmoking. But there, he was among kindred spirits. The Irish have always been partial to a drink, a smoke and a bit of 'the crack'. Not so the Californians. Clean living goes a long way in LA, where they're fitness obsessed and long ago embraced the no smoking, no drinking, no drugs, clean living credo with, as always, a vengeance. When Californians subscribe to a fashion, they subscribe heart, body and soul. The free-lovin' drug culture of the sixties and seventies was replaced with the backlash in the eighties. Californians were the new Puritans. By the time Neeson was established there, he had to be a covert smoker, drinker and curry-eater. All the aforementioned vices were best carried out in privacy.

But there was another reason for this recent conversion to healthy living. With bizarre and tragic coincidence, he had just put to bed the hillbilly thriller, *Next of Kin*, when he got the phone call in the middle of the night that every son dreads.

His father, Barney Neeson, had died suddenly in his sleep. It was February 1989. Neeson went home to bury him. 'I had to go home very quickly and sort out all this stuff and of course it was sad because he went very suddenly, but we had such a wonderful time. All these relations, great-aunts, uncles, cousins, they were all there, taking a drink to him, remembering him. It was a beautiful celebration of his life.

'All these wonderful women were coming up to me, saying, "And do you know me, young Liam?" and I'd say no and they'd say, "Sure, I used to rock you on my knee when you were just this high," and I'd say, "Now I know you!"

'The Irish attitude to death is terribly healthy. There's an attitude to tragedy and joy that goes hand in hand. Us Irish can easily become so fucking morbid and twisted and yet in a second, you can throw all that right off. You never see it more than at a wake. Everyone is toasting the departed's health, singing their praises, singing anything.

'I didn't even get drunk at my father's wake, I was too busy taking it all in and buying everyone else a drink. Mr father never drank at all. Mind you, I've made up for the both of us in the past. There's a way of getting over it – it's all to do with your meals. You never drink on an empty stomach, or if you do, you have to have a decent meal after it. Like the politicians do – drink themselves into oblivion with a fine meal.

'I'd been told by a few people that you never really grow up until one of your parents dies, and that was certainly true for me. Suddenly I was no longer my father's child, I was the keeper of the flame. As the only boy, that was the role that fell to me. In a way, that helps you with the early days and weeks of grief. It fell to me to organise family affairs, be industrious. But then, when you've expended your energy on that, there comes a time when you slow down and the full weight of it hits you.

'For me it was when I'd returned to LA and I was lying in my bed and I felt I should telephone my sister to see how she was coping.

Then it hit me, the weight of it shunted down on me a bit more. It didn't quite crush me, but it came close.'

There are many men who would not be able to make such a confession, from the heart, so soon after the trauma of losing their father. Neeson was always ready to feel his emotions, and be honest about them. 'Being open helps you deal with them. If you shut them away, they're only going to boil away inside and erupt later, in some weird way.'

He took solace in the fact that, though he'd veered so far out of the path his father had mapped out for him, he had made the old man very happy. 'I know he was terribly proud of me. That helps. Death like that, the death of your father, it leaves you with a legacy. It's when you know for sure that there is nothing to fear but fear itself. I live by that now.'

And he would use it as a lesson: 'I was at his funeral, carrying my father's coffin and this man – he's known my father all his life, lived in this small town all his life, and my father's father and his father's father before him grew up together and he's come to pay his respects to my father and he sidles up to me and says, "I hear you've been working with Clint Eastwood, Liam."

'And I'm carrying my father's coffin. There's a side of me wants to put it down and punch this guy but at the same time there's another side which is standing back laughing at the absolute absurdity of this situation. A side which is thinking, Yes, my father would have loved this. He would have laughed at it. It is funny.

'After the funeral, I was listening to the priests telling wonderful stories about him. Like the time he was driving along the motorway to Belfast and got pulled over by the police. For driving too slowly!

'That was him all right. He ambled through life like a snail. Sure, sometimes that could be infuriating. When you're young and full of fire and enthusiasm and you want to see things, do things, be things, move on, grab experiences. And there's the man in whose mould you are made, tootling along in the slow lane. But losing him made me remember something – how important it is to stop and smell the roses. That was my father. And now I'm aware that's something I haven't been doing enough of.'

It also made him aware of how vital a happy and fulfilling permanent relationship was – like the marriage shared for over forty years by his parents. But old habits are hard to break. Neeson was still, despite an increasing propensity to be seen in public with the most eligible women in town, a self-confessed loner who liked it that way.

'I guess I'm a bit of a mystery to LA. When you live there, on your own, people assume you're on a quest to find the right girl and having no luck. So they think, We must invite Liam over for lunch or a barbecue and line him up with a nice girl. It's a terrible position to be in. You don't want to offend – people have only got your best interests at heart. But that kind of set-up is so forced, and embarrassing.

'The trouble is, I really like being on my own. I'm good at it. It's precious to me. You get used to having your own time and your own space and you think, How would it be if I had to share this with someone on a permanent basis? It might be fine for a while, it usually is. But people change.

'Sure, sometimes I get lonesome, but there's a difference between that and actually being lonely. That's a terrible place to visit, but I have to say, it doesn't happen to me. I learned years ago how to be all right on my own. It suits me fine. It's a habit I'm trying to wean myself out of. I am aware that if you closet yourself away *too* much, it can be unhealthy. You retreat deep inside yourself and all sorts of negative things can come out of that.

'The other thing you discover about yourself, of course, is how frighteningly easy it is to get out of the practice of being with a woman. I've happily gone for months without dating anyone at all. Then when you come to it, it's an eye-opener. You've got out of the habit. Your hands shake, you feel sick with nerves. That's happened to me. I've found myself looking in the mirror an hour before a new date and thinking, Is it too late to cancel? It's all right once you get into it, but the nerves beforehand – it's as bad as it gets before a performance. Worse!'

Eat your heart out, girls.

13

Girls, Girls, Girls (and the older woman or two)

'I lead a simple life and that's the way I like it. I don't even own a car. I'm concentrating on the career and I know it sounds corny but the only thing I'd love to have – to be able to afford to buy – is a nice house back home for the folks.'

He wasn't long in Hollywood before Liam Neeson achieved that particular dream. Today, his mother Kitty lives in a luxury ground-floor apartment in an exclusive executive-style block in the centre of her native Ballymena. What Neeson wanted, Neeson got.

Not so his mother. She wanted nothing more than to see her Liam happily married, settled, with the prospect of his own family round the corner. He was downhill on the way to forty now and she was beginning to be concerned.

'I know she wanted to see me settled down,' he admitted sheepishly. 'When she'd spot me in the gossip columns with a girl on my arm she'd be straight out with the pen and paper and sending me a letter with the newspaper clipping asking, "Just who is this young lady?"'

'Ever the optimist!'

Neeson had been ostensibly single since the short, sharp shock of his split with Julia Roberts. Rumour was that he'd become hooked on playing the field, dabbling with a relationship here, a few dates there, but no firm commitment to any one girl. This Lothario reputation annoyed him so much he went on record saying it was not the case. 'I don't fool around. I had a strict moral upbringing. It left its mark.'

The affair with Julia Roberts certainly left its mark on a British

journalist who had become extremely close to Neeson since meeting
him the year before he migrated to Hollywood. They became lovers
and continued the relationship when he moved to LA in 1987. After a
romantic stay with Neeson at his Venice Beach home, the woman was
shocked in mid-flight on her return journey when she happened to
glance at a newspaper being read by the man sitting next to her.

Other passengers were startled when she let out a horrified scream.
'My boyfriend's living with Julia Roberts!' Her eyes had alighted on
a headline in the gossip column declaring Liam Neeson's love for the
hottest legs in Hollywood. He was not her boyfriend any longer.

'I wonder if he ever was,' she later mused ruefully to friends.
'Transatlantic love affairs are never easy to conduct but it was
perfect for Liam. He could get up to absolutely anything he wanted
– and obviously did.'

Although heartbroken, she ultimately forgave him. 'Frankly, if
you're going to lose out to another woman, it might as well be Julia
Roberts.'

Neeson had always been slightly sheepish about past lovers,
preferring them to disappear from whence they came after the affair
was over and nurse the memory of it to themselves. Astonishingly,
they all did, demonstrating a kind of wounded loyalty that only the
rarest of loves can inspire. Which suited him fine.

He wanted the world, and especially Kitty, to know he wasn't
leaping into bed with a different girl every night. It wouldn't do
his public image much good in these moralistic, AIDS-scared days.
Trouble was, he would get his picture in the papers all the time with
a different girl on his arm, seemingly week in week out.

In Hollywood, that's the name of the game, but back in Ballymena
they were coming up to Kitty Neeson in the Tower Centre and saying,
'So Liam's got himself a nice new girlfriend, this actress from *Dynasty*
is it? What's her name? And will this be the right lassie now?' And
Kitty Neeson was not amused because she hadn't even seen this
particular newspaper and who knew what the lassie was like or who
she was, because Liam had said nothing to her.

Catch 22. On the one hand, he was still answerable to his mother,
still concerned for her feelings; on the other hand, it did little harm
to be seen with a host of gorgeous women and not just any old
gorgeous women but recognisable names, the bigger the better.
This tactic certainly worked as a career move. Link your name
with someone famous and it would stick. People remembered. It

worked with films, when he hopped from one genre to another with what looked like insatiable thirst for experience. Neeson and de Niro. Neeson and Rourke. Neeson and Cher. Neeson and Diane Keaton. Neeson and Darryl Hannah. Neeson and Patrick Swayze. Now it was Liam Neeson in lights, in his own right.

Now he'd attained a certain measure of success and recognition, he wanted more: 'It's time to move the career up another notch.' Up there with those names he's referred to time and again, the big boys, Mel and Kevin and Harrison.

So what did Neeson have that they hadn't? Or what didn't he have that they all did? Simple, a wife. Being single had several plus points in his favour. He could play the field, be seen as desirable, thereby becoming even more so. To be seen escorting the great and the good and the downright gorgeous women of this world could only enhance his eligible status. Directors, take note.

There was just one problem. How did you separate the perception of sensitive, still-searching eligible bachelor from randy superstud? Tricky one that, better play devil's advocate. To the press – and equally as important, to his mother, Kitty – he took the decent chap line. While not trying to convince anyone he was a saint, he could subtly get across the message he just hadn't found the right girl yet. And it was all *his* fault . . .

'Sure, I love women. I want to get married and have kids one day. But I'm not that confident when it comes to making the first moves. And I'm a lazy sod. I'm not one for the champagne and roses.'

But he had been, quite noticeably, alone for years before this sudden spate of public appearances with a selection of glamorous dates. He was still not willing to make any commitment, it seemed. 'I'm single, very single but that doesn't mean I'm a Warren Beatty, it just means I'm free. I don't have the added weight of responsibility of a wife and family so I can concentrate on work.'

How many of us get to middle age and can honestly say we've never been in love? For a man who conveyed such inner depth and sensitivity, who had the (acting) ability to wear his heart on his sleeve, how was it he'd never managed to fall head-over-heels?

Sceptics might posit the question: was Liam Neeson in love with himself?

'I'm just footloose and fancy free. I'm not owned by anybody. I don't get lonely because I've always kind of been on my own. Certainly, for the first five or six years in this business, as regards relationships, I was alone. Why not? I'm good at being on my own and I like it. My own space is really precious to me.

'I like relationships on the phone. I keep in touch with some girlfriends that way. On the phone, they're easy to talk to . . .'

The truth is, not since Don Juan had there been a celluloid hero who owed as much to as many women in his life. And with Liam Neeson, you have to go right back to the beginning to see where the pattern took root.

Brought up with three sisters and a strong mother, he learned very early how to handle women. They were his protectors, mother hens clucking round him, fussing over him.

Neeson himself admitted he was most at home in the company of women. 'I've always loved women. My three sisters were always bringing their girlfriends home; the place would be crowded out with girls, all a few years older than me, discussing quite openly their problems, their love lives, their emotions. It was always kind of intimate, girls' talk. When you're used to being in a room full of women like that, guys become really boring.'

When he left the collective bosom of his family to make his own way in the world, he found other women willing to step in and become his guardian angels. In Hollywood, there would be Diane Keaton, Barbra Streisand, Kate Capshaw and Natasha Richardson, all of them ready to take him by the hand and help him negotiate the rocky road to success.

He had always expressed a taste for older women. They were alert, not simply to his raw sexuality, but also to that sensitivity, the little-boyishness that brought out the mother in them. In fact, that was the last thing most women wanted to do with Liam Neeson, but it certainly helped hook them in.

One ex-lover, an actress from his London days, said: 'Liam's penchant was always for older, more sophisticated, experienced actresses who coached him in sexual politics because they taught him it was not merely okay but actually attractive when he revealed his more vulnerable, gentler side. Under their approval, he learned how to explore and express his emotions, because he knew it affected them, it turned them on. It was more than most men were willing to offer. It made intelligent, sexy women feel they were communicating on a much deeper level than normal.

'That in turn made Liam seem outstanding, rare among men. He was a kindred spirit as well as a lover. It intrigued and captivated.'

Despite previous insistence that he was an intensely private person and any decent man's love life should remain private out of respect for the woman involved, now Neeson found it expedient to back up this more sympathetic theory. Knowing that legions of women read magazines, he was happy to expound on his own personal philosophy of love to them.

'I've often been accused of flirting. But in fact, I'm very shy when it comes to actually chatting women up. I'd never make a lounge lizard in a million years. The fact is, I didn't go out with a lot of ladies because work ate up most of my time. Then you have to make time for yourself to switch off from work. What's left over is not a lot. Besides, when I'm heavily involved in work, I like to be on my own. It's easier that way. There's just me and the mirror to take it out on.'

Wouldn't we all love an equable, considerate, responsible man like that, ladies? With each considered interview, Neeson knew he was gaining more votes.

He knew he had a receptive ear – and frequently other bits of the body too – when he was in any woman's company. Very occasionally he misjudged it: one well-known LA-based writer was incensed to hear why she'd been selected out of a pool of several journalists to meet Neeson.

'The rumour was that he'd put the word to his publicist that he'd prefer to be interviewed by women. He felt he'd not come across in the few interviews he'd done with male reporters. I went along prepared to switch off from this manipulative smooth-talker. But he beamed me this sweet smile, looked right into my eyes and . . . smooth-talked me.

'I couldn't even hate myself afterwards. But when I looked at his press cuttings, I saw the interviews he'd done with men were totally different in tone. He was very much more one of the lads with them. With the women it was all oozing sex. I'm afraid I was just another lamb to the slaughter.'

He certainly had the right effect on most of the women who met and wrote about him in those LA years. One took great glee in reporting how she'd been invited back to his Hollywood Hills pad – only the third person, he claimed, and she had no reason to disbelieve him – to be allowed to do so in as many years.

During their prolonged interview session, the undeniably gorgeous writer asked why he had picked such a low-key hideaway hole to live in? Was it to retreat to, came the loaded question, when women started throwing themselves at him?

To the romantic strains of Van Morrison in the background, Neeson gave his measured reply: 'Why would women want to throw themselves at me?'

'Because,' came the inviting reply, 'you're sexy.'

'Well,' Neeson countered, smiling passably shyly, 'if I am, they don't tell me. But sure, we're always attracted to things we don't trust, or that we're wary of. And' – a big winsome grin here – 'actors have been rogues and vagabonds for centuries. Outlawed by society. Being an outlaw is sexy, I guess.'

But to be approaching forty and still single in Hollywood presented a bit of a problem for Neeson. People began speculating. What was wrong with the guy? Sexual problems? Emotional hysteric? Was there something *missing*? Neeson knew he had to knock down any potentially scurrilous speculation before it took root.

It wasn't that there was anything wrong, you understand, it was all down to his old friend, timing. Thus far, the moment just hadn't been right. 'Marriage and a family? Some day, aye. But I'm a great believer in things happening at their proper time. Generally speaking, I think women come into their own in their late twenties, whereas men don't seem to get their shit together until their early forties. I'm going to rely on that.'

Meanwhile, there were still the joys of older women. In 1990, while promoting his latest film, *The Big Man*, Neeson made an uncustomary public slip to a reporter when he confessed: 'I do actually have a new girlfriend. We don't live together, we're just a nice old-fashioned boyfriend and girlfriend. I've always had strict morals and as I get older, I'm becoming increasingly more strict with myself.'

But he saved the best for last. His reference to her was, if nothing else, to the point.

What words would you dream up to describe your new love in one simple phrase? Stunning, lovely, gorgeous, sexy, intelligent, capable, successful, rich, kind, soft? The true lover is spoilt for choice, really. Not Neeson.

He described her thus: 'She's a Bronx Jewess.'

He could have been unkinder, you suppose. He could have said, 'She's much older than me.' Or, 'She's not classically beautiful.'

She was Barbra Streisand.

Was it indeed, that rarest of events, Neeson letting his guard slip for a moment, giving an insight into his normally private love life? Or did he know that no reporter worth their salt could fail to realise this was word from the man himself that the latest Hollywood rumours were true. It would hardly harm any actor's career for people to know that one of the most powerful women in the industry was also in his arms. Streisand, at the time, was directing and starring in her latest opus, *Prince of Tides*.

Irish actor Peter Caffrey paid a visit to Neeson's home at this time. He was invited by Neeson to accompany him to Streisand's Malibu home where, in her private cinema, she gave them a preview of the upcoming movie.

A friend says: 'Liam was quite keen for people to know he was with Streisand. But he also knew that she didn't want the press intruding on her love life. She likes to keep that very low profile. She had no need to parade him or any other man round places where they would have their picture taken. It was all conducted well away from the spotlight, invariably at her homes.

'But by taking a friend like Pete to meet her, the word was bound to get out. Pete was impressed. Who wouldn't be? He said Streisand was all over Liam like a raincoat. They slipped away at the end of the screening and didn't surface till late next day. It was quite clear what she saw in Liam and it wasn't just his acting potential.'

He began to be seen around town with an array of stunning girls. Let the pictures tell the story. Then he could put the word out via friends – and himself, in interviews, because the press were fascinated now – to countermand them. He claimed he found the image foist upon him, that of a Celtic gigolo, annoying. He let it be known to a garrulous friend, his dialect coach Tod Todoroff, that he was 'tired of people writing about my love life'.

Todoroff was happy to talk. 'I keep saying to him, "Well, you have to change your love life. If you stop having these three-month intense affairs with famous actresses, then they wouldn't write about it."

'The trouble is, there's no doubt Liam is in the top three per cent of the most charming men on earth. Women simply respond to him. He doesn't even know he's doing it. He simply loves women and they tune in to that. When he's with a woman it's automatic, all his lights go on.'

There was a genuine downside to all this attention focused on his amorous exploits. Neeson was disconcerted to find himself defined suddenly, not by his acting merit, but by the string of lovely leading ladies he dated.

It may or may not have been his original intention to attract the attention of the gossip columnists, paparazzi and tabloid reporters and, via them, the studio heads, but if so, it now seemed to have back-fired on him. And it did so when he reached out for the biggest star in the Hollywood heavens, Brooke Shields. Her acting credentials were slim, but Brooke was one of the most publicity-worthy girls in town.

There had always been speculation about her love life. Was she still a virgin at thirty? Could she possibly have a thing going with stars like Michael Jackson and André Agassi? Now there she was fluttering in front of the cameras with surely the most masculine of men, Liam Neeson, and even sporting a huge diamond on her engagement finger. A friendship ring, she called it, coyly.

The press were falling over themselves to get the exclusive – wedding bells at last for Brooke? Neeson, however, was going under in this tidal wave of press attention. It wasn't turning out the way he had wanted it at all. 'It got wa-ay too much, real intrusive stuff.'

When it hammered on the door of his home, he knew it was time to call it a day. 'I was lying in bed one morning when I heard this knock at the door.' For a man who had invited so few to his precious sanctuary, he leapt to the obvious conclusion. 'I thought it was a messenger with some scripts. I jumped up and went to answer the door in my underwear. As you do . . . and there's this guy standing there saying, "I'm from the *National Enquirer*. Could you give us a statement about Brooke?"'

Neeson's retort to the reporter is not on record. But the hapless journalist must eternally be kicking himself for not getting a snatch picture of Neeson in his underwear.

Ten minutes later, someone else was on the phone – his personal home number, no less – claiming to be Brooke's assistant and suggesting that it might be in their best interests if they co-operated with the press and talked about the romance. Starting with Liam. And starting right now. 'You could practically hear the tape recorder whirring on the other end of the line.'

It was too late to stop the ball rolling now. His constant denial to the press of any information about the Shields romance had a knock-on effect. The press went to town postulating possible scenarios. The whispers turned Chinese and grew to encompass an engagement, the exchange of vows, talk of babies. And the rumours flew far and wide, eventually reaching the family back home in Ballymena.

Kitty Neeson called to find out the truth behind the gossip. On no account, she was told, should she talk to anyone, not friends, not neighbours and especially not to the press. No one was to be trusted. All it took was for one unscrupulous reporter to weazle his way into some Ballymenian's confidence over a few pints down the pub and wham! Before you knew it, it would be WHAT NEESON MUM THINKS OF LIAM'S LOVERS, all over the front page.

Neeson had pulled the shutters down even more firmly than before. Kitty and the rest of the family stayed tight-lipped.

But Neeson's claim to have been stunned by all the press interest was perhaps a mite disingenuous. What had he expected, when he'd elected to woo some of the world's most beautiful and newsworthy women in public? That photographers would pack away their cameras and say, 'Oh, well, Liam, seeing as it's you and you just hate publicity . . .'? Hardly. He was coming out of all this just fine, still heroic, always so protective of his girls.

He generated even more column inches when he noisily repudiated his public liaisons were publicity ploys. 'Listen, the women I've been involved with, I love dearly. But suddenly you're stuck with this tag: Liam Neeson, the guy who used to go out with Julia Roberts. Or "the guy who has befriended Brooke Shields"' – note the careful choice of words on this one – 'and it's like – where have twenty-two years of acting work gone?'

Brooke Shields did not appear to have her heart broken when the affair fizzled out after a few months. But Irish singer Sinead O'Connor was devastated when her own brief fling with Neeson was abruptly terminated.

The controversial shaven-headed singer was renowned for wearing her heart on her sleeve. When she fell for a man, she fell hard, and exposed her pain and heartache in her songs. Although they shared an Irish heritage and background, the same Celtic introspection and indigestion, she was a rare departure from Neeson's norm in love and lust with her bald head and strident political views. Yet still she manifested the curious mix of strength and vulnerability that he seemed to bring out in all the women in his life.

An Irish friend of the unlikely couple revealed: 'Sinead was completely smitten with Liam after they met in New York. He seemed really taken with her too for a few weeks, but he very quickly switched off. He let her down gently, but she was incredibly cut up about it.

The thing with Sinead is she's incredibly needy and Liam couldn't handle that.'

He was much more comfortable being coquettish. It was instinctive and infallible. All a woman had to do to switch on Neeson's flirt button was be there. He turned his focus – and flirting – on to any woman in the vicinity. He was never abashed to do this in front of other people, either. Friends, family, even reporters witnessed this phenomenon in action. 'It was,' says one friend, 'as if Liam had to prove he was the most attractive man in the world. He never switched off when there was a woman around.'

Given that he invariably met with interviewers over a restaurant meal, the nearest – always willing – victim was inevitably a waitress. Unperturbed that he was breaking off the flow of the interview, and simultaneously aware that his every move would be noted down, written up and published for the world to read, he chatted up a waitress in practically every venue he was interviewed in.

The chat-ups are almost puerile in their simplicity. First the opening gambit: 'Darlin', you must be part Irish.' Then the flattery: 'You're not? Well, you look it. There must be some Irish in your family, sure?' Then he would gently extricate the history of the family tree back six generations where, sure enough, great-great-great granny was half-Irish on her mother's side. And the waitress, charmed into complete emotional submission, would retreat in a lovestruck daze.

Anyone witnessing this scenario could be left in no doubt whatsoever that here was one of the world's sexiest men. As one remarked: 'Whether or not he appreciated the pilgrim soul in the waitress or not, he clearly appreciated her long legs.'

Even male friends were staggered by the consummate ease with which Neeson magnetised women to him. Richard Graham says: 'Women have always gone potty over him. He's not a man's man, not in the least. He's very private and very sensitive. Women relate to that. They're intrigued by it. He simply gets on better in the company of women.'

And Todoroff expands on that surefire chat-up technique: 'He has *the* world's greatest line. So simple, but so effective: "Darlin', would you fancy comin' up for a wee cup of tea?"'

Etchings are such a tired and hoary old line, after all. Says Todoroff: 'So cosy. And then, once they're inside, the door is locked. It's "You're mine now!"'

However, according to people who have witnessed the phenomenon in action, Neeson still had one fateful flaw. 'He bores easy. It's all white heat and intense passion – and then he wants to move on. Basically, he's not your average middle-aged man. He's more like a mercurial eighteen-year-old. He jumps into relationships so impetuously. It makes him nuts. At first there's a mutual intoxication. He calls up and says, "This is it. We're talking about having kids." Yet a few weeks later, "It's over."'

It was a point Neeson himself, despite being tight-lipped about most aspects of his love life, was willing to concede. 'No matter how wonderful it is to begin with, you always kind of wise up. I would always wake up in the morning and think, Hold on. This is wrong.'

As if to put salve on the wound, Neeson excused his behaviour by referring to it in the lyricism of W.B. Yeats: 'The sweet sickness had passed.'

'Well, after all,' says an ex-lover, 'for all his pontificating about feelings and sensitivity, Liam Neeson is still a man.'

Others would contend, and he would definitely wish it believed, that he was new man. Insatiable flirting apart, of course, you'd never see much Neanderthal behaviour from Liam Neeson. He always knew he was different because he actually cared about women. Though how this aligned with his hectic track record was hard to reconcile.

'Men,' he proclaimed, 'are generally assholes. Women have grown in leaps and bounds over the past thirty years. They've found their voice – and their right to speak it. And long may it continue. Men are so shit-scared of the women's movement that they've got no voice any more. Their heroes are still the Clint Eastwood types, strong, moody, silent, all that crap. That's still the image that makes a man a man.

'Take American football as an example. It's all rules. Here's the front line. Here's the battle line. It's all about knocking down your fuckin' opponent. Men have always been and still are bound by straight lines, boxed in, playing games about pitched battle and getting off on it.

'I think men are really scared and confused. The only way they know how to be is to be an asshole. Confront them with anything emotional and they're off. "Fuck this, I'm not listening to this. I'm out the door." They can't confront feelings. They have to deny them. It's a sign of great weakness, I think. Of course, women are the opposite, they like to be in touch with their feelings, they explore them.

'I once read an article which made the point that for generations, men were denied access to their feelings. The dictum was, "You mustn't cry, it's not manly." The only thing they were allowed to feel was . . . their cock!'

Ever since the trauma of his confessional about masturbation in his mid teens, Neeson had this thing about the male sex organs. His own, naturally. 'Well, it's a weird sensation to look down and see this strange thing, this tackle hanging there. It's like, "Jeez, what *is* this thing?"'

It had long preoccupied him. And a considerable amount of people who've come into contact with him. The legend that travelled all the way from Dublin to Tinseltown last year received official recognition from an association calling themselves the Hung Jury. In order to attain membership to this exclusive club, would-be applicants had first to measure up to a certain physical criteria that involved a twelve-inch ruler.

Now some 2,000 strong, other legends in their own lunchboxes are Frank Sinatra, Dolph Lundgren and Kiss singer Gene Simmonds. Recently, members voted Liam Neeson to be elected with honorary status in their midst. Averred one: 'Well, everyone knows Neeson needs a yard stick!'

Apocryphal? Even if it was, it couldn't do his reputation as the world's sexiest star any harm.

And although few girlfriends ever volunteered any inside info on Neeson's performance between the sheets – another valuable aspect of remaining friends with ex-lovers. They never betray you with a kiss 'n' sell – a couple recently came out of the closet with one voice.

'There are two things,' reveals the first, from an affair several years ago, 'that stand out about Liam Neeson – one is his enormous . . . how can I put this? "allure" – it's positively gargantuan. The other is his boundless ambition.'

The second lover, from an affair in the early nineties, confirms, 'Liam is the most generously endowed man I've ever come across. What's he like in bed? Does it really matter? When you're that well endowed, you're nine-tenths of the way there. No girl is going to protest at his sexual technique with equipment like that.'

It is testimony to their fidelity to him as a friend that no ex-girlfriends will reveal anything adverse about Neeson as a sexual athlete. Perhaps there is no room for criticism. Perhaps he is, as the legend proclaims, the world's greatest lover. Equipped with the perfect physique, the perfect technique and an insatiable appetite for variety, Neeson is the answer to any red-blooded girl's dreams.

According to one well-known New York socialite, with whom Neeson had a colourful relationship, he loves to talk about sex. Which is why, she confessed to friends, he spent considerable time running up a sizeable phone bill. 'Liam really doesn't like to get close to people. He likes to be separate, he's not really comfortable as half of a couple. He likes to keep you at arm's length. That's why he's so into sexy phone calls.'

His friend Richard Graham reveals how even his own elderly mother fell prey to Neeson's effusive sexy charm over the phone. 'The first time he called me at home, she answered the phone to him. She only spoke to him for about sixty seconds but when she handed me the phone she said, "Oh God, that's the first time my knees have trembled in forty-five years!"'

When Graham's fiancée, a nurse, lived in a communal nursing hostel, Neeson's home phone number was freely passed around among the staff. Off duty, the other nurses would queue up to use the payphone to call Neeson's home. Just to listen to his voice on the answering machine.

Maybe the mere sound of those melting Irish tones can reduce a woman on the receiving end to a quivering mass. Or is there more? According to a close friend, who insists on remaining anonymous for fear of jeopardising the friendship she retains with Neeson to this day, he pursued her with suggestive and eventually explicit sexy calls for months.

'It was an incredible experience. It had never happened to me before, although I've got girlfriends who have regular phone sex with their boyfriends. But the thing about this was we hadn't got it on when he started ringing me. I'd met him, sure, he'd flirted like crazy, yes, but this came out of the blue.

'It was an incredible turn-on. Liam's talk is actually the sexiest thing about him – that voice and the slow, pensive way he speaks. The excitement was in not knowing when, if ever, anything was actually going to happen between us.'

They have remained friends to this day. 'Liam likes to stay friends. It's his pattern. I guess it's an ego thing. He knows we're still here and we still care about him in one way or another.'

She was surprised, however, when he married in 1994. 'I was staggered that he actually took the plunge. He was never the sort to get too close, or too involved. But then, of course, it was Natasha Richardson.'

One writer who got close to him proclaimed: 'He is stoically determined to make it. But he hides it well; you'll never see ambition burning naked in Liam's eyes, he keeps that flame within. Come on, he's an actor.

'But if you get close to Liam – as close as it's possible to get, because believe me, he doesn't let people in – you get to know that he'll put anything down if it stands in his way. But no one stands in Liam's way because he charms them to step aside. And not only do they do it, they find themselves wishing him well on his way.

'Natasha is perfect for Liam. Bright, beautiful – but not *too* beautiful, she reinforces his "thinking man" image. Have you noticed how they always wear wire-rimmed specs? Lends just the right air of intellectuality. She's well known and respected in an area that *he* had long traded in for commercial success. Well, it couldn't fail, could it?

'And the thing about Natasha was she didn't give up. She wanted Liam and she had the confidence to pursue it when he wouldn't commit at first. He'd been backing off women who were too keen for twenty years, he had it down to a fine art. But there was a combination of factors that made it work for Natasha.

'He'd been in Hollywood seven years and done plenty but at the same time done nothing of huge merit. He really hadn't made it, not in the way he wanted to. People saw him as having little real depth. Natasha had class, credibility and contacts in an area where he didn't.

'The timing was perfect. He knew *Schindler* was coming up and his name was in the frame but he didn't have the weight for it. Doing *Anna Christie* on Broadway opposite Natasha would give him the required weight.

'And of course, in the nineties, we are looking at the decade of real values: love, fidelity, sharing and caring. The time of the power couple, so in love, happily married – is now.

'Some tactician, Liam.'

14

Reaching The Dark Places Within

'I saw Darkman as a guy striving to keep the yin and yang of his soul together. He's always suppressing something, trying to quell the raging beast within.

'I can relate to that. You know, you're sitting at a restaurant table or in a traffic jam or waiting for an elevator, and there's an outward side of you that has to present itself as a normal human being.

'But inside you're dying to stab somebody.

'Especially here in Los Angeles.'

In his next film, *Darkman*, Neeson really got his teeth into his favourite kind of character – the tormented outsider, racked with inner pain, hunted like a wounded animal, doomed by his own plight, yet ferocious in his determination to avenge. It was precisely the kind of tortured role he excelled in. But how much of himself did he bring to Darkman? Just what was it that lay buried deep inside the genial giant Irishman that he should sometimes feel the urge to cut someone down in a frenzied knife attack?

'It was great to know that this guy really could lose his temper. He has some secret the world doesn't know, this terrible unbelievable rage. He wants to keep it harnessed, but sometimes he loses that battle. I felt real empathy for the guy.'

Darkman? Or Neeson himself? Did Darkman reach the parts of Liam Neeson that other roles failed to reach? As always, he was giving nothing away, but his fascination with Darkman was plain to see.

'I loved his sheer drama. He moves ʼthrough the entire range of emotions from timid romance to rage and despair, a character who changes so completely and becomes, both physically and emotionally, another being altogether. It was a real acting challenge. I had to maintain a rage, yet hold on to some control and contain certain emotions. I was faced with trying to project the emotions I was trying to protect.'

Director Sam Raimi saw something of this conflict when he picked Neeson for the part. He said: 'Liam's range is astonishing. He could transform himself from this warm and giving man, a paragon of virtue and control, into a demented beast fuelled on anger and spitting rage. He could bridge that gap so you never even noticed it was there.'

For Neeson, portraying a character with two diametrically opposed facets to his nature was no problem. 'I was lured by his turmoil, the idea that he could no longer fit into mainstream society. Because he's decided to become this avenging angel, he's had to pay the price: solitude and the loss of his relationships.'

All that must have struck a deep chord within him. 'I can't have a relationship while I'm working on something like *Darkman*. I have to train physically and mentally for something as demanding as this. I trained for it like an athlete – focus on the fixed point ahead there and make sure you get to it.

'So I don't find it difficult to stay in character while filming, even though there are great gaps when you're not actually acting. When the work's at hand, I can't be bothered going out. Social life? Forget it. This was a monastic experience.

'No matter what the film is, I mostly keep to myself because what I'm there for is to get the work done.'

Such sentiments of complete dedication to work, to the total exclusion of any personal life, are what have always made Liam Neeson different. The film playing inside his head has always sustained him. Only when the final credits roll does he think about life outside.

It was something that was not lost on director Raimi: 'Liam has an inner dignity deep within himself. He has soul. And he's curiously out of time. It's like he really belongs in the past, somewhere around 1850, but he's got stuck in this timewarp and somehow found himself in the 1990s.'

Darkman from the Dark Ages? Whatever Raimi's perceptions about Neeson, this film, in particular, consumed his leading man. The script revolved around a scientist, Peyton Westlake, who is on the threshold of a miraculous scientific breakthrough, pioneering synthetic skin. Sadly, before he can enlighten the world with his discovery, he's set upon by thugs and horrifically burned in an even nastier acid bath than the one that turns Jack Nicholson into the Joker, and left for dead. In archetypal anti-hero fashion, he plucks himself from death's door and escapes from hospital to wreak his bloody revenge.

His horrendous scarring meant Neeson had to spend an incapacitating three to five hours a day sitting rigid in Make-up, a stiflingly boring exercise that required the patience of Job – or Liam Neeson. He claimed he was not perturbed by the lengthy and debilitating process.

'It was no problem for me, I was trained as a boxer. I got really fit, did my yoga, in order to be able to sit in a make-up chair for hours before dawn, conserving my energy for the time when I got out of that chair and had to start the day acting. Sure, it was demanding but it was a great challenge. It gave me a buzz to be coming out of that trailer after a five-hour make-up session when the crew were just turning up to breakfast.

'And I was intrigued by playing beneath a ton of prosthetic make-up. I liked the idea of exploring the emotions involved in playing behind the mask. I accepted the make-up as being my own skin and I was convinced the audience would too.'

Neeson was undoubtedly not in this one for the glamour. Wrapping his strapping physique and his prosthetic face in suppurating bandages and a floor-length black cloak, it looked hardly likely that the world's sexiest man would score points with his brigade of female fans for this one.

In fact, he found the camouflage did not in the slightest deter his die-hard female following. 'Actually when I had the make-up, the cloak and the hat on, I felt really handsome. I mean, when I look in the mirror with my normal everyday face, I never see Mel Gibson anyway, so this was a real experience.

'I felt really cool and sexy, very swashbuckling. It was interesting, it had a marked effect on women that I really never would have predicted. On set sometimes the crew would bring wives or girlfriends and female journalists would come along to check out the film in progress. When I had all the gear on, it seemed to do something for them. A couple of times, when I was in full make-up, I was slipped telephone numbers. But I was too nervous to follow them up. I was scared that I'd take this stuff off and they'd go, "Oh, yuk. He's Irish and just look at him, would you!"'

Self-deprecation taken a step too far? Actress Frances McDormand, who played Westlake's girlfriend in the film, remarked: 'Aw, come on. Those girls gave him their numbers precisely because they knew what was under that stuff.'

She knew it, they knew it. Neeson knew it too. He just didn't want people to know he knew it. Arrogance was a trait he had always deplored. Much better, and much more powerful a tool, is to project humility and to have the confidence, the single-minded determination and the belief in self, tucked away beneath the surface.

In *Darkman*, he was able to see another fantasy fulfilled. He managed to grab himself a slice of action man – a niche he'd always secretly fancied himself in. In one scene, the eponymous misfit hero is seen dangling precariously from a helicopter as it zooms through the towering edifices of downtown LA. Suddenly he's launched precipitously through the plate-glass window of an office block, sending shards of glass flying over the aghast office workers.

Neeson pulled off the stunt with panache, offering his profuse apologies for the untimely intrusion, before being whisked out again on his airborne travels. This particular scene was classic comic strip hero action. Had it not been for the broken nose and crooked teeth, Liam Neeson might have found himself happily in the role of Superman – heroic, vulnerable and above all unfailingly courteous. It was an ambition he tucked away, waiting until the right character came along. With his unconventionally handsome looks, he knew it would have to be a slightly battered hero. Someone, perhaps, more like Rob Roy . . .

Still dreaming of the distant future when he would star as an all-action conquering hero – and he would, he knew it, it was just a matter of biding his time, building up his repertoire and his image – Liam was particularly excited by *Darkman*. Not only was he the male lead, he believed it would turn out to be 'a wonderful action romantic fantasy'. Great faith. Misplaced as it turned out. *Darkman* was destined to become a cult movie, but, yet again, another flop at the box office.

Neeson was hugely disappointed. He had desperately wanted to make a sequel to explore the part – and himself – further: 'If there was a sequel,' he said, 'that inner struggle could be developed so you could really examine it in a deeper, psychological vein.'

There would be no sequel. *Darkman* did not generate enough revenue. *Darkman 2, The Thought Processes*, was never on the agenda.

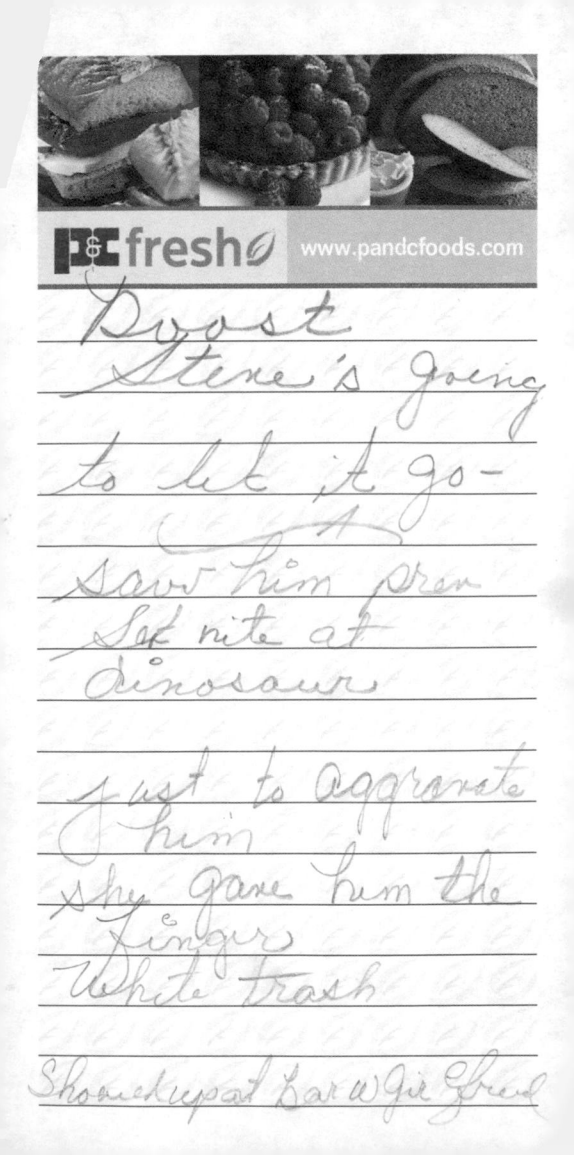

Boost
Steve's going
to let it go —
saw him prov
Sat nite at
dinosaur

just to aggravate
him
she gave him the
finger
White trash

Showed up at bar w/a friend

But after the film opened to half-full houses, Neeson retained a sense of irony about it all. The publicity campaign focused on huge billboard posters which went up all over America, demanding of the public: 'Who Is Darkman?' Americans responded in their inimitable way with graffiti proclaiming variously: Mike Tyson, or Spike Lee, and in New York, Mayor David Dinkins. No one scrawled the name Liam Neeson.

He was big enough to see the funny side of it. 'I always knew that if it wasn't a good movie, I could distance myself from it; after all, I was covered up for ninety per cent of the picture. But if it was good, I was ready to be unmasked. I could stand up and say, Yes, I was Darkman!'

Sam Raimi had no regrets about picking Neeson for the part, and he recalled one moment during filming that encapsulated the sheer professionalism that made Neeson stand head and shoulders above other actors. In one scene Darkman had to struggle through a torrential downpour, completely drenched, and forage through rubbish in a desperate search for clothes to protect him from the driving rain.

Raimi recalled, 'We flooded this alley with five inches of murky water. Liam had to battle his way through the murk, clutching this coat he'd found, then fall into the water. I thought he might be a bit dubious – the water was real grimy-looking, so I was explaining that the alley had been steam-cleaned when out of the corner of my eye, I see a rat as big as my head swim by.

'I looked back at Liam, praying he hadn't seen it, when he looks me straight in the eye, without a flicker of emotion, and says, "Great-looking mechanical rat. Let's do it."'

One thing Liam Neeson could never be accused of was prima donna behaviour. Raimi confirms, 'He's popular with directors – hell, he's popular with everyone for that lazy Irish charm. It comes with the package, being a Celt.'

There was not much lazy about the career moves Neeson was making now. As he had referred to in his training for *Darkman*, he had called on his boxing background to give him the strength and stamina to undertake the film. Now he was fighting fit and going for the championship: 'I felt I was just at the point where I could pick and choose. Some of the stuff I'd done was shite but when I looked back on it I thought, So? It got me here, I'm ready now, readier than I've ever been.'

Liam Neeson was on the up 'n' up. More success, more confidence, more confidence, more success. Life was coming full circle, on a par with those forty-year-old dreams. Liam Neeson was in Hollywood and had been solidly working since his arrival three years before.

So what was it that made him so different to all the other fêted and rated Irish actors who crossed the Atlantic in their bid for fame and fortune? The others, by and large, had discovered that America was not quite the land of golden opportunity it had been painted.

Patrick Bergin would make a big Hollywood splash in 1991 with *Sleeping with the Enemy* (ironically – for Neeson – starring opposite Julia Roberts), only to disappear without trace. Gabriel Byrne, Neeson's main competitor all those years ago back in Dublin and every Irish actor's hot tip to make it, would finally concede defeat too. *Hello Again* (1987) was almost goodbye to his Hollywood career before it even got off the ground. It nosedived even further that year with *Siesta* – which was what it induced in most of the audience. Even Byrne said of it, 'Some people think it's the greatest film they ever saw. But most of them are medicated.' Although at least he met the woman he would marry, actress Ellen Barkin, through it. Even if to commend him, there was the brilliant Cohn Brothers' *Miller's Crossing* (1990) and *Into the West* (1992, again with Barkin), ultimately Byrne would find his place behind the camera rather than in front of it, producing films, notably *In the Name of the Father*.

It was curious to note, however, that both he and Neeson pursued, as far as they could, the philosophy that work begets work, opting to throw themselves at full tilt into a series of movies that might best have been left at the drawing-board stage. But whereas this route would lead to a relative dead-end for Byrne, it had opened on to a six-lane freeway for Neeson. And it seemed he was on cruise control in the fast lane, too.

The only other Irish actor to make the grade was Pierce Brosnan, who hit a winning streak early with the bubblegumshoe series *Remington Steele*. But it seemed as if he too had peaked too soon when all went quiet on the Brosnan front. In fact, he was battling personal crises following the illness and untimely death from cancer of his wife Cassandra. When he resurfaced, it was as a pastiche of himself in *Mrs Doubtfire*. He came good eventually, though, landing, in 1994, the plum role of Bond, James Bond, Mark 5.

If the road to success was rocky for American-born actors, then for the Celtic brigade it was a virtual impasse unless they took what came their way, no matter how leaden. Like Byrne, Bergin and all the Irish others, Neeson had little in the beginning apart from a whole lot of hope. Or did he have some unquantifiable extra he brought to his quest? He alone found himself working solidly, even if it was in a series of lacklustre films. But even if they were turkeys, they were still vehicles which had star billing, big names, big budgets and great publicity value.

So why, among his theatrically trained cohorts, had he plumped for what they unanimously would have referred to as the sell-out? Lack of discrimination? Lack of vision? Or perhaps the opposite, vision on a panoramic scale? Perhaps Liam Neeson was the one, the only one, who viewed life through macrocosmic glasses.

'Actors have to keep practising. Somebody like Bobby Duvall was able to arrive at the comfort and ease of acting by doing zillions of films, most of them bullshit. But always learning something. You always do. You always learn *something*.'

He had always been straightforward, down-to-earth ambitious. Other people had lofty ideals. He had dreams he was determined to pursue with deadly accuracy. He had anticipated there would be long years of slogging it out on the Hollywood circuit, living frugally, keeping just the right kind of presentation going, talking to the right people at the right time with the right kind of self-effacing, charming message. Hard work, right enough.

To the nihilist, Neeson's path through Hollywood might have looked like Belfast at the height of the Troubles: scarred, pockmarked and blitzed with gaping holes. There they were in plenty: big-budget box-office deaths (*The Bounty, Duet For One, The Good Mother, High Spirits*), small-budget flops (*The Innocent, Lamb, The Big Man*) and fifth lead in moderate successes (*The Mission*). There were others that even Neeson would like to forget, like *Satisfaction* and *The Dead Pool*, which he 'felt sick to be associated with'. It had been his biggest hit to date, but so far as critical filmgoers were concerned, it was a dud.

He knew that, where he came from, where the acting was valid and valuable only by dint of giving your all to a product which would make people stop and engage the cognitive processes, his Hollywood work was as nought. He knew most of his Irish and British counterparts would shrug their shoulders and say, 'If the suit fits, wear it, boy. But remember, you are in the Emperor's clothes.'

It was all incredibly infra dig if you were classically, theatrically trained. He had been faced with the age-old dilemma – starve in a garret for your art or take the money and run. He'd always been a runner.

He was prepared for the brickbats from old colleagues who had stayed in their safe environment, pursuing their art rather than the Golden Grail. He had taken great pains to pre-empt their volleys, always claiming he had done what he did purely to pay his bills – and of course, those of his poor aul' folks back home who had sacrificed all for him.

Gerry McKeown, who had set young Liam on the path to acting, had this to say: 'If you look at Liam's work, it's not a fairytale story. There were sideways steps into things he normally wouldn't have entertained but it was all part of a bigger picture.

'Liam wanted to act and I think he realised very quickly you're not going to be handed Hamlet on a plate. So he did what he could and kept moving. A lot of the things he did, particularly when he went into film, were to get his name around.

'But I'll guarantee he still enjoyed one aspect of it, no matter what the quality of the end product – he would have still loved the acting. He came to life when he was in character. He stepped outside of himself and into where he wanted to be, where he knew he would be ultimately.'

They saw what he had done, and they respected it. It was his choice when offered the ultimatum: your money or your life. He would have both, and, hopefully, eventually shoot the highwayman that was Hollywood.

His friend Richard Graham revealed: 'Liam was always very ambitious. Acting is not just his career, it's an obsession. He says himself that without it, he'd shrivel up and die.'

And John Irvin, who worked with Neeson on *The Big Man*, backs this up, saying, 'Liam is extremely wary, like a boxer looking over his gloves, waiting for an opening.

'He's a long-distance runner, pacing himself, knowing he's got to go the distance so he's nurtured his career along nicely. It's well built, solid, interesting and varied.

'You can take some of the things he says, though, with a pinch of salt. He talks all the time about Costner and Cruise and Gere being the main men, and how he'd like to be up there with them. Forget it. Liam is in a good position. He gets a wide variety of roles. He's discriminating, intelligent and shrewd – and he has always made strategic blows to put himself in that position of power.'

Power was always the quest. Now he was within fingertip touch of it and he wasn't letting go. His Hollywood career might not be a knockout, but he was going to take it to the final round . . . and win on points.

15

Art Not Without Ambition

'I've never gone in for any kind of analysis, even though I know LA is the place for it. Everyone has their own pet shrink. I don't need any of that. Acting does it for me.

'You have to plumb the depths of your soul. Just by the range of people you get to play, it can totally alter your life and your way of thinking. One minute you're a coal miner, the next you're an AIDS victim. Believe me, that gives you perspective, it broadens the mind.

'I don't understand why everyone in the world doesn't want to be an actor. You get to stand up there in front of other people, saying someone else's words. It's fucking great.'

Neeson was now poised to take a major influence in his own life, his boxing, to the big screen. In director David Leland's *The Big Man*, he would play a bareknuckle boxer. There would be no pulling punches with this one, either. It was the role he had been groomed for, pitching for, since boxing and drama had crossed over in his teens.

He was also drawn to the film because he felt a very real affinity with the character he was to play, ex-miner turned boxer Danny Scoular, macho and tough on the outside but vulnerable in the extreme behind the bravado. He acknowledged the inevitable comparisons between himself and Scoular.

'The physical similarities are obvious. I'm a big guy, he was a big guy. I'm a physical actor, he worked his body for a living. But I felt empathy for the guy. There's a sequence at the start of the film that brings home the two complementary and yet contrasting sides of him. It opens with him on the picket line, vociferous, angry, on strike and yelling about it.

'Then you cut to him in the wee house and he's stood there doing the ironing, this great big guy looking real awkward. He's used to risking life and limb digging a hole a mile underground and here he is with this iron in his hand. You really feel for him.

'I know about the bravado that goes with being a boxer. I used to be one. People said I had a good left hand but deep down, I was scared of it all. I'd work hard at keeping up this veneer that I enjoyed what I was doing but it was a lie and one I didn't know how to get out of. So I had to carry on with it until there was a time and a reason for me to stop, that wasn't just the way I felt about it.'

His points defeat in the All Irish Championship at seventeen had given him his out clause without him losing face. For all those years he had boxed on, hating what he was doing, despising himself for it – but he carried on regardless. Liam Neeson's middle name should surely be Tenacity, even in the face of all odds. Now, twenty years on, he was able to put that experience to good use.

'So I took my own impressions and married them to Danny. I thought, maybe Danny felt like I did. Maybe he was no natural fighter, he's just got carried along with it. Maybe someone had seen him chin a guy outside a pub once when he was eighteen and it sort of took off from there. The word went round, "Watch out for the Big Man, he can look after himself." Then the whispers have turned him into a hero and it's "Watch out, he's a killer."

'And the irony is, maybe that was the only fight he'd ever had but he didn't deny the myth that built around him because it's kind of flattering in its way. But in his heart, he knows it's not what he's really about.'

He brought this understanding to the film's big fight scenes. Married to his knockout punch and the physique he had doggedly built up in the gym, it was a prizewinning performance.

As was ever his way, Neeson had invested heart, body and soul in his preparation but in this case there was a preponderance of body. It was not stipulated that he should add weight, but it was a prerequisite that he add bulk for the role, so he would look a credible heavyweight against his opponent, the real-life heavyweight boxer-turned-actor Rab Afleck who, Neeson noted somewhat wanly, was 'built like a brick outhouse – and then add three garages'.

The daily workout he had by now adopted with something akin to religious fervour was brought forward from its normal pre-dawn start at 3 a.m., to a catatonia-inducing 2 a.m.

The results, female studio staff observed admiringly, were worth it. Neeson was thrilled to be back in top boxing fitness. He found his punch was as dexterous as ever and his aim as true. For fear of actually knocking Afleck's head off, he started by pulling short his punches. But after a month's intensive training, his eye and reach were so precision-perfect he could pull up his shots just a fraction short of cannoning Afleck to the floor. He also found he could control what he scathingly called 'the Clint Eastwood stuff', those controlled blows that skim the skin without doing any damage to the recipient.

The resultant fight scenes, complete with smashed knuckles and battered, bleeding faces, were gruesomely true to life, eliciting considerable shock and horror from all who witnessed them. The pivotal fight in the film – a particularly brutal bout between Scoular and Cutty Dawson, played by Afleck, would prove to be the most controversial.

Neeson justified it thus: 'The whole point about the film is that Danny must go through this black hole of violence in order to pull himself out the other side and survive. He relinquishes every shred of dignity. Then he can begin to put himself together again, in a different way. It's all about the humanity and innate dignity of solid working class battling for their very existence. The fight is a metaphor for that struggle.'

Unabashed and, as it turned out, unbashed too, despite some very explicit scenes where he appeared bloody, battered and bruised, he said, 'I wasn't hurt at all, during five weeks of filming. Off set, Rab Afleck and I would spar and work out together. There was a good bond between us.'

When criticised for the brutality of the picture, Neeson took an uncharacteristically adamant stance, responding as if a personal slight had been cast at his continuing love for the sport. 'I love boxing. I know it's getting hammered over the head these days, but personally, I'll defend it to the death.'

The Big Man had another big effect on Neeson. Though he was at best reluctant, at most completely intractable when it came to talking about politics, the political theme of this film – about how miners were deprived of their livelihood and ultimately their dignity by ruthless governments – moved him to speak out for once.

'What Thatcher did to Great Britain and Ireland is horrendous. But what she could never do is break the backs of the people.

She couldn't crucify their spirit, the heart that "little" people have in the face of huge odds. That is what *The Big Man* was concerned with, that spirit and that heart.'

In the purposes of publicising the film, this was a rare breach of personal protocol by Neeson. As one of Ireland's leading lights in the entertainment world, he had often been asked to evaluate the political situation at home. He had steadfastly refused to be drawn on the issue. The most he would ever elicit was a terse: 'You can't possibly give a quick, three-line summary of the situation. After all, you're looking at a history of troubles that stretch back seven hundred years.'

But no reporter of any merit would ask for a three-line summation. People were asking for his opinion. He had one and doubtless still does; but he won't give it to anyone who might pass it on and write it up large. He has his reputation and his family to protect. Talking politics, especially when you're Irish, creates problems. People side either with you or against you. And Neeson has always hated conflict.

He was fully aware that there are elements in Northern Ireland, around Ballymena, who need only the slightest excuse to target victims, say relatives of some opinionated person in the public eye. Neeson might well be opinionated, impassioned about the politics back home, but you will never get him to talk about it. Like most things he cares about, he will hold them close to his chest. With the notable exception, of course, of his work.

Director David Leland appreciated this loyalty and steadfastness in Neeson. 'He is a steady actor and completely dependable. You know he will produce the goods you're looking for. With Liam, you know where you are. He served up the right stuff every time.'

Neeson, it was unanimously agreed, was an all-round knock-out performer, but the film went down in the first round. Based on William McIlvanney's bestselling book, the movie was torn apart, especially by critical Scots who saw its portrayal as a denial of the precise depiction in the book.

Neeson took great personal umbrage over the critical assault. Always touchy about criticism at the best of times, on this occasion he was sufficiently incensed to make his feelings publicly known.

'I was so disappointed by the critical reaction. I think it's a fabulous film. It had an expanse, an epicness to it, it was very brave and I thought it worked. But the critics! I think it was the

Daily Telegraph which said the only country where a film like this would find an audience is Romania! Just out-and-out hatred.'

The bottom line was yet another Neeson vehicle had failed to gain public approval. But if nothing else, after the completion of this one, Neeson's own presence could no longer go unnoticed. As the eponymous Big Man, he would henceforward have a big reputation to match. Even if it was in the way he least expected.

Despite his protestations at the time that he was 'only really big in Ballymena', people were starting to notice that Neeson was big everywhere.

One long-time fan, a writer whom Neeson had charmed into submission some years before, was moved to write a piece suggesting she had insider knowledge of, at the very least, Neeson's inside leg measurement.

She reported: 'Liam's moody visage has seen him voted sexiest man alive by a bevy of admiring beauties: Mirren, Streisand, Julia Roberts . . . and moi!' Rather uncoyly, she adds the innuendo that would thereafter spread like wildfire whenever Neeson's name was mentioned: 'The recent success of his movie *Big Man* has given rise to monstrous innuendos . . . of which, I assure you, I have no knowledge.'

Maybe, maybe not. One thing was for sure: henceforward, Neeson would be renowned for yet another leg-end.

But after *The Big Man*, he felt drained. It was time to lie low, conserve energy, recharge batteries. The onslaught of two lead roles and all those 2 a.m. training sessions had taken their toll. 'I'd finished *Darkman* on a Saturday night and flew to Scotland to shoot *The Big Man* forty-eight hours later. We filmed in a Glasgow tramway for five solid weeks. After that, I needed to step back.' He didn't work for most of 1990. He needed no excuse. 'Sometimes,' he said, 'it's good to just sit back and watch the paint dry on walls.'

Certainly, nothing much seems to faze him. On a trip to London around this time, he was standing at a tube station when an incident took place that might have panicked lesser men.

First you have to ask, why was Liam Neeson standing on a tube platform, when he was a Hollywood star with his name up in lights every five minutes? Who else with half a dozen movies to his name would take the tube, instead of a limo, or at the very least, a London taxi?

But no, Neeson was travelling by public transport. Old habits die hard, even when you've got a tidy fortune in the bank. In fact, he was testing out a favourite theory, that when you stroll down a London street, unless you're Margaret Thatcher or the Queen, no one's going to take a blind bit of notice of you.

'That's what I love about London. You really can be anonymous. Even if people recognise you, they'll look at you quizzically, wonder just where they've seen you before. Think maybe you've been on the television, or was it in the supermarket last week? And then go off home to think about it. If people do approach you, they're very polite – but it's rare.'

On this day, someone did approach Neeson. An old man, impeccably dressed in suit, tie and silk scarf, staggered up and tugged Neeson's jacket sleeve. He was having a suspected heart attack. The man with Neeson, an acquaintance he'd just bumped into on the platform, was paralysed by the horror of it. 'It was obvious this man was going to splutter and crumple and die in front of us. He's mumbling to Neeson, "Please can you help me? I'm so sorry."'

The man did not die. Neeson, helped by another bystander, carried the old man upstairs, into the lift and out on to the street, where he suggested getting him to hospital. The old man did not want an ambulance. He wanted to go home. So Neeson ran out into the road waving at cars. A taxi stopped. Neeson helped him on his way.

And the moral of this tale? If you're ever going to collapse at anyone's feet, make sure they're Liam Neeson's. But then, we girls have always known this to be the case.

In Britain he could pass unnoticed, ambling along at his own pace. It was a different story across the Atlantic where, in order to keep his name in the Hollywood frame, his presence very much had to be observed in public. Combined with the frenetic pace at which he had been working since his arrival, there were moments when those pressures just got too much.

'You can't compare LA with anywhere in the world. Someone once said to me, treat LA like a moment in time, and the more I think about it, that's exactly it. You can't put your finger on the pulse of LA, it's too fast.

'So I go home and shut it all out. I'm there in my house right beside the beach in Venice and it's like being on holiday, the sun is always shining, you're by the seaside and it's just as well they send the stretch limo in the morning or you'd never get to work.'

Despite his predilection for public transport back in Britain, Liam

Neeson was earning enough Hollywood movie money to warrant a platinum Amex. Here, he was not backwards about flashing it, either.

When picking up the restaurant tab for one very attractive and successful dinner date, Neeson not only presented his glittering testimony to success with a flourish, but expected her to admire it. 'Nice colour, isn't it?' His sophisticated date, unused to such ostentation, was unable to prevent her perfectly arched eyebrows from raising just a fraction. Neeson was unperturbed. Naturally, he hadn't wanted one himself, but 'My business manager insisted. I've never had so much plastic in my life.'

His personal favourite, he confessed, was the one with the stage-coach embossed on it. The logo of the Wells Fargo Bank. Especially since he tried to present it, on his recent trip back home, to some dinky store in Ireland. They refused it. Wells Fargo? Well, wasn't that a cowboy fillum, then, and not a bank, sure?

And there he was, he related, pleading, 'No, no, it's a real bank. Honest, I promise.'

'But now I just go, "Get that, baby, I wannit now!"'

Amazing what success could do for a man. Despite his penchant for displaying the symbols of his nouveax riches, Neeson was always insistent that megabucks had never been his motivation. But if they came his way he wouldn't say no because, with charitable magnanimity, he'd like to invest it in worthy causes.

He was a self-confessed fan of actor-turned-director Robert Redford, who'd set up the Sundance Campaign, pumping money into the movie industry with an avowal to make popular, intelligent films. 'The idea of nurturing raw talent that might otherwise go nowhere is very appealing. I'd love to see that kind of expansion in Ireland, go back there and start up something, maybe summer schools to give those kids extra incentive and instruction.

'Hungry actors deserve a chance. Too many of them fall by the wayside because of lack of opportunity, not lack of talent. There are lots of budding actors, directors and writers out there who don't get the breaks because of lack of chances. I always think, There but for the grace of God, go I.' *Her casket has the Claddagh symbol on it*

'Anyway, I won't be holing up like some reclusive Howard Hughes or Harrison Ford on a ranch in the desert.'

No its at a farm in N.Y. State! 2 homes in fact in Millbrook N.Y where Natasha was buried in 2009. She was buried from St Peters Episcopalian church March 22, 2009

16

Never Mind The Quality . . .

'I remember watching an interview with Dana Delaney and the interviewer was asking about her love life and she said, if she were in a room with James Woods and Willem Dafoe and Liam Neeson . . . there wouldn't be room for anything else!

'Well, I blushed.

'So, if I'm ever in a room with James Woods and Willem Dafoe we'll be kind of going . . .' And here, Neeson's eyes alight on what you assume is an imaginary figure opposite him. Scanning the physique up and down, his eyes come to rest at what is approximately crotch level . . . 'Checkin' each other out.

'I was sorely tempted to ring up an ex-girlfriend and say, "Have you said anything about our sex life?"'

He'd been in LA, in films, for five years. His tenth was coming up. True to form, he'd picked the kind of role he'd never tackled before, just to throw off the scent, anyone who might be trying to pigeonhole him. Versatility was still his middle name. Or perhaps that should be 'over-enthusiastic'? Because he still wasn't picking the greatest of vehicles to star in.

In *Under Suspicion*, a twisting and turning thriller set in the 1950s, he played a dissipated detective who found himself entangled with a devious heiress played by hot actress Laura San Giacomo, fresh from her successes in *sex, lies and videotape*, and *Pretty Woman*. This was undeniably a better script than he'd latterly been working on. It was just a pity, critics remarked, that the plot had more holes in it than a string vest. It was largely Neeson's charisma that carried the film. His presence was magnetic, distracting the audience from the fact that the plot was palpable nonsense.

He had long since realised that the magic potion of good acting, better scripts and the best marketing were the ingredients for
a hit movie. But the recipe was far from infallible because even then,
sometimes it turned up a dud.

None the less, his acting had remained the same, consistently
good, no matter how decrepit the vehicle he was appearing in. So,
a wiser man than he had been years ago when he first arrived in
LA with six weeks' money and a lifetime of hopes and dreams, he
now felt confident enough to criticise the industry he worked in.
It was, he knew, an industry run by moneymen with one unanimous goal: to make more money.

Increasingly disheartened by the way the whole business was run,
he lamented that the Hollywood machine was, 'a real sad state of
affairs, a spiral descending into total blandness. When movies are
regarded first and foremost as a business, the value of a good
strong narrative is too often ignored. I will always believe that
what people want to see is a good story, ably acted out. And if
a film touches your emotions in some way, that's the icing on the
cake.'

He would continue to seek out roles that afforded him the chance
to do both, act his heart out and touch the hearts of those who
watched him. And why not? He had worked with some of the
biggest names and the best. He had amassed a considerable bank
balance and achieved his goal of buying a nice place for his mother
back home. And he was still hungry.

One critic was moved to comment that 'Neeson's performances
have often been the saving grace in otherwise graceless films.' That
hit home. He'd brought something of himself to the camera, fleshed
out characters which might otherwise have been cardboard cutouts.
There was a unique tenderness and romance in Neeson which was
evident on screen that no other leading player could bring to a role,
but which, clearly, had not yet been fully explored.

Although most of the films he'd done so far had been less than
the successes they were held up to be, he was full of hope for the
future. Indeed, he was positively buoyant when it came to his next
picture, *Shining Through*, a thriller starring Michael Douglas and
one of Hollywood's favourite girls, Melanie Griffith. He'd stepped
back down to third lead in this, but names didn't come much
bigger than Griffith and Douglas, both of whom were virtually
guaranteed box-office smashes.

But, as Neeson was to discover, a guarantee is sometimes only worth the paper it's printed on. The film was hailed as one of the funniest bad movies ever made, with a ludicrously silly script and dialogue that had audiences choking on their choc ices with hysterics.

Secretary Griffith is sent by Douglas into Nazi Germany as a spy in the guise of a nanny. There, she takes her young charges, who just happen to be the children of a leading Nazi, to search for secret documents belonging to her Jewish relatives. She naturally succeeds and emerges victorious, having made her escape from the clutches of the baddies in a voluminous white ballgown, which miraculously stayed pristine despite her marathon slog through mud and slush all the way from Berlin to Potsdam, fifteen miles away.

All this is done in retrospect, with Griffith as a granny in her dotage aged around ninety with prosthetic wrinkles to match, doing a voiceover in breathless Shirley Temple tones.

Neeson, with his avowal to uphold good stories and strong, meaningful scripts, must surely have winced at lines like, 'Mein Gott, you've got guts.' And, 'By late October 1941, London was reeling under a hailstorm of German bombs called the Blitz, and life in America was energised with the knowledge of what was inevitable.'

He himself played a Nazi architect who designs concentration camps, then turns on his employers. A curious premonitory echo of another Nazi-aligned role that would later come his way and take him to far greater heights?

True to form, he had spent considerable time studying slice-of-history films to evoke the mood of the time. He had lately been intrigued by 'this incredible video of one of Hitler's 1936 rallies. Millions of people and the look of awe and euphoria on their faces is really something. Looking back, of course, we can see the evil in all of it, but that's because we know what happened. What they saw then was this guy putting food on their table and making the country strong.'

With such a fascination, it was only a matter of time before he landed a war film. Although it was curious that just before it was announced he would be starring in *Shining Through*, he declared to a reporter: 'I'm just dying to play one of those stiff-collared, close-cropped Gestapo agents. A real slimeball. That would be fun.'

Fun, it was. For the audiences. Though sadly, that was not what it had been intended to be.

Perhaps it was his continuing appearance in risible films that audiences rejected, and worthy films that no one wanted to watch, that finally made Neeson begin to design a different way forward. He had long been a voracious reader. He had come across many books screaming out to be made into films. Good stories, good plots, good dialogue. But somewhere between the printed page and the big screen, most of them got mangled by the middleman – Hollywood.

He was not just beginning to wonder, he actually knew he could do it better himself. He was simply biding his time, watching, listening, learning, putting his all into just one thing: work. There was no room for anything outside, at least, nothing that would sideline him from the job in hand. At night, still, he went home alone, to plot out his progress. 'When I don't have work immediately scheduled, I just come back and read.'

In his chequered career it was inevitable that at some point Neeson would meet up with a Woody Allen movie. He had come to the director's notice through his performance opposite Diane Keaton in *The Good Mother*. The pair had become friends and the actress had introduced them. Allen had marked his card and henceforward kept his eye open for the right role for Neeson.

He found it in *Husbands and Wives*. So keen was Neeson to work with Woody that he turned down the chance to star in what turned out to be a big money box-office bonanza, *Patriot Games*, with Harrison Ford. It wasn't the first time he'd turned down a film that ended up as a monumental success. Two years previously he'd turned his back on *Pretty Woman*, which not only shot his ex-lover Julia Roberts to superstardom, but also revived the then flailing career of Richard Gere. Later, he dismissed his failure to spot a surefire winner with a peremptory, 'Films like *Pretty Woman* insult the intelligence. The script was manipulated into a neat little Madonna/whore package.'

But he could hardly be kicking himself this time for turning down *Patriot Games*. *Husbands and Wives* was classic Woody Allen, and though it did not score nearly as highly with the mass market as did *Patriot Games*, it was still a worthy contribution to his CV.

The part Neeson played gives a great screen example of why he is so attractive to so many women. Amid a maelstrom of neuroses, Neeson plays the only sane character, a passionate, romantic Irishman. To female filmgoers, this was true-to-type Liam Neeson, the heart-throb with a heart. You could practically hear the palpitations in the audience as his dulcet Irish tones envelop the woman he loves, wrapping her with his sincerity: 'I'm from a different era.' Here he was the good old-fashioned romantic hero, the stuff of millions of women's Mills and Boon dreams. The fan club continued to swell, if not positively pulsate.

This was not a big role – which many felt was a crying shame – but Allen's speciality was never the sane and down-to-earth character and Neeson still managed to make his customary impact. Allen praised him, commenting: 'He's incapable of saying a line that doesn't sound natural.'

It was simply a pity that, with eerie prescience, *Husbands and Wives* should no sooner hit the streets than Woody Allen's own marital fiasco knocked all his work for six.

Simultaneously, Neeson was walking the path that would lead to his own husband and wife situation. The Woody film had brought him, for a prolonged period during filming, to New York. Here he met Natasha Richardson, already someone else's wife, but ready to be freed by the overpowering romance of this Irishman from another time and another place. A man himself free – at least, from the usual Hollywood neuroses. A man, thus far, in love only with his work.

Yet that was not how it looked to the rest of the world. When in New York, he took some time out to socialise. Contrary to his previous low-profile form, and his avowal that he liked nothing better than to curl up at home alone with a good book, Neeson was suddenly very conspicuous at paparazzi-beleaguered spots with glamorous women like Jennifer Gray and Lisa Shapiro.

Yet whenever, as was inevitable, he was questioned about his public appearances with such gorgeous and well-known ladies, his answer was uniformly the same: he was tired of the press intrusion into his personal life. 'I'm never going to say anything about it. It just messes me up. You talk for about ten seconds on your current relationship and sure enough, that's what appears in the papers. Suddenly it's Liam Neeson with all these famous actresses in heavy black print. It's not what it's really all about at all.' But it didn't half keep your name in the public eye.

Next up was *Leap of Faith*, completed in August 1992, with Steve Martin and Debra Winger. Neeson played the sheriff of a drought-ridden Texan town, whose domain is shaken by the explosive arrival of Steve Martin as a conman-evangelist. Seeing through what are, to him, obviously faked 'miracles', the sheriff is transformed when a real bolt from the blue shakes up his world. 'It's a nice kind of moral fable,' says Neeson. 'People do change.'

He himself had changed his tune. No longer pontificating about how valuable, how worthy and how exciting were his previous ventures, he was playing this one absolutely straight. He'd had his fingers burned too often when he'd enthused at length about a film only to see it end up a joke or a flop. Or both. Time, then, for honesty. 'I did *Leap of Faith* for very political reasons,' he admitted with candour. 'I'd come to realise that the way to crack Hollywood is with a successful box-office film. This fitted the bill.'

With a $30 million budget, big names like Martin and Winger, and a massive publicity machine ready to leap into overdrive, Paramount were banking on *Leap of Faith* as *the* Christmas blockbuster.

As a bonus, Neeson got to play the role that had long been prophesied for him, the Gary Cooper character: solid, dependable, the upright, clean-cut all-American sheriff, the ultimate good guy with the badge of respectability. It was, he conceded, 'a strong male role'.

This time, he was right, It was his most surefooted step into the fray to join the A-team. He felt by now, quite rightly, that he had done his apprenticeship in supporting roles – *Next of Kin*, opposite Swayze, *The Dead Pool*, opposite Eastwood and *Shining Through* opposite Michael Douglas. Now he could be one of them.

But his motivation was much more altruistic than mere megafame and fortune: 'I want to see how far I can take this, not just because I want to be a big movie star. It's a step towards that real power, the power that would free me to do what I really want and that's to develop scripts I believe in. I want to be able to go to the studios and say, "Here's a great project and I want you to do it with me."'

He knew that was, even now, still a long shot, especially when he was yet a relative stranger in town, even if there were six years and twice as many movies as that under his belt. To the long-time players who had worked themselves into positions of real power in the Hollywood hierarchy, as much as to the precocious studio heads who had made it by their mid twenties and burnt out ten years later, Liam Neeson was still an outsider and, worse, a foreigner.

He knew there were some who would say: 'What the heck does he know about the movie business? Lofty ideals come low on the list here. It's a billion-dollar industry and it's about making billions.'

He knew his handicap was not just his solid traditional theatre background, but his very Irishness, that air about him, that accent. So now he was making deliberate steps to play the archetypal red-blooded male roles so revered by those who adore stereotypes – middle America. It had all been a tightly constructed game plan, all those support roles opposite leading players to get the name in the frame, then the artful roles like Darkman and now, a jump back into mainstream with a view to a blockbuster. And a killing.

The movie moguls could no longer fail to be aware of his net worth as an actor. Liam Neeson, as a star, was very bankable indeed. There was his powerful screen presence, his indubitable acting talent, his versatility and, of course, his sheer promotability. All those column inches generated by his liaisons with famous actresses helped fuel the publicity machine that turns a big movie into a blockbuster.

He was still at pains to point out that this was not the case – at least not with the last mentioned. But then, he would say that, wouldn't he? And the heroic, romantic suit of armour that women fall in love with would be seriously dented. The fact remained that all the free publicity linking his name to Tinseltown's loveliest leading ladies had not detracted from his image as Hollywood's latest Lothario. His burgeoning status as a bit of a stud on the quiet and his fabled libido had greatly endeared him to the gossip columnists.

He was now the first to admit he enjoyed the spoils of what Hollywood had brought him, the pool, the jacuzzi, the Ford Bronco and now, the new apartment in Manhattan. But his mind was made up. He would, from now on, spend more time in New York, home traditionally of the American theatre and Broadway, more than of the film industry.

Out at last went the holier-than-holy image, the purported non-smoker and non-drinker. There was always a bottle of decent wine sitting proudly on the table these days and he puffed away at Marlboro Lights non-stop. Los Angeleans would be aghast and fumigating the room before he even took his first drag, but here in New York, smoking, drinking, dining out with a series of gorgeous girls was all quite permissible.

He was not quite ready to transform into a roué but it was almost as if he was paving the way for a role as one; a role that he would very shortly be chasing. That of another bon viveur and sybarite, Oskar Schindler.

Meanwhile, there was work to be done. As if to counterbalance the sell-out commerciality of *Leap of Faith*, Neeson then lined up the lyrical, esoteric and extremely low-budget – by Hollywood standards – screen adaptation of Edith Wharton's novella, *Ethan Frome*. If ever there was evidence that actors should never be confused with the sum of parts they play, then *Ethan Frome* proved it for Neeson.

In what many agree is his finest acting hour, as the eponymous Frome, he created a shambling gait and the distracted air of the afflicted but he never played it as a cliché. He lived the role and was totally transformed.

He had envisaged the part as his for a very long time, since he heard there might be a film of the book in the offing. He had his agent put his name out with a very strong message that he wished to be considered as a contender. When the script was delivered to him, he took it and shut out the world. The door was closed, the curtains drawn, the phone taken off the hook until he had savoured every line.

The following day he arranged to meet director John Madden to discuss the part. There was no point in wasting time on this one. He wanted it, badly. He said, 'I loved the whole project, the book, the script, all of it. I knew it was zero money, but I felt it was something I could comfortably do.'

'It was quite clear that he had fallen in love with the script,' says Madden. 'Even though he had only had it in his possession for a few hours he had absorbed it. He got up in the middle of lunch and walked across the restaurant in the kind of crippled shuffling gait that was unequivocably Frome.'

To get an actor of such theatrical stature, and such a Hollywood high profile as Neeson, and for such a small paypacket, was a coup for the film-makers. But more than that, what captivated everyone was the compelling intensity and pure emotion which Neeson brought to the role. He could convey, the cast and crew noted with awe, a range of emotions so deep and so powerful with a poignant glance, a wistful smile. Neeson's expressions were invested with such pain the camera could barely bring itself to move off him.

Enthused Madden, 'He's got one of those faces that is transparent to the camera. You can actually *see* his feelings – and very clearly. With Liam, you know the wheels are turning all the time – but you never ever see them. He always knows exactly what he's doing, he's in control but we're not privy to that. We just see the end effect, it's both hypnotic and powerful.'

Ever the meticulous craftsman, the one place Neeson had consistently fallen down was in his accents. Never quite managing to escape the soft Northern Irish brogue had in the past led him to produce some strangled vowels and curious hybrids. He had always been defensive about this, adamant that a contrived accent could overwhelm the character.

In *Ethan Frome* then, yet again, he opted for the Irish burr. Why? Obvious, really. This being nineteenth-century New England, invaded several decades before by a tidal wave of Irish immigrants, 'The older residents still sounded like they just got off the boat.'

But where he fell down on accents, Neeson made up for in characterisation. He was in a quandary. He was Irish and that Celtic moodiness and romance brought its own power to the screen yet simultaneously it was being Irish that had impeded his progress to some extent.

John Madden confirmed, 'Liam has tremendous physical magnetism. But what has held him back is his foreignness. He's not typical. He's not American nor is he the rare kind of foreign star, like Australian Mel Gibson, who can convince audiences he's American.

'The evidence that he can so easily slip into another time and another place is what marks him out from the other Hollywood lead players today. Tom Hanks is the only other contender for the outsider, the imbecile – but then, he's done so many of those parts they're marked out for him. Every one of Neeson's outsiders is vastly different.'

Frome, the ardent and heedless young New England farmer who is trapped in a loveless marriage and gradually crucified both physically and spiritually by the life which imprisons him, has a brief moment of exultant glory in love with a young housemaid Mattie Silver, played stunningly by Patricia Arquette; but they are ultimately doomed, careering to suicide on a toboggan ride that leaves them both tragically crippled. Neeson knew it was a story that had immense impact on those who read it and now that he had brought Frome to life on film, he was sure it would have the same effect on those who witnessed it. He was absolutely right.

Critics hailed it as 'a characterisation of genuinely tragic stature'. They did add the rider that his quasi-American accent was 'interestingly eccentric'.

Neeson was more prosaic: 'Everybody remembers *Ethan Frome* as that tragic love story with the toboggan ride; it's like *Of Mice and Men*, it's a story you don't forget.'

He had reason to quote the comparison with Steinbeck's oeuvre, of course. He could never forget that it was in *Of Mice and Men* at the Abbey in Dublin that he had been spotted by John Boorman for his movie debut in *Excalibur*. The rest was history but he was still writing it . . .

After playing a worthy part in a literary film, he recalled with nostalgia the halcyon days when he revelled in the pure art of performing and in a story worth telling. It was his bête noire. He still couldn't put it down. All those years of Hollywood froth were now thrown into light relief by a magnum opus on a minimum budget like *Ethan Frome*. If it could be done like this, why could it not be done on a larger scale? Neeson's voice was becoming louder: 'This business has always been about and still is about telling stories. A lot of these executives with their Armani suits and ponytails sometimes have to be reminded that drama depends upon the spoken word. I'm not saying actors should be treated as gods, they shouldn't be, not at all. But we do have something to offer.'

With the notable exception of his Irish accent, which no amount of dialogue coaching could eradicate, Neeson had by now slipped comfortably into a niche as one of America's most in-demand film actors. But he had also been determined to hold on to something else. The outsider's distance meant he could not, would not, let himself be sucked into the microcosm that was Hollywood movie madness. The beast that fed on itself could do just that. He would stand back and watch.

He preferred to study film-making as an art form, having been initiated into looking at the English theatre in this way, all those years before, as a student of Gerry McKeown. Those early years of learning had stood him in grand stead. He still clung to the oral tradition and culture of his Celtic background and he lived in fear that this era was on its way to extinction. 'It's not just in America that kids don't read books any more.'

But hope still sprung eternal. After all, he himself was an aficionado of film's instant gratification, gluing himself to the screen at the Ballymena State cinema every week for years on end, opting for the straight-between-the-eyes hit of someone else's imagery above the more ponderous transports of books. He did not discover literature himself until late into his teens. 'I was sixteen or seventeen before I truly discovered D.H. Lawrence, George Eliot, the enduring writers.'

For Neeson, the truly great days of performing appeared to have died along with such luminaries as Laurence Olivier and Ralph Richardson. Time for a revival then? And who better to lead the backlash against bubblegum movies, to invest in products that do not insult the intelligence of audiences, that stretch the acting abilities of performers, than Liam Neeson, an actor who lived and breathed his craft. At forty, he had grown into the mantle left behind by those greats. Where once he was picked for his youth and fresh vigour – John Boorman said when he chose him for Sir Gawain in *Excalibur* that he wanted Neeson for his 'raw, inexperienced energy' – now he had the experience to take an overview, to know exactly what kind of energy and authority to channel into each role.

But Hollywood was not ready for him yet in any capacity other than acting. So what next? Having made film the dominant medium in his working life for ten years, Neeson increasingly felt the urge to return to the stage. He had, he relayed, become pragmatic about his direction. Experience had mellowed the burning desire to make it in movies, now he was listening to his heart, not his ambition.

'Henry Fonda once said something about movie-making that I took on board in a big way, "Screen acting is learning to wait." I can understand that. It's learning how to conserve your energy and release it in little spurts when it's called for. I love the process, but there comes a time when you long to get back to the solid application of energy, the concentration through an intense work that takes all of you over at one time.'

He found it in Eugene O'Neill's 1921 play, *Anna Christie*. He made his Broadway debut at the Roundabout Theatre in January 1993, playing Matt Burke, the Irish coal stoker who ignites the fire of a new passion in Anna Christie and forgives her wanton past.

His performance was spellbinding. Back in the métier where he felt truly at home, from whence he had been missing for so long, he brought with him all those years of frustration and misdirection.

Critics noted that Neeson played Burke with 'an animal-like intensity'. There were moments in his performance that shook the audience to its core. When he finds out that Anna Christie has been a whore, he lets out a moan of incandescent pain 'that seems to shake every bone and cell of his muscular six-foot-four-inch body'.

It won him a Tony nomination.

One friend who watched the transformation in him was moved to remark, 'Playing in *Anna Christie* revitalised Liam. People raved about him, nominated him for awards, told him he was a great actor again and no one had actually said that to him since the days of the Abbey Theatre. It rejuvenated him.'

Neeson was defensive about his radical change of direction, however. When asked to take an objective look at his career change, he got quite shirty about it. 'I haven't a clue how my career has shaped up. Nor do I care. Some people are more suited to some roles than others. Everyone has their own appeal. Even Olivier had to deal with that.

'I simply respond to good material. That stems from my rep theatre background. There, one day you're playing an old man, the next you're the young juvenile lead, and the day after that you're back row chorus in a Greek tragedy.

'With *Anna Christie*, we were all focused. It was of the moment. Through all those days of rehearsal, all the speculation about films literally disappeared. In my head it was as if LA had been erased – razed to the ground.'

Director David Levaux applauded Neeson's stance and added his own affidavit: 'Liam is both direct and emotional, that's the way he responds to things. He's always in search of passion, because he has such a well of it within himself. But he's not chasing it in a wild or sentimental way. In a way, he's in pursuit of passion where the real attraction is the actual pursuit itself.' Things were ever thus. With work and with women.

Ironically, because it was *Anna Christie* which brought together, with spectacular synchronicity, the two loves of his life – theatre and the woman he would marry – Neeson almost turned down the chance to do the play, script unseen, when Richardson first approached him with the suggestion. Reputedly, he came back with an underwhelmed, 'Uh . . . maybe.' And instructions to let him think about it.

He was noncommittal at that point because, 'I'd come to America to do Hollywood movies, not theatre. You don't want to commit to something like that because you're hoping that someday, somebody like Steven Spielberg will cast you in a film.'

He knew, at that juncture, that Steven Spielberg was casting for the biggest and personally most important film of his glittering career: *Schindler's List*, based on the Thomas Keneally book to which he had bought the rights a decade before. Neeson knew because he had tried out for the part in front of Spielberg himself some eight weeks before in September 1992. And subsequently heard nothing.

He was miffed. He wanted the part so badly, yes, he could practically taste it. He had pulled out all the stops, even going so far as to turn up in full Schindler-style wardrobe – double-breasted forties suit, shiny new haircut and trilby. He had given the screen test all he had plus the costume in case that wasn't enough. Then nothing.

He knew Spielberg was concerned about getting exactly the right person for this, the project he had nurtured for so long. He tried to make light of it, 'I knew he was seeing other people. Quite right too.' But it irked him. He had not come this far, over this length of time, to miss out on the one he wanted right now. The big one. And he was convinced, he just knew, he would be so right for it.

Spielberg, however, was not convinced. Physically, yes, Neeson was big, like Schindler – but he was much leaner and more muscular. Spielberg firmly believed that Schindler, being a bon viveur with a capacious appetite for all things, especially women, wine and gourmet food, would be carrying considerable avoirdupois in his middle age. He had envisaged Schindler as a charismatic, lumbering bear of a man, with gargantuan tastes and the body to match. Neeson was good, but was he Schindler? It was some dilemma. Until Neeson worked out how to play the situation to his advantage . . .

He knew, because there were few secrets in this business, that Spielberg was as yet noncommittal over who to pick for the part. He had never been one to sit around waiting for the phone to ring. He decided, as always, to act. But this time, he would act in something that could only enhance his credibility as a heavyweight.

Neeson wondered if his track record in films might actually jeopardise his chances of this meaty and mighty part. However, appearing on Broadway in *Anna Christie* would earn him reviews in the serious journals, would get the weight of theatre critics behind him, help him steer a clear route away from the gossip-column image he had been lately saddled with.

It was certainly a possibility. But he knew too, that things had a habit of blowing up in your face. What if, the minute he said yes to the play, the call from Spielberg came through. He had always known the value of travelling light and travelling fast. It had served him well in the past. Now he had been invited to make a commitment and, film work apart, he had *never* been good with commitment.

David Levaux's revival of *Anna Christie* was set to go with English actress Natasha Richardson in the Garbo-esque title role, and Anne Mear and Rip Torn in the supporting roles. They were all class acts, and Neeson knew it. Still, he was torn, undecided. Richardson stepped up the pressure. Colleagues say she was desperate to do the play with him. Rumour had it that she called him on a monthly, then a weekly basis, stepping up the momentum, trying to get him to agree. She was as charming and persuasive as he was. He had met his match.

He succumbed. And as soon as he stepped into rehearsals, he knew he had done the right thing. It was an incredible euphoria to be back treading the boards, hearing the roar of rapturous, spine-tingling applause ringing in your ears. He had almost forgotten what it felt like.

'Doing the play made me feel like I'd been to Tibet and spent three weeks with some incredible guru. You remember why you got into acting in the first place. To get back and recharge your batteries with those genius writers just fills your soul.'

Anna Christie was the ace up Neeson's sleeve, yet he was still playing his remaining cards close to his chest. When he was asked about his decision to return to the stage, he put it down to the laissez-faire attitude to life he had expounded before – and which people seemed to lap up. 'It's like Zen philosophy, you know if you go grabbin' after something, it will always be one step ahead of you. But if you step back, it will come to you.'

If you billed it, he would come. Liam Neeson got top billing on Broadway. Spielberg came.

17

Top Of The Hit List

'I think if Steven had told me, "I'm giving you this part because you're a womaniser and a big drinker," I would have said, "You can go fuck yourself. I'm going back to do a play."'

Oskar Schindler was a German Catholic profiteer who, while he grew rich on the spoils of war and exploited the workforce of Polish Jews at this Krakow-based enamelware factory, was at the same time so moved by the plight of his workers that he saved 1,300 of them from the Nazi death camps. This 'list' of Jews whom he had rescued pledged undying allegiance to their employer and rallied round to support him in later life when his own fortunes floundered.

After he died, in 1974, he was officially honoured by the Israeli government at the Jerusalem Holocaust memorial, Yad Vashem.

His was a complicated and controversial story which needed the most adroit handling. Already, Spielberg's great dream of bringing the book to the screen had taken ten years to come to fruition, largely because of script problems. Screenwriter Kurt Luedtke, who had a laudable track record with scripts for *Out of Africa* and *Absence of Malice*, had spent four years on the project and only progressed as far as page thirty.

Finally, in desperation, Spielberg turned to the talented writer Steven Zaillian who had previously produced plaudit-winning scripts for films such as *Awakenings* and *Searching for Bobby Fischer*. He successfully created a script Spielberg was happy with. The project was up and running at last but it had survived only because of Spielberg's continuing dedication to and belief in the project.

Now he was ready, the casting presented as much of a problem as the script had. Neeson was good, but was he right? He was too skinny for a start but that could be fixed. De Niro had piled on three stone for *Raging Bull*, Dennis Quaid did it for *Great Balls of Fire* – so could Neeson.

Yet still he couldn't decide. As was so often the case, it was a woman who played the catalyst which spurred Neeson along his way. Spielberg's actress wife Kate Capshaw neatly swung the balance in Neeson's favour with a well-timed whisper in her husband's ear.

It happened thus: *Anna Christie* was a riproaring runaway success. Neeson turned in a towering performance as Matt, positively smouldering as he took Natasha Richardson in his arms. It was *the* play to see in town and New Yorkers were queueing round the block for tickets. Paul Newman, Gregory Peck and other acting luminaries came, saw and were conquered. Directors, too, were checking out Neeson's performance. First there was Francis Ford Coppola, followed hotly by Steven Spielberg, his wife and her mother.

When the curtain fell for the third time after the standing ovations the show would go on backstage where the celebrity well-wishers congregated in Neeson's packed dressing room to pop a few celebratory corks and offer their congratulations.

On the evening Spielberg attended, his mother-in-law was so moved by the tear-jerking final scene she was still mopping her eyes when they arrived in Neeson's dressing room. Seeing the elderly lady's distress, Neeson spontaneously put his arm around her in a big bear hug and comforted her. It was enough.

In the car going home that evening, Kate Capshaw turned to Spielberg and said, 'Do you know, that's exactly what Schindler would have done.' The part was his. Kiss me, Kate.

Spielberg announced his choice and lauded Neeson for the requisite 'naïve optimism'. He also praised his 'cigarettes and cognac' voice. The less cautious might have remarked on some rather more obvious resemblances, viz. the penchant for a succession of pretty women. But Neeson was quick to scotch this one before anyone started voicing such scurrilous assumptions. You need to knock those rumours on the head when you're playing a serious role.

Once he had committed to Neeson, Spielberg was determined to give his star the grand entrance that befitted a man of Schindler's stature. He told Neeson, 'I'm going to give you the best introduction in a movie that any actor has ever had.'

After that, it was down to him. Still, Neeson was ever the realist. He knew the film would be publicised par excellence. It was already widely hyped that this was the ultimate Spielberg epic. Forget *Jurassic Park, ET, Jaws*. All mere stepping stones on the way to this one, his apogee, even if they had grossed millions in revenue and entertained as many cinemagoers.

Now he planned to move away from pure fantasy entertainment and the sensational special effects that had been his trademark, ensuring him awestruck audiences around the world. *Schindler's List* was to be cinema vérité although, naturally, it would include a modicum of his previous prize-winning, crowd-pulling tactics for dramatic effect.

His inspired vision was a film which would traverse the great divide between fiction and documentary. His quest, to create the ultimate drama-doc. Many had tried this genre, some had pulled it off, although never on the immense scale that Spielberg envisaged. He sought to combine those normally mutually exclusive elements, raising public consciousness about the horrors of the Holocaust and putting bums on seats around the world. He would reach out to a generation who knew the futility and horror of war, and a generation that did not. But he would show them.

As a by-product, there was no getting away from it, a magnum opus of this scope and resonance seemed set to turn Liam Neeson into a global household name. Neeson remained phlegmatic. He had seen ostensibly watertight ships sink before. And develop barnacles.

Several factors stood in its way. The relatively low budget – $23 million – the black and white cinematography, the documentary feel, the potentially yawn-inducing length of three hours, the fact that Schindler was a complex anti-hero and perhaps, above all, the considerable public doubts that Spielberg could actually create a grown-up movie. It was a gamble for everyone concerned, but particularly for star and director, both of whose names would be firmly anchored for ever to this ship if it went under.

Neeson himself felt it was relatively non-commercial and he was prepared to go on record stating his concerns. 'I don't think it's going to be a Hollywood career enhancer, the main reason being I don't play an all-American hero. It's not Wyatt Earp. It's set against the Holocaust and I play a guy with a German accent. It's not going to turn me into Kevin Costner.'

The sensible money, however, was saying that was precisely what it would do. After Schindler, Liam Neeson would rocket right up there into the stratosphere, landing squarely on that territory that was Hollywood's shortlist of universally appealing leading men.

He was determined, at least, not to lose out on his hunky status. There was the delicate issue of weight gain. Spielberg wanted him to gain, gain, gain, as befitted his own vision of the sybaritic Schindler. Neeson begged to differ. He was reluctant to lose the fine physique he'd for years so lovingly lavished all that time, sweat and tears on in the gym.

Was it all down to vanity? Friends say no: 'It's a European attitude. What he's saying is not so much, "Look at me I'm in terrific shape and that feeds my ego," but more, "I really don't need to alter my physiognomy to carry off this role. I can bring the weight to the part." The flab is an accessory, a prop, it's easily dispensable.'

Neeson stood his ground. He had his own reasons and he believed them to be completely valid. 'People in the forties looked older, maybe twenty or thirty years so, and bigger than they do now. Schindler was a robust man who looked old beyond his years, as they did then.

'Personally, doing eight shows a week in *Anna Christie* had left me a little lean. Steven gave me some of that weight gain stuff body builders use. Well, it made me sick. And I thought, if I succeed, people were only going to say, "Jesus, that guy Neeson's put on weight!" It wouldn't necessarily marry me to the part. That was my argument. Well, it worked out. You know what I mean?'

The cast of *Anna Christie*, playing to a sell-out full house on Sunday night, had barely gone to bed before Neeson flew to Poland and *Schindler's List* the following day. He scarcely had time to draw breath, never mind put down the play that had taken him to such triumphant heights, but who was he to say no to this crippling deadline? He had worked to similarly crushing schedules before. Liam Neeson was the actor who would be there, on time, prep done, even if the deadline was Alaska, yesterday. He prided himself on it. He had spent six years with his bags packed by the back door for just such opportunities.

So it was only hours later that he found himself on set, sinking in snow that engulfed him halfway up to the knee, at Auschwitz. Now all he had to do was psych himself into a role for which he had had no time to do the mandatory research that normally characterised all his work. He needed to enter into the spirit of Schindler, from nowhere. He had to *feel* it.

'There in front of me were all those familiar bleak rows of huts, death huts. But of course, they were interspersed with all the usual clutter of a movie in progress: caravans, cables, trailers. On one level I knew I was standing in front of a sacred monument, but on the other hand, in my jetlagged frame of mind, there I was on yet another film set.

'It was freezing cold, snow up to the knees in places, there were all these people and dogs around and there was me, in this wonderful fur-lined jacket. Two different worlds.'

Neeson was uncomfortable with the way he had plunged himself into the deep end without vital preparation time to step inside Schindler's immaculately polished shoes. He turned to one of the co-producers, Branko Lustig, who nodded at Neeson and solemnly intoned, 'Horrible, isn't it?'

Neeson was trying, but had not yet been able to soak up the atmosphere, nor the heart of darkness. 'I suppose so. But I haven't been able to feel it yet.'

Branko stood for a second, considering. Then he turned back to Neeson and wordlessly removed his glove, rolled his jacket and shirt sleeve up to his elbow, thereby baring his arm in the freezing cold to the actor. It was a moment that would stay with Neeson for a very long time.

'There it was, the tattooed number. He said, "I was born here. In Auschwitz."'

For Neeson, it was the turning point. Now he felt it, the horror. Now he could progress, be Schindler.

It was interesting to note, too, that on this film Neeson broke with the habits of a lifetime and actually participated in life off set. Whereas he had previously always been regarded as stand-offish – although his intention was simply to keep himself to himself and please, no offence taken – with *Schindler's List*, he actively mingled with cast and crew, passing the time of day with them instead of retiring to his trailer to concentrate, read and chainsmoke. Nor did he now leave the set immediately after the day's shoot, preferring to enjoy his own solace. Here, he joined the team in socialising in local bars and restaurants.

As always, there was a work-orientated motivation behind his sudden sociable madness. Schindler, after all, was a bon viveur and raconteur who enjoyed both a colourful social life and an audience. Although Neeson was not likely to step out of line and hold court to an enrapt cast, he was willing to join in. 'I felt that Schindler would have done that. And I felt, too, that every minute spent making this film was precious. I wasn't going to waste any of it.'

In addition, he was concerned for the feelings of some of the Jewish cast, for whom the revival of the Holocaust had deep personal repercussions. 'If the Israeli actresses were coming back after a horrible day, I always made sure of being around in the foyer to buy them a drink or a coffee or just to give someone a hug, instead of fucking off to my room – because some of them felt unbearably vulnerable.'

He himself was also deeply affected by Spielberg's treatment of the wholesale slaughter perpetrated in Nazi Germany. The film stood up as testimony to both the director's and the cast's passion about the events it unfolded. And also to history because it actually happened. This was not just a story. It was real life.

There was no quest to step inside the souls of the characters they were playing here. That would have been too much to bear. 'The approach was, "The day's work is finished. Let's hang the characters on a peg and see you tomorrow." Certainly, we spent lots of time discussing the characters, but there was no Method acting bullshit.'

But the carnage got under Neeson's skin enough for him regularly to attend mass in Krakow Cathedral, which actually survived the war and in which all sorts of feelings were evoked for Neeson.

'You'd see all these old people coming out to church on these freezing cold mornings and there's a real beauty to that faith. Then you'd think, I wonder what they were doing fifty years ago. Who they shot? But what's the answer to that? Maybe it was all just a test to see what is good and what is evil and how it can blossom at any moment and then fade.'

This film, above all he had worked on, would stay with Neeson. 'It's just as terrifying today. The violence is so cold. The Nazis put their final solution into operation with the same precision it takes to build a car, a perfectly executed Mercedes Benz. But in this case, they took their clipboards and their notes and numbers and went to murder innocent people.'

He had come a long way from the days, not so long before, that he had confessed to want 'to play a shaven-headed jackbooted Nazi. A real slimeball. That would be fun.' Fun was not what it was all about at all.

Neeson quite rightly won as much acclaim for the film as he had done for *Anna Christie*. Critics adored his performance, which led to a worthy Oscar nomination, although he lost out to Tom Hanks for his role in the more topical AIDS-themed *Philadelphia*.

They were devastated by this outrage back home in Ballymena. They talked about nothing else in the pubs and the shopping centre and the streets, for days. 'And sure that was an Almighty sin they didn't give our Liam the Oscar.'

Neeson had a premonition it would go to Hanks. When his mother Kitty had asked if she could attend the Oscar ceremony with him, he put her off, saying it was a waste of time. Yet he took time to attend the post-Oscars party where – a rare event for Neeson – he almost came to blows in a contretemps with a photographer who tried to snap him with Natasha Richardson. The pair were still hotly denying any romance and Neeson clearly did not want any pictorial evidence to the contrary.

Meanwhile, back in Ballymena, where they were lamenting the lack of statuettes for Kitty's mantelpiece, she shrugged off her disappointment, saying it would be far more of an accolade to be named Irishman of the Year – which he was set to be, at an upcoming ceremony in New York. Now that one, she proudly admitted, she would be going to, along with her lad.

It would be one of these rare moments when Neeson laid claim to his heritage. At all other times, he liked to downplay his role as an Irishman in New York. 'I keep away from those clans and kins. Ed McMahon once asked me to ride in a coach down Hollywood Boulevard for St Patrick's Day. You couldn't pay me to do that stuff.'

And he was not devastated by not winning the Oscar to which so many believed he was richly entitled. 'Sure, it's great to get accolades and stuff but it's not a cure for cancer, is it?' For Neeson himself, the applause and praise would have to do for now. At least he could enjoy that, after all those years without the requisite rewards for consistently good performances, even if some of them were in lethal vehicles. Friends noted that, 'For the first time in years, people were saying again what a great, a fine actor he was. It did his ego no end of good.'

So he regained the status he had enjoyed in the English and Irish theatre, and now enjoyed it in the film world, too. But Neeson had always wanted a bigger portion of the pie. He still wanted to have these accolades married to massive commercial success. *Schindler* merely whetted his appetite, giving him a taste for more.

He wanted to be the Colossus who would straddle the yawning chasm between culture and commerce.

He had won the first round, now it was on to the next. He was still – crazy after all those years though it seemed – chasing the huge commercial hit. He talked wistfully of the mainstream box-office smash, *The Fugitive*, which played in 1993 to packed houses everywhere. 'Wonderful script, wonderful piece of work by Ford and Tommy Lee Jones. I would have loved that.'

He knew there was still something missing from his repertoire. He still had not made it to the all-action adventure screen hero, so he determined that now, at last, he would. True to form, he did his homework first, insisting on being sent the script for every putative film in the offing 'even the ones I wasn't up for and wouldn't be right for'.

The reason was straightforward. He wanted to train himself to spot a potential winner a mile off. He wanted that elusive sense, born of both intuition and experience, that would let him know for sure he'd picked a solid gold cert.

As usual, once he set his mind to something, 'Now I could look at any given script and say, "This is the usual schlock, right. Here's the car chase. Yup, this is the guy who did it." There's no way I would want to be involved in most of these movies but by sifting through them I can now recognise a movie that's going to be a hit. And I'm right about seven times out of ten.'

All those years of holing himself up with a good book have paid off. He could skim-read through a pile of manuscripts a mile high and automatically spot the duds, of which there are plenty. It's the nugget of gold in the dirt that he's panning for. And when he gets it, he wants control of it, that's the ultimate goal. He's made no bones about it for a long time. Now he's as near as dammit in possession of that power he's been pitching at for so long. No one could ever doubt his tenacity, either, he's always been a stayer.

These days, if he spots a book or a script that seems to him to be right up his street, he'll keep plugging away at it, putting the word out, having his agent make those calls. He saw it work for Spielberg who clung on for years, through seemingly endless problems, to his dream of making *Schindler's List*. Neeson knows he is no Spielberg; he has, as yet, none of the director's facilities at his disposal, but he has faith and endurance by the bucketload. And a few of his own pet projects up his sleeve too.

According to one Hollywood source, he has been keeping track of a particular script, on Michael Collins, founder of the Irish Republican Brotherhood, for some time. More than that, Neeson was moved to drop in, to several interviews, how he had been reading this fascinating book on . . . Michael Collins, knowing his interest would make it into print and be noted in high places. What's the point of giving interviews if you can't use the media in return?

This particular script, by writer/director Neil Jordan – with whom Neeson struck up a lasting friendship way back on *Excalibur*, and who directed him in *High Spirits* – is currently languishing in dry dock. 'But Liam knows it will surface again. And he'll be pitching for it.'

The truth is, Neeson had been working hand in hand with Jordan on the project for years. His 'plants' to the press were merely to generate interest in an idea that had long since been pollinated but was still waiting to bud. 'I had known Neil for years. We were going to do a Michael Collins project with David Puttnam years ago.'

He had never lost sight of it. He knew that one day, if and when it came to fruition, it would be his. And by that time, hopefully, he'd be big enough to have major input into it himself. That time may be now. Since the ceasefire was called in Northern Ireland last year, it was suggested to Neil Jordan that it might be a timely moment to put in a call to Paramount Studios, with whom the script had been languishing without much hope. He did. It was. Talks are currently underway. As Neeson knows, everything comes to he who waits.

It helps, of course, being Irish. He's never been one to rush into battle, claymore swinging wildly and battering down the opposition. Quite the reverse; he's always favoured the considered tactical move. Which is why, last year, he decided to sell the Hollywood Hills home in which he'd hermitted himself in his few precious hours of free time for over five years. The 1950s 'sleazy bungalow' realised its asking price of nearly $500,000. Neeson was happy to know it went to people who would appreciate its bookish ambiance. Novelists Judith and Garfield Reeves-Stevens would be suitable heirs to the home he'd loved for so long. They're also executive editors of a US sci-fi TV series, *Phantom 2040*.

Neeson was headed for his New York base, a SoHo loft he also bought last year, so he could keep his feet on the ground on the east coast, while his fingers are still in the Hollywood pie in LA. Yes, of course he's available for Broadway plays. Yes, he can still do another Tinseltown film.

And we should pay tribute, too, to the hunger, the grit, that his Irish background affords him. He is aware of it in himself, though he prefers to illustrate it by referring to one of his fellow countrymen, Richard Harris. Then it could never be construed as those greatest, in Neeson's book, of all evils – arrogance and blatant self-promotion. However, if he lays claim to it vicariously, perhaps no one will notice the true destination of the deflected glory.

A tale he is most fond of relating concerns his compatriot and how tenacious the now-reformed hellraiser had been in his quest to land the part of King Arthur in *Camelot*. 'Do you know what he had to do? Just about everything in the book – and a few extra chapters besides. He found out where the head of the studio was dining out and he'd dress up as a waiter, bold as you like, and approach him at the table. Then he'd present this silver salver with a flourish. And inside, instead of food, there was this note which read, "Look no further, I'm your King Arthur"!

'God bless his socks, I really admire that man!'

Talent will out, of course, but it was probably perseverance that swung it for Richard Harris, who was justly given the role and executed a superb performance in the 1967 film opposite Vanessa Redgrave as his Lady Guinevere.

Nearly thirty years on, Neeson is still a great admirer of the Harris tactics which, to all intents and purposes, have changed little.

'When I last bumped into him, he was telling me he was begging and wheedling with Warner Brothers to give him a screen test for their new movie. They weren't having any of it. They wanted Paul Newman or Gene Hackman, but Richard wouldn't take no for an answer. He kept on and on until finally they gave in and gave him a screen test. Probably to get him off their backs!

'But of course, he was sensational. He just blew them away. And they rightly gave him the part. He won it through sheer belligerence. Without that, his talent would have just gone unseen.'

If there is a moral here, it is that persistence pays off. No matter how many doors you have closed in your face, no matter how many rebuffs or rebuttals, you just have to hang on in there.

Neeson had always known there was no such thing as a free lunch, especially not in his line of work. 'That process is never going to stop for Richard and me. It's as simple as that. If a role is coming up between Kevin Costner and me, it's going to be Costner every time. Nothing's going to change that. Certainly not *Schindler's List*.'

But maybe *Rob Roy*, which was his next-but-one project and surely the most apposite role for him so far. Another Celtic legend, a conquering, romantic hero of huge stature and charisma.

The part might have been written for him

18

Onwards And Upwards*

'Sex is the most pleasant thing you can do, as a human being. It's the most basic, primal instinct. Anything else we do might be fun but we're intellectualising what we're here for – which is to procreate. Have sex, reproduce.

'I sometimes feel these urges. I love seeing pregnant women, I drool at the mouth. But you want it to be with the right person, you want it to last. For years, I was surrounded by people having babies. Then you realise, well, it was just all those cold nights coming in . . .'

They fell in lust during *Anna Christie*. Natasha fell harder and faster than he. Six months after their debut Broadway performance together, the relationship had progressed far enough for her to be looking for some form of commitment from him, despite the fact they had been separated for most of this time, he in the frozen wastes of Poland filming *Schindler*, she back at home in New York. As always he was immersed in the project in hand, and in his role. But he was sufficiently mindful of the beautiful blonde to remember – just in time – her mid-May birthday.

She was thirty, something of a milestone in a woman's life. She was newly alone, in the process of divorce from her husband of two years, producer Robert Fox. A heartfelt gesture from the new man in her life would be much appreciated. A call to Interflora for a display of her favourite white lilies, perhaps, or a sentimental gift ordered by long-distance phone and delivered via Bloomingdales.

*New occasions teach new duties: Time makes ancient
  good uncouth;
They must upward still, and onward, who would keep abreast
  of Truth.
                    James Russell Lowell, 'The Present Crisis' (1845)

Neeson did not manage either. Instead, he whacked off a last-minute fax from the set: 'You're catching up with me. Lots of love, Oskar.'

Some women might have let it pass. He was thousands of miles away, deep in work. She knew how he operated; he was no longer Liam, he was Schindler. He had even signed himself thus.

But Richardson was made of sterner stuff. She was not being fobbed off like this. How dare he? She winged back by return a fax terse in its brevity but redolent with feeling: 'This is like a letter from a buddy. What *is* our relationship?'

Neeson was pulled up short. He knew she was right. He also knew she was feeling both hurt and incensed by his frivolous dismissal of her birthday and their romance. More importantly, he realised he *cared* what she felt.

It was a turning point in their relationship. Suitably chastened, he sat down to write a more appropriate reply, outlining his feelings for her. But he found himself writing a retaliatory diatribe on the fleeting nature of showbiz love affairs: how inevitable it is for heightened passions to ignite between two leading players, and how equally inevitable it is for the ensuing affairs to fizzle out.

It was not what he had intended to write at all. He had automatically slipped back into a familiar place. He had adopted this line before. It was based on his own experiences. None of his famous affairs with actresses had worked out. It was a philosophy that had both protected him and prevented him from further, deeper involvement on many occasions.

This time, he didn't want that. He didn't want to pull away. He put his inherent pessimism to one side for a moment and looked at the facts. He was not getting any younger. Here was a woman, beautiful, bright, talented, accomplished, aware, adult, with the strength to stand up to him, challenge his dominance, go the distance, make it work. A woman who absolutely adored him.

He felt suddenly old and cynical. His recalcitrance to commit and his long-indulged desire to take the easy way out, to escape commitment, suddenly compared badly and sadly with the gifts she offered him. He took stock.

'I'd patted myself on the back for actually remembering her birthday in time and sending this hasty note with a little witticism. And there she was, hurt because it wasn't personal, it was flippant. Then I realised, I'm forty years of age – what do I believe in?

'And that was when I knew I really loved this person. I thought yes, this is real and genuine, this has to be protected.'

He opened the door for Richardson. She leapt in, zooming to be by his side on the *Schindler* set. Onlookers noted her visit breathed new life into him.

She was a force to be reckoned with. The daughter of Vanessa Redgrave and director Tony Richardson, granddaughter of Sir Michael Redgrave and Rachel Kempson, she had inherited the talents of both these great theatrical dynasties and established herself as a classical actress of renown. Where Neeson was a veteran of schlock mini-series and US bubblegum movies, her pedigree was pure thespian platinum. Trained at the Central School of Speech and Drama in London, she launched into theatre with stunning performances as Helena in *A Midsummer Night's Dream* and Ophelia in *Hamlet* at the Young Vic. She was Shakespeare and Chekhov to Neeson's Cher and Clint Eastwood.

But she adored him. And she was not walking into this one blind. She knew exactly what she was getting into when she got involved with Liam Neeson. She wanted it. That was that.

She revealed: 'How could I not know? Every time I picked up a newspaper, I was warned about Liam. His reputation preceded him by a long way. It's scary when someone has that kind of label and then you find yourself falling in love with him. You think, Am I crazy or what?

'But he was so funny, incredibly funny and so incredibly kind. What struck me was his absolute genuineness. He was so much *who he was*, I couldn't quite believe it.

'And what no one realised was that it took a lot longer than people thought. We were both cautious. We took our time. When everyone assumed we were in love, we actually weren't at that point. We fell in love later. Well, he certainly fell in love with me later . . .'

She worked at making it happen. She knew how to mesmerise, how to capture the hearts and minds of audiences with her spell-binding performances. It was not so difficult.

One Friday night, Neeson and co-star Ralph Fiennes took her to their favourite local restaurant where staff downed tools after all meals had been served to perform a singalong round the piano for the diners. The cast were particularly fond of the place because it provided welcome light relief after interminable days of recreating

Holocaust doom and gloom. Fiennes recalls: 'There was a joie de vivre there that was very attractive.'

Natasha, never one to stand waiting in the wings, entered right into the spirit of things. She enjoyed centre stage, it was her rightful place. She grabbed the microphone off a singing waiter and launched into an evocative rendition of 'Maybe This Time', from *Cabaret*, very much in the spirit of Nazi Germany.

Fiennes was among those who watched her, entranced: 'She was stunning, unequivocally the star of the evening. Liam was so happy, just watching her.'

So when he had completed *Schindler*, it was only natural that he should come home to Natasha. They were now very much together. And they were due to work together in the upcoming *Nell*, the first production from Jodie Foster's own film company, Egg Pictures. They would be together, day and night, throughout the duration of filming. If ever there was going to be a crunch time, this was it. It was as close to living with someone as he had ever got.

He played an Irish doctor, Jerome Lovell, who relinquishes a big city practice to work in the backwoods of North Carolina, and discovers the feral child-woman Nell, living alone in a remote cabin in the forest, unaware of the outside world. The role echoed sentiments very close to his own.

Jodie Foster observed: 'Liam wanted to do *Nell* for the same reason this character, the doctor, is fascinated by Nell herself. He asks the question: "Can you live completely alone, cut off from the outside world, and survive?"'

Neeson had always cherished his own space, indulged his need to shut off and cut off from situations and relationships that drained him. Despite (or because of?) his newly established closeness with Natasha, he still found the need to break away during filming *Nell*. He found his escape in fishing. Encouraged by the props mistress, Ellen Freund, who had taken up fishing seriously after working on Robert Redford's fly-fishing epic, *A River Runs Through It*, he would take off for hours after dusk to go fishing. She taught him how to cast a line, how to reel in. He was hooked.

Freund noted how, even on night shoots, when Neeson was not called on for a scene, he would sit on the set houseboat, casting his line out into the blackness of the night and the water, savouring the peace and solitude.

On the occasions where he was joined by other fishing fanatics, he would still manage to retreat into his own world. He admitted, 'I went out one Sunday with a couple of other guys; up at five in the morning at first light, it was stunning with the mists all round. We were on this boat threading worms and little lizards on hooks and chucking them into the lake. It was raining too, never stopped for five hours. I never caught a thing, but I came back completely refreshed, rejuvenated. And the whole time we were out there, we maybe said ten words between the three of us.'

Jodie Foster, always a sharp observer of behaviour, saw how Neeson's propensity for space and silence worked in his favour with Natasha. Theirs was truly an attraction of completely complementary opposites. 'Natasha is a real talker, while Liam prepares to take off, be alone on some rock somewhere with his Walkman on, in his own little world.

'Natasha is cosmopolitan, sociable and socialised, cynical, a real smart brain. Liam is much more animal. He lives in the messy world of instinct. When he does talk, he'll tell you a story, the way the Irish do, maybe about him being in some play. You want to ask all these questions he's left unanswered. You ask a simple one like, "Why did you do it?" and he'll say "I don't know."

'It's like, "Has he *really* done all these things without thinking about them?" And the answer to that one is: probably. Natasha is very, very aware, she knows her reasons and he's standing there going, "Hey, I caught a fish *this* big!"

'Liam is a big strong guy and he's able to be totally non-intellectual. He doesn't feel the need to analyse everything. He feels something, he asks no questions. He just feels it and admits it. He doesn't try to kill things by bringing a bunch of language to it.'

Nell's director, Michael Apted agreed: 'There's nothing elitist or frightening about Liam. There's an *ordinariness* about him people like and feel at ease with. We did some test screenings for *Nell* and the lower down the demographics, the more people like Liam. The higher up the scale, the more people go for Jodie.'

Others who worked with him saw the big soft guy become even more mellow when Natasha was around. *Nell* producer Renee Missel noted: 'There is an innate goodness and gentleness in Liam. He comes from the heart.' When they worked together on *Nell*, she noted, Neeson and Natasha fitted together, these two seemingly polaric opposites, like pieces of a jigsaw. 'They learned to appreciate and honour each other's rhythms, each other's way.'

During filming they lived together, sharing a rented house. Natasha slipped readily and easily into the role of hostess. Neeson had never been one to throw dinner parties or get involved in a cosy domestic set-up. Natasha did both and with considerable panache. She organised regular dinners for friends among the cast, over which she would preside, with Neeson always seated on her right as head of table, her other half.

Her domesticity on these occasions did not extend as far as cooking; the food was ordered to be sent in from outside caterers. The happy couple could then play – a novelty for Neeson – the relaxed and gregarious host and hostess.

To those who attended, it seemed Natasha played the gregarious half while Neeson landed the relaxed role. Richardson, effusive and witty, would hold court while Neeson sat quietly by her side, basking in her reflected limelight.

Jodie Foster recalled: 'I watched him watching her tell stories. You can see he gets such a kick out of the way she can turn a phrase. She's so very English, witty, dry, literary. While Liam tells simple stories the Irish way. He acts them out. It's like, "Then I turned round like *this*" accompanied by a gesture.'

From the way he gazed in ardent devotion at his eloquent lover, Foster was left in no doubt that by then he was completely enamoured of Richardson: 'You could see he totally loved her.' She had talents he didn't. There was her great articulacy, so much in evidence, engaging all who met her. In this partnership, he had no need to feel inept any more, for not being that way himself. She could perform on his behalf in that area. He had her to do it instead.

He brought to her, in contrast, his romanticism, his sensitivity, his kindness, gentleness and that irresistible animal magnetism. Where his own articulacy was lacking, he compensated for it in physical ways. He was Spencer Tracy to her Katharine Hepburn. It was a great and passionate coupling.

In *Nell*, Doctor Lovell finds himself gradually falling in love with the character played by Richardson, the psychologist who sees Nell at first as an experiment before coming round to side with Lovell in trying to protect her from exposure to society and science.

As with *Anna Christie*, their performances became blurred and indistinguishable from real life. By now Neeson knew he loved Natasha too. She was always the marrying kind, keen to have a family, settle into the type of at-home, Waltons-style set-up she had been deprived of in her own upbringing as her parents went their own separate ways, pursued their own careers, put work before family. Vanessa Redgrave, by her own admission 'was not there for the children', too busy with her all-consuming twin passions in life – acting and politics.

So it was that Natasha wanted all the old-fashioned, traditional things, a solid marriage, a settled family, which she felt had been denied her. A ring on her finger was first on the agenda.

Neeson, in contrast, had long fought shy of the notion of marriage, not even getting near the stage in any relationship where it was contemplated. His upbringing had been the antithesis of Natasha's. Solid, secure, family with a capital F. He'd been there, lived it, done the jigsaw. That was what deterred him. He was neither appalled nor repelled by the notion, it simply had never attracted him, never been that important. 'It was never the golden light at the end of my life. I was too caught up in getting into the film industry, getting on with this business. That was what *was* important.'

But now he had met a woman with a greater need for the institutions of marriage and family than he. A woman with whom he was now in love. It was a fait accompli. Marry her or lose her.

He proposed over dinner in a downtown Manhattan Chinese restaurant, shortly after the completion of filming on *Nell*. Thus far the relationship had been shrouded in secrecy despite, or more likely due to, the constant press speculation. Neeson had been customarily wary of saying a word. Richardson was more fulsome, proclaiming to the press that Liam was 'pure animal passion', an indication of her devotion and hopes for the future.

He might have wanted his proposal to be private, their engagement to remain a secret for a while longer, but their cover was blown that very night. A couple sitting at the next table overheard the intimate conversation and blew the whistle to the press next day.

Neither star would admit nor deny the situation when their agents were besieged with calls for a statement. It was left to Kitty Neeson, this time with Liam's full approval, to provide the requisite confirmation. 'Natasha and Liam are very much in love,' she reported, 'and yes, they will marry.'

They determined that the wedding would not be as public property as the engagement. Strict security measures were to be enforced. All family and friends were sworn to the utmost secrecy over details. At the beginning of 1994, they took the first step towards married

life, investing $4 million *MILLBROOK N.Y* in a beautiful 1810 farmhouse, in its own
rolling grounds, in upstate New York. With its perfect setting and
wide-open porch, Neeson described it as 'Just like something out of the
Waltons'. Surrounded by a high security fence and shrouded by trees,
it was also the perfect place for privacy. The couple decided they would
be married there. Arrangements were made to fly the whole Neeson
clan over for the ceremony, to take place on Sunday 3 July. *1994*

Back in Ballymena, Kitty was spotted out shopping for new shoes.
She said she wanted a smart pair for she was soon off to America to
visit Liam. She made no mention, not a whisper, of the wedding. But
other locals knew it was imminent. At his tiny gift shop in Cushendall,
Pat McCambridge was asked by Neeson's sister Rosaleen to provide
suggestions for a wedding gift. He suggested – and supplied – some
exquisite Waterford crystal. For his own gift to the lad he had
known since he was knee high, he chose an oil painting of the
Lurig Mountain, by a local artist.

He said: 'We all knew the wedding was just round the corner. We
knew exactly when Kitty and the sisters were going away. But no
one would have breathed a word. It took Liam a long time to find
his bride. We all wanted the day to be perfect for the both of them.
There was no amount of money offered by the press – and there
was plenty that did offer – could have tempted any of us to whisper
anything that might ruin their day. We look after our own.'

The couple were already exchanging gifts of their own. For
Natasha's thirty-first birthday, just six weeks before the wedding,
there was no repeat of the gaffe with the offhand fax, which Neeson
had almost come to grief over the year before. This time he made
amends, with another note of a much more intimate nature. He
scripted out, right down to the last detail, their honeymoon itinerary
and left it, a love note, under her pillow.

In return, for his forty-second *FORTY-FIrst* birthday three weeks later, she
presented him with a long-coveted Harley Davidson Springer Softail
– 1989 vintage, a classic. Her hopes were that he would take off on
it when need be, but mostly it would keep him at home, getting his
hands dirty. *He had an accident in 2003 on this bike + was found crawling on roadway – Broken pelvis*

And so they were married in front of a glittering crowd of
stars, close friends and family. It was, as the couple had insisted,
a thoroughly hush-hush affair. Until the last minute. Just forty-eight
hours before the wedding, someone leaked information to the news
broadcast cable station CNN. The press was on hand and on

red alert. Neeson countermanded them. He had a landscape firm erect – with considerable urgency – a new, higher fence around the property and plant new trees to further screen it from view. Then he doubled the number of security men to repel all uninvited would-be boarders on the day.

The hasty preventive measures worked. No photographer, nor TV crew, nor intrepid hack managed to break through the ranks. The wedding went ahead, despite the last-minute flurry of activity, in blissful peace and privacy.

Neeson made his groom's speech proclaiming his incredulity at finding such luck and such a bride. The bride said all she had to say in a romantic and heartfelt rendering of – what else? – the groom's favourite, a Van Morrison song.

Their happiness was complete. Ralph Fiennes was among the quests and was moved to observe that throughout the ceremony and the celebrations, he felt Neeson had finally arrived where he belonged. 'You knew this was exactly right for Liam, exactly now.'

The honeymoon was just as Neeson had spelt it out to his then bride-to-be in her birthday love letter. A few days in that most romantic of cities, Venice, where they strolled hand in hand, visiting the art galleries and taking a trip down the canals in a gondola. Then it was on to the south of France where they were snapped by paparazzi, gazing into one another's eyes, oblivious to the clicking camera lenses, completely in love.

It was, however, only a brief respite from work. Neeson then flew, the following month, to Scotland to start filming Michael Caton-Jones's $25 million epic, *Rob Roy*, while Natasha flew on, over the Atlantic, back to New York where she was scheduled to oversee a benefit première of *Blue Sky*, the last film executed by her late father, who had died in 1991.

Although he had only been married for a few short weeks, Neeson welcomed the parting: 'I need my own space. I'd go mad if I didn't have it.' He also acknowledged the need to work. He had been looking forward to this, his role as the Celtic all-action adventure hero, for a very long time.

It had taken him nearly thirty films to get here, but now he was well and truly enthroned as king of all he surveyed. On the set, at Fort William in the Scottish Highlands, the crew noticed he had the stature and bearing of a true leader of men. They believed in him, intrinsically, as the living embodiment and recreation of this Scots legend, Rob Roy. The self-effacing gentle giant had crept off into the shadows. In his place stood a towering Celtic hero.

Rob Roy's director, Michael Caton-Jones, had absolutely no doubt he had picked the right man for the part. No one but Neeson could have filled Rob Roy's giant shoes. 'Liam,' he said, 'has that rare combination of deep romanticism and a hardness of being. You can't invent that stuff. Liam understands it in his bones. It's evolved in him from a million tiny things in his background, his own personal history and the history of the world he was raised in: the bracing cold winds, the way the clouds move, the manner of the Scots and the Irish, the way they react with one another.'

He cited, by example, the peculiar way the Celts address each other, using insult and abuse as a term of affection – incomprehensible to the 'more civilised' and reticent English. 'You start off with "Fuck you", and get warmer. To most people, that seems a rather extreme way of behaving. But Liam understands it innately.'

He recognised, too, the familiar path he and his star had trodden, that enabled them to bring the common, populist touch to their work: 'Liam and I don't come from a Britain that's Shakespeare or Merchant Ivory. We're both working-class boys who've scuffed our way up.'

Neeson had that much in common, too, with Sean Connery, the Celtic superstar he was now, surely, poised to overtake. Though you could never suggest that to Neeson himself. Although the quality scripts he had worked to get for so long were now virtually plopping on his doormat daily, he still preferred to downplay his own talent, deferring to the greats. Of whom Connery was certainly one. Sadly – and perhaps mindful of this situation – Connery turned down a role in Rob Roy, thus precluding audiences from actually seeing the Celtic crown being handed over on screen from one generation to the next.

Neeson acknowledged the maestro's supremacy: 'I remember watching him in *The Wind and the Lion*, playing this swarthy Moroccan prince. It was a very swashbuckling part, all flowing robes and swords flashing. He's kidnapped the beautiful heroine, Candice Bergen, and comes out with this ridiculous line, "I am Prince Afdad Muhammed Alfuz and you are my prisoner!"

'Completely silly, but it's Connery saying it and you go along with it because he can do anything.

'I remember him saying once, "I can't change my accent. I wouldn't know who I was if I did." I respect that.'

Neeson has come to know himself and to know the parts that suit him: men from a different era, flawed heroes who rise to greatness despite themselves. Rob Roy, Oskar Schindler, Ethan Frome, men from another time and another place but with a code of honour and a code of conduct that is timeless. Men like Liam Neeson himself.

As *The Big Man* director David Leland once commented, Neeson is something of an anachronism.

And Neeson himself agreed: 'We live in an age where information is flying at you from every direction, it's like a barrage. Gimme peace! Like, there's all this technology everywhere, feeding you things you don't really need to know. TV programmes: How did Superman fly? Watch next Tuesday and we'll tell you.

'Don't do that! It's like asking a magician how he takes a rabbit out of a hat. It's a trick. It's amazing. Leave it that way! Lord knows, there's no mystery left in life.'

He will never change on this. Ever reticent, discreet, he will always remain something of an enigma – a fact he recently willingly endorsed: 'I think you should always keep something back, a little bit of the mystery.' It was always, until Natasha, his philosophy with women: 'I always believed, even during courtship, you let the wind blow between you. Keep something back for yourself.'

And perhaps it still is. Today, his is the life he always dreamed he would have: 1995 will see him starring with Meryl Streep in *Before and After*, the story of a couple who face their son's trial for murder. There is a strong chance, too, that he will play Oscar Wilde in a bio-pic of the flamboyant homosexual Irish dramatist, wit and writer, opposite the screen's current hottest young heart-throb, Hugh Grant, playing the part of his lover. And finally, after fifteen years of believing in the story and backing it all the way, his pet project with Neil Jordon on Michael Collins looks set to take off, following the ceasefire in Northern Ireland.

No one could argue that Neeson has left behind him for ever the 'dross movies' and their home, Hollywood. He can afford, now, to look back in anger, to be disparaging about the place in which he felt trapped, building his career.

'Los Angeles is such a fascist place. In Ireland, the pub was always the social centre of the world, a great meeting place, a godsend to go to. In LA, if you're seen to go alone into a bar it's "Do we have a little problem here?"

'And God spare us the anti-smoking brigade! The insidiousness of it! The air there is this yellow cotton wool of shit and people come up to you and say, "Do you mind putting that cigarette out?"

'It's wonderful, people keeping fit, but I'm from the European school. I smoke too much but at least I run fifteen miles a week. But in LA people jog for two hours a day and they think they're morally right. That's when you want to choke people . . .'

London too, is 'stale and bleak'. So the Neesons are ensconced now in New York, the hippest, most happening place for metropolitan art, theatre, culture of all kinds. There is a second home, a first base for now, while they get their country retreat in shape: the central two-bedroom apartment with inspirational views over Central Park and the Manhattan skyline, packed with books and ethnic objets d'art, many of them picked up by Tony Richardson on his global travels, and handed down to Natasha.

It is a far cry from Corlea Gardens, but only a two-hour drive in his brand-new four-wheel-drive Mercedes Gelandewagen to their farmhouse.

He still has his dreams, of course, but now they are come full circle. Now he has attained wealth and a wife, kudos and star status, the dreams have returned to the earth and the roots from whence he came. He wants to farm. Or at least, to live in the style of a farmer. On his own prime New York farmland, he will have planted some good Irish potatoes and grow his own organic crop. Beyond that, there is the artistic vision – to plant spring perennials, meadowsweet, a copse here and there of billowing trees – that he might awake every morning to an Impressionist vision of a blaze of fresh and vibrant, living colour.

The barn and outbuildings stand ready and waiting for the influx of crop activity. But, as ever, Neeson will get round to it in his own time, and in his own way.

For now, the barn has its own use. It houses his punchbag. He still has that Irish temper, but now he knows where to take it. No longer does he have to retreat from a relationship to deal with it. Natasha knows that and Natasha understands. That's what makes her different.

He concedes these days that he has met his match: 'I know now that all my life I avoided conflict with women. Maybe I thought they were going to leave or maybe I was scared of how far my anger would go. But with Natasha, we don't have flare-ups. Sure, a couple of times we've maybe had angry words, but afterwards, it's all smoothed out. And she's still here! I actually realise I feel better for that. It's like, wow, this is a huge achievement.

'When we disagree, it's over little things. She's always getting on at me for reading alone in bed. She says, "Why can't you come and read down here with me?" Well, I just can't. When I was a kid, that little house was so small, the only place to go to be on your own and get peace was bed. I had to do it, had to be on my own.'

Natasha, forced on such occasions, somewhat reluctantly, into her own space, will not be on her own much longer. Within three months of their July 1994 wedding she proudly announced to friends that she was pregnant.

She had always wanted Neeson's baby. She was thirty-one. She saw no reason to wait once they were wed. Neeson, however, was not quite as exultant as the expansive mum-to-be.

'I know I'll help out with the nappy changing and all that. I'm kind of good that way. I'm the type of guy who enjoys washing dishes. Great therapy. But whether I can honestly say I'm overjoyed at the thought. . . I'm not. It's like, "What's the surface of the moon like?" I don't know. I've never been there before.'

But a journey into the unknown has never thwarted him before. No one can be in any doubt that Liam Neeson will carry on taking those long, loping strides through his life and his glittering career. And all the while smiling enigmatically to himself.

As of 2009 - he has 2 sons. Micheal 13 Daniel 12 They were married for almost 15 years before she hit her head after falling and striking her head while learning to ski in Canada.
She died March 18, 2009, age 45 at Lennox Hill hospital in New York City after becoming unconcious and unresponsive while hospitalized in Canada.
He was 59 in June 2009
He admitted he was born in 1850

He became an American citizen
in September 2009.
He said that he is so
overcome to still be
receiving messages of
Condolence from so many
people in America.

He is close friend
with Ralph Fiennes (actor)

FILMOGRAPHY

EXCALIBUR	1981	NEXT OF KIN	1989
KRULL	1983	THE BIG MAN	1990
THE BOUNTY	1984	DARKMAN	1990
THE INNOCENT	1984	UNDER SUSPICION	1991
LAMB	1985	SHINING THROUGH	1992
THE MISSION	1985	HUSBANDS AND WIVES	1992
A PRAYER FOR THE DYING	1987	LEAP OF FAITH	1992
DUET FOR ONE	1987	RUBY CAIRO	1993
SUSPECT	1987	SCHINDLER'S LIST	1993
THE DEAD POOL	1988	ETHAN FROME	1993
THE GOOD MOTHER	1988	NELL	1994
aka THE PRICE OF PASSION		ROB ROY	1995
WHO FRAMED ROGER RABBIT?	1988		
HIGH SPIRITS	1988		

a movie w/ Pierce Brosnan (2009)
- The Other Man (2008)
- Taken
- Chloe (made in Canada
& he was working on it
when Natasha Died (2009)

TELEVISION

ELLIS ISLAND	1985
IF TOMORROW COMES	1985
A WOMAN OF SUBSTANCE	1985
HOLD THE DREAM	1986
SWORN TO SILENCE	1986
SWEET AS YOU ARE	1987

LIST OF ILLUSTRATIONS

Section one

Liam Neeson. Open, honest, the kind of face you can trust
(Bonnie Schiffman, Retna Pictures)

Kitty Neeson
(Belfast Telegraph Newspapers Ltd)

The enigmatic smile hinted at, even at seventeen
(Belfast Telegraph Newspapers)

As Michael Lamb, with Hugh O'Conor, in *Lamb*
(The Kobal Collection)

As Danny Scoular, *The Big Man*
(Rex Features)

No, you can't come in. I'm a private kinda guy
(Rex Features)

Section two

Liam alone: that inimitable look of the soul in torment
(The Douglas Brothers, Retna Pictures)

With Helen Mirren
(All Action)

With Natasha Richardson. 'If anyone's got what it takes, Natasha has'
(Nick Elgar, London Features International)

No, I'm not giving up – they're such a great prop for these moody introspective
shots
(Sebastien Raymond, Rex Features)

With *Nell*, Jodie Foster
(London Features International)

As Oskar Schindler. 'I'm going to give you an entrance in a movie that no one's
ever had before'
(London Features International)